MY POLAR FLIGHTS
by Umberto Nobile

In May 1926 the whole world was astonished to learn that a small airship, the *Norge,* under the command of the Italian engineer and explorer General Umberto Nobile had flown from Rome to the North Pole and from the North Pole across hitherto unexplored lands to Alaska.

On this journey, which is known in the history of polar expeditions as the "Amundsen–Ellsworth–Nobile Transpolar Flight" (Roald Amundsen initiated the expedition, the American Lincoln Ellsworth backed it), the northern Polar Sea was discovered and crossed by man for the first time.

Two years later Nobile, commanding the airship *Italia,* explored unknown regions of the north and on May 2, 1928, reached the Pole for a second time. On the flight, after fighting for thirty hours against storms, the *Italia,* overcome by the forces of nature, crashed on the pack ice.

This book, written by Nobile himself, tells for the first time the full story of the daring venture of the *Norge* and the thrilling drama

(Continued on back flap)

MY POLAR FLIGHTS

AN ACCOUNT OF THE VOYAGES
OF THE AIRSHIPS *ITALIA* AND *NORGE*

by

UMBERTO NOBILE

Translated by Frances Fleetwood

G. P. Putnam's Sons   New York

CONTENTS

page

Preface

PART I THE FIRST CROSSING OF THE ARCTIC
          OCEAN

The Preliminaries of the Expedition   15
On the Eve of the Flight   23
The Flight from Rome to the Svalbard   34
From King's Bay to the Pole   49
In the Unexplored Zone   65
Over the Bering Straits   71
The End of the Flight   78
Returning Home   86

PART II THE TRAGEDY OF THE *ITALIA*

Origin and Preparation of the Expedition   99
The Flight from Milan to King's Bay   112
At King's Bay   124
The Flight to Severnaya Zemlya   129
The Voyage to the Pole   139
The Catastrophe   148
Adrift on the Pack   157
The Courage of Despair   169
"Both Parties will Die!"   180
Six in the Red Tent   190
The Miracle of the Radio   198
Manna from Heaven   214
An Aeroplane lands on the Pack   223
On the *Città di Milano*   234
The End of the Drama   250

page

APPENDIX TO PART I

The Danger of Icing 273
The Dirigible *N.1* 274
The Landing-sack 275

INDEX:

General 277
Geographical 284

ILLUSTRATIONS

(all following page 128)

Umberto Nobile

The *Norge* over Leningrad

The forepart of the pilot's cabin in the *Italia*

The *Italia* setting off from Stolp for King's Bay

The *Italia* inside the hangar at King's Bay

Malmgren, Mariano and Nobile on board the *Italia* at Vadsö

Zappi, Mariano and Viglieri at King's Bay

The Arctic Ocean near the North Pole

Dropping the flag at the Pole

The Red Tent

The flying-boat S.55 lands near the *Città di Milano* at Virgo Bay

On the ice pack

Viglieri, Behounek and Nobile at the arrival of Lundborg

Zappi climbs on board the *Krassin*

The *Krassin* beside the Red Tent

PREFACE

Nearly 35 years ago, on the initiative of a great Polar explorer, Roald Amundsen, the *N.1*, a small Italian airship which had been renamed *Norge* and was flying the Norwegian flag, set out from Rome and with 6 Italians on board, 8 Norwegians, an American and a Swede, reached the North Pole. Thence it continued across the vast unknown region extending between the Pole and the northern coast of the American continent, and after 169 hours of flight it landed at Teller in Alaska, a tiny Eskimo village. Thus was ascertained the existence of a frozen sea in the region till then inaccessible to man, and the first crossing of it achieved.

Two years later the first scientific Arctic exploration by air was organized in Italy, with the *Italia*—a sister-ship of the *Norge*. Its members were 16 Italians with 2 foreign scientists, a Swede and a Czechoslovak.

The *Italia*, after a hazardous flight across Europe, arrived at King's Bay in the Spitsbergen islands, and there began a series of exploring flights in regions hitherto unknown to man. In one of these, a non-stop voyage lasting 3 days, we explored the region of Severnaya Zemlya (Northern Land). A third and last flight was made across the unexplored district east of Spitsbergen and north of Greenland. Having reached the Pole by this novel route, the *Italia* started to return to its base, still over unknown ground between the 25th and 40th meridians of longitude east of Greenwich. For 30 hours on end the airship struggled against a persistent storm. Suddenly, when it was in its 131st flying-hour of exploration and only an hour or two away from its base, the catastrophe occurred: the *Italia*, probably because of very sudden ice formation, crashed on the pack. This was the beginning of a fearful, dramatic adventure, which caught the imagination of the whole world, and about which hundreds of books have been published in many languages.

This book tells of the triumphant *Norge* expedition, and the no less memorable, if unlucky, one of the *Italia*. I have already told the stories in two separate books, both long since out of print. But here the facts of the two expeditions, inter-connected as they were in reality, have been united in a single narrative. In this I have omitted not only a few marginal episodes which, after this lapse of time, no longer seemed to me of any importance, but also everything concerning the technical and scientific preparation of both expeditions.[1] The latter, so far as the *Italia* is concerned, is given in full in the book *Die Vorbereitungen und die wissenschaftlichen Ergebnisse der Polarexpedition der "Italia"*.[2]

The new generation in my own country and others ought not to be left in ignorance of the vicissitudes of the *Norge* and *Italia* expeditions. After a third of a century their daring has not yet been surpassed, and they will remain in the history of Polar exploration. The former expedition, which officially took the name AMUNDSEN–ELLSWORTH–NOBILE TRANSPOLAR FLIGHT, can boast of having been probably the first to reach the North Pole by air, and certainly the first to cross the Arctic Ocean. In the second, we organized and carried out the first scientific aerial expedition in these regions.

Two years ago an American submarine, the *Nautilus*, propelled by atomic power, crossed the Arctic Ocean from the Bering Straits to Spitsbergen, following more or less the route of the *Norge*, but in the opposite direction. Its commander on that historic voyage, Captain William R. Anderson, has authorized me to quote the following passage from a letter he wrote to me:

"From your courageous flight over the polar ice pack in 1926 it was established that there was no land between Alaska and Spitsbergen. Without this knowledge, found by you and confirmed by the aerial expeditions that followed you, we would not have known enough to undertake our voyage."

[1] I have also omitted the very painful story of the intrigues and attacks perpetrated against the expedition. Any reader who is interested can find the full and documented tale of them in the book *Posso dire la Verità*, which I published in 1945, when for the first time it was possible to reveal it to the Italian public.

[2] Justus Perthes (Gotha), 1929.

Today it is easy to fly to the North Pole. Regular airlines, equipped with powerful machines, link the European continent with North America and Japan across the Arctic; but our young people should know that it was two airships which, built in Italy to fly in Mediterranean skies, first hazarded the voyage from Rome to the Bering Straits and the region of Severnaya Zemlya.

UMBERTO NOBILE

PART ONE

THE FIRST CROSSING OF THE ARCTIC OCEAN

THE PRELIMINARIES OF THE
EXPEDITION

A Telegram from Amundsen

ON July 15th, 1925, unexpectedly, I received a telegram from Roald Amundsen, in which the famous explorer suggested meeting me in Rome for "an important and secret conference".

A few months previously Amundsen had returned from an expedition in which he had unsuccessfully tried to reach the North Pole with 2 Dornier Wal seaplanes, built in Italy at Marina di Pisa. When one of them was damaged, both had been obliged to alight on the ice north of the Spitsbergen islands, in 87° 40' latitude N. Twenty-five days later, abandoning the wrecked machine on the pack, Amundsen and his 5 companions had all crowded into the other and flown back to their starting-point at King's Bay.

Having failed in this attempt to reach the Pole by seaplane, Amundsen had thought of an airship—the advantages of which over an aeroplane as a means of polar exploration were obvious even to a layman.

I myself had been thinking for some time about the possibility of using a dirigible to explore the Arctic regions, and I was convinced that, with one of my own ships, it might very well be successful. At that time I was a colonel of the Aeronautical Engineers, and for some years had been in charge of the military factory of Aeronautical Constructions in the Giulio Cesare Avenue, near the Tiber, in Rome.

This has been done away with today, and replaced by ugly blocks of flats, but in those days its workshops were busily employed in the construction of airships for the Navy and the Army. Starting with a tiny dirigible, the *Mr*—the smallest semi-rigid ever built in the world—with which I used to take off and land, single-handed, in a courtyard of the barracks beside our workshops, I had developed the *N.1* airship, built for the Navy— the prototype of a new series, of which a second and improved example was then under construction.

Two days after the first telegram there came a second in which Amundsen asked me if I could come to Norway, as some circumstances had arisen which prevented him from visiting Italy. I set off. On July 25th I was in Oslo. That very afternoon and next day I met Amundsen in his villa, in the presence of Riiser-Larsen and a representative of the Aeroclub of Norway. We sketched out the general lines of our enterprise and laid down the objective to be achieved—which, in Amundsen's view, should be to cross the Arctic circle from Spitsbergen to Point Barrow, on the northern coast of Alaska. Starting from Rome, the airship would fly up to King's Bay (latitude, approximately 79° N.), where we would have to establish a refuelling base. From King's Bay we would strike direct for the Pole, and beyond it explore for the first time an immense region which had never been seen by man, stretching as far as the American coast.

For this venture I maintained that the suitable ship was another example of the N-type, which, as I have said, was then being built in our workshops. Having made it lighter by comparison with the prototype, its useful load would be sufficient to give it the necessary range. But Amundsen insisted that the expedition should be made in the following spring. Now, in 8 months it would have been impossible to finish building the new dirigible, equip it, and get it ready. We would have to use a ship that was already available, and there was only the *N.1*.

The Agreement with the Italian Government

We decided upon the venture. A daring decision indeed, bearing in mind that at the very same time the Germans were planning a Polar expedition with an almost identical route, for which a committee of scientists and experts headed by Nansen thought it necessary to use a Zeppelin of 4,768,000 cu. ft.—seven times larger than *N.1*.

The Aeroclub of Norway definitely undertook the financial organization of the expedition, as soon as the American Lincoln Ellsworth had promised his personal contribution of $120,000. But even before this an agreement had been made in Rome, on September 1st, 1925, between the Italian Government and the Aeroclub of Norway, represented by Amundsen, by which the Aeroclub acquired the airship *N.1* for the Polar expedition, after the structural modifications which I thought necessary for the projected flight had been completed. The document also laid down the details of our individual participation in the enterprise, stipulating that we Italians should be responsible for piloting the airship, preparing everything for the flight itself, including the refuelling bases to be set up at King's Bay and anywhere else that was necessary. The Aeroclub's task would be to help us prepare the bases, and to supply Polar clothing, provisions and all that would be needed in case of a forced descent on the ice: tents, sledges, knapsacks, skis, firearms.

The signing of this agreement was Mussolini's first act as Minister for Aviation—which seemed to us a good omen. Once it was settled Amundsen went to give a long lecture tour in America, from which he was due to return only in the following spring, and join us in King's Bay to come aboard the airship. While Amundsen left for America, we Italians and the Aeroclub of Norway, each on our own side, settled down to the feverish and continuous hard work of preparing the expedition.

The Route Across Europe

Once the agreement had been signed, my first problem was to plan the route we should follow in order to reach King's Bay from Rome—a long flight, and not without its difficulties. It could not be made in a single stage: one or more halts would be necessary for refuelling with petrol and hydrogen.

I at once thought of the possibility of crossing Russia, where the large old hangar at Leningrad was probably still in existence. It was the nearest hangar to Spitsbergen, and would enable us to cross the stormy Barents Sea in the most favourable conditions. What is more, we could reach it directly from Rome.

But I was not sure whether the Leningrad hangar would be put at our disposal; so, as an alternative, I thought of making a stop in England. Therefore, on the way back from Norway, I went to London and called on the Air Ministry, to ask permission to use one of the English hangars. The English authorities readily agreed, and suggested the airfield at Pulham, which was perfectly equipped. Thence we could have continued to King's Bay along the west coast of Norway, stopping to refuel at Trondheim if necessary.

Later, when we knew that we should be able to use the Leningrad hangar, since the Aeroclub of Norway had expressed the wish that the airship should stop for a day at Oslo, I finally chose the route Rome-Pulham-Oslo-Leningrad-King's Bay. In all, over 4,000 miles, without counting any detours. It worked out, in fact, to nearly 4,500 miles.

My First Journey to Russia

Early in January, 1926, accepting an invitation sent to me through the Soviet Embassy in Rome, I went to Russia to ascertain the condition of the hangar at Gatschina near Leningrad, and to make arrangements with the Soviet authorities.

I had never been to Russia before.

I arrived in Leningrad on a grey, rainy day in mid-winter. The sight of the great city—depopulated, drab; its half-ruined palaces still showing traces of their former splendour; its inhabitants poorly clad, with faces careworn from long suffering; its vast number of beggars—all made an unhappy impression upon me. But four months later, when I returned with the airship, things were different: the city appeared less desolate, the people happier and their poverty less in evidence. On both occasions I was struck by the number and size of the bookshops and the pharmacies.

The Russian authorities were most courteous. General Zinovieff, Commander-in-Chief of the Air Force in Leningrad, accompanied me on my visit to the hangar at Gatschina. It was a grandiose wooden building, disused for years. A great many repairs would be necessary, and during the winter months it would not be easy to make them with the requisite speed.

We held a conference at the office of the Agent for Foreign Affairs, as the local representative of the Commissariat for Foreign Affairs was then called. There were present, with the Italian Consul Bombieri—who gave me most valuable help during my stay in Leningrad—General Zinovieff and an engineer from the construction services. They worked out that the cost of repairing the hangar would be at least 25,000 roubles; but the Agent for Foreign Affairs expressed his conviction that the Soviet Government would make itself responsible for this. However, I would have to go to Moscow for a definite ruling on this point. I went there.

I was a guest of the Italian Ambassador, Count Manzoni; and, accompanied by him, I went to see the Assistant Secretary for Foreign Affairs, who at that time was Litvinoff. He declared that the Soviet Government would do everything in its power to assist our enterprise; and in fact next day, at a meeting held in the office of the Air Chief Marshal, it was announced that the Soviet Government would repair the hangar at its own expense by April 15th, and would supply all the materials and personnel that I thought necessary.

These promises were all faithfully carried out; actually, the Russians did much more for us than they had agreed to do.

Meteorological Conditions in the Arctic

The meteorological problem presented many unknown factors. It was even difficult to gather statistical data about the various regions we intended to cross.

For the Polar regions I could draw upon the observations made by the expeditions of Nansen and the Duke of the Abruzzi. Taking as a whole the data supplied by Nansen, it appeared that the most favourable conditions would be in April and May, preferably from mid-April to mid-May, when there were very few foggy days (two or three out of thirty). Our crossing was, in fact, made between May 11th and 13th, but, contrary to our expectations, we found thick fog, lasting nearly 16 hours and stretching for over 750 miles along our route. Fortunately, as other observers had noted before us, the height of this fog did not exceed 3,000 ft., so that we could easily fly above it. The temperature, at the height we were flying, did not drop below 9·5° F.

If storms are rare in the Arctic Ocean, the territories surrounding it—particularly the Barents Sea, Franz Josef Land, Novaya Zemlya, and the Bering Straits—are frequently swept by terrible cyclones that produce winds of hurricane force.

The Barents Sea, above all, is considered one of the stormiest in the world. From statistics we calculated that on Bear Island, situated about half-way between Norway and Spitsbergen, the average wind-speed during April is over 30 ft. to the second; while at Leningrad it is little more than 12 ft., in London 15, in Oslo 6, and in Rome 9.

As for the Bering Straits, it was quite useless to worry about them. To expect on leaving Spitsbergen to have good weather not only for crossing the Pole but for landing in Alaska, would have been too much. The essential was that our wireless on board should work well, so that we could pick up news from the weather stations in Alaska, and select the route to follow for the last part of our journey accordingly.

But as it turned out, in the unexplored regions beyond the Pole our wireless—which until then had been extremely useful— ceased to function.

The Reconstruction of the Airship

The *N.1*, in its original condition, was not suitable for the Polar flight we had planned. With a volume of only 654,000 cu. ft., its lift would have been at most 48,500 lb. Subtracting its intrinsic weight, which when I took the ship over from the Navy was 29,540 lb. and a further 8,800 lb. for equipment, ballast, provisions, and a crew of 16, there would have remained 10,140 lb. for petrol and oil—entirely inadequate for the flight. It suffices to remember that at a cruising speed of 50 m.p.h. the engines would consume 3·3 lb. for each half-mile traversed in calm air, and that in round numbers the distance across the Arctic Ocean would be 2,500 miles.

I had designed the *N.1* in 1921, but only 2 years later, on my return from America, did I obtain the authorization to build it. To reduce the expenses of construction to a minimum, I had been obliged to use materials already in store, which were not the most suitable, and consequently the main frame was heavier than necessary. I may add that the airship, originally intended to carry from 20 to 25 passengers, had been provided with many comforts —among other things, a saloon, a kitchen, and even an elegantly decorated bedroom. It all looked very nice, but it added to the weight.

It was therefore essential to lighten the ship, to gain the 3,500 lb. of petrol that were lacking: a difficult task, because at the same time various parts of the ship would have to be strengthened to resist the stresses it would undergo at the mooring-masts, which were not in use in Italy.

We had to carry out long, meticulous, patient work, lasting several months; but in the end it was successful. Early in the new year, having finished the work and reassembled the airship, I checked its basic weight: I had the satisfaction of finding that it had been reduced by 3,500 lb., just as I had proposed.

The Preparation of the Bases

In Oslo, at Vadsö on the northern coast of Norway, and at King's Bay in the Spitsbergen islands, we had to create outright the whole organization necessary for receiving the airship, re-fuelling it with hydrogen and petrol, and carrying out any repairs that might be necessary.

The Oslo base, being simply intended to satisfy the desire of the Norwegian people to see the dirigible, was not particularly important in itself. Still, we had to install a mooring-mast, with all the accessory services and requisite materials.

More important was the refuelling base at Vadsö, and still more so that in King's Bay. The preparation of the materials to be sent to these two bases was made in Rome with the greatest care and lavishness; so that when the time came we should have at our disposal everything which at the last moment might appear necessary.

The wisdom of these precautions was shown by the fact that at

King's Bay we had to change one of the engines, replace the rudder, and repair the lower part of the keel.

The mooring-masts at King's Bay and Vadsö were entirely built in Italy. The Vadsö mast was set up under the supervision of our chief technician Rossi, helped by three of our workmen.

To King's Bay, where both mast and hangar, designed by us in Italy, were built by the Aeroclub of Norway, I sent several officers and workmen, and, to make meteorological observations, my brother, Amedeo, a doctor in physics.

ON THE EVE OF THE FLIGHT

Members of the Expedition: The Norwegians and Others

A CHARACTERISTIC of our expedition was the heterogeneous composition of its crew: Italians, Norwegians, Americans, Russians, Swedes. This naturally gave rise to difficulties, not the least of them being that of communicating with one another.

In the control cabin of the *Norge* the official language, so to speak, was English; but there were times when English did not suffice to make my orders clear, and then I spoke Italian. In moments of crisis, when there was not an instant to lose, and orders had to be executed immediately, my Italian must have been accompanied by very expressive gestures; otherwise, I cannot explain how I managed to make myself understood.

Another difficulty was that the Norwegians knew nothing about dirigibles, except for Riiser-Larsen, who had made a few flights in an English rigid airship; so I had to instruct and train them. And there was only a month in which to do it.

Five Norwegians, besides Amundsen, were to take part in the Polar flight: Riiser-Larsen, Wisting, Horgen, Gottwaldt and Omdal; but Gottwaldt was to supervise the wireless, and Omdal was an engine mechanic. There remained 3 to man the elevator and the rudder: Riiser-Larsen, Wisting and Horgen.

Many people in Italy thought it dangerous for me to set out without having on board an Italian officer who was used to our dirigibles. Certainly, the presence of another expert pilot would have enabled me to rest from time to time, sparing me an uninterrupted vigil of 32 hours between Rome and Pulham, and another 44 hours between Pulham and Gatschina. But, all things considered, I do not regret it. When responsibility is concentrated in a single person, who knows that the others will carry out his orders without the slightest hesitation, his attention is sharpened, his decisions are made swiftly and swiftly carried into effect. This happened several times during our flight: there were moments when a single instant of indecision would have been fatal.

The Norwegians on board—always calm, punctilious and disciplined—performed their duties splendidly. Once an order had been given, one could be certain that they would carry it out scrupulously. If their inexperience prevented me from using them on the ground, for overhauling and handling the ship, this was of no consequence, as I had foreseen it and sent some expert Italian officers to Russia and Spitsbergen. But on board Horgen, Wisting, and even Gottwaldt when the radio service left him free, were indefatigable helmsmen. Riiser-Larsen, assisted by Horgen, was our navigator, occupied with reading the navigation charts, checking speed and drift, measuring the height of the sun, and determining our position. They achieved this task very well.

The meteorologist on board throughout the flight was Finn Malmgren, a Swede who had been with Amundsen on his expedition in the *Maud.* The wireless operator was a young Russian, whose rugged exterior belied his gentle nature: Olomkin. During the flight in Europe, under Gottwaldt's supervision, he kept us in constant communication with the European station receiving the weather code messages, which were then decoded by Malmgren. But at the last moment in Spitsbergen he was replaced by a Norwegian operator.

To complete the list of the Norwegian members of the expedition I must mention the journalist Ramm, who slithered quietly with his typewriter into the back of the control cabin and gave us no trouble, although he weighed over 14 stone.

My Italian Comrades

When I returned to Italy after my journey to Russia, my first thought was to choose the Italians who were to accompany me on the expedition. It was not an easy choice. To check up the vital organs of the ship in flight, and if necessary repair them, I would have to rely solely upon Italian workmen. Therefore I must select from among the most expert—those who through long experience in our workshops and in flight knew each individual piece of the airship's structure, and how it would behave in the air. Nor was that all: they must also possess the necessary physical and mental qualities to stand up to the discomforts, risks and unknown factors of our voyage. They must be hardened against fatigue, indifferent to danger, calm, resolute, and at the same time enthusiastic about the enterprise. I must have the most complete confidence in them and they in turn must have the blindest faith in me, who had prepared the flight and would now have to lead it.

So—naturally—the choice fell on those who were nearest to me, whom I had known for years and had personally seen working in difficult conditions.

They were: Cecioni, Arduino, Caratti, Pomella, Alessandrini. But, lest one of them should fall ill or be hindered by family worries, I selected 4 other men as reserves.

Here are some brief notes on these five comrades of mine, who contributed so largely towards the success of the expedition:

NATALE CECIONI, 39, a Florentine. A very resourceful man, who could turn his hand to anything; he had 20 years' experience in the workshops, and 15 as an engine mechanic in flight.

When I sent for him, to ask if he would like to come with me, he said simply and unhesitatingly "Yes!", nor did he ever have a moment's doubt subsequently, even when (as he told me afterwards) his friends tried to dissuade him.

During the whole journey he was tireless. Sometimes he grumbled, often he made rude remarks in his Florentine dialect, but he was always at his post, whether on the ground or on board.

One of Cecioni's characteristics was not to trouble in the least whether the person he was talking to understood his dialect. Whilst he worked, I heard him talking in Tuscan to English workmen, Russian soldiers—and even to the Eskimos. The best of it was, that they really did understand him, since the work got done without any difficulty. He was tall, solidly built—weighed

15 stone and a half. It was not surprising, therefore, if during the Polar flight he was continually grousing that he had not enough to eat: "We're dying of hunger here!" How many times, during those three days in the air, did that phrase not ring in my ears!

ETTORE ARDUINO, from Verona; first-grade engine mechanic, with a dozen years' flying experience, decorated for military valour, serious, taciturn.

He was my reserve chief engineer. If Cecioni needed rest, or had fallen ill and been left behind during the journey, Arduino would have taken his place.

Always calm and serene, he went quietly about his tasks. I never heard him grumble, criticize or complain. During the flight he too was untiring.

ATTILIO CARATTI, 30, from Brescia, an experienced airship mechanic—the only one who went off without leaving a wife and family behind him.

I sent Caratti up for a medical examination, the same as the others, but the report was unfavourable. He was quite healthy, but there was a history of trouble: the previous year he had suffered from acute rheumatism in his joints, which might have suddenly attacked him during a long flight in a very severe climate.

I called him into my office and told him that on medical advice, in his own interests and those of the expedition, I was obliged to do without him. Caratti, standing rigidly to attention, did not blench—but his eyes reddened and shone with tears. I made up my mind: against the doctor's advice, Caratti joined the expedition.

VINCENZO POMELLA. A Southerner, with blue eyes and thick fair hair. He had been working for many years in my workshops. A first-rate motor mechanic.

No need to expatiate on how he behaved during the flight: his pluck and physical endurance were unequalled. It suffices to say that during our crossing of the Arctic Ocean the stern engine, under his control, worked uninterruptedly, regularly . . . and for 71 hours on end.

RENATO ALESSANDRINI, a Roman: rigger.

I had known him for years. For years he had worked in the assembling of our airships. He climbed around everywhere like a squirrel, worked for hours and hours in impossible positions, in places which anyone else would have found inaccessible. His intelligence was as lively and supple as his limbs. He knew our ship inside out, having worked for months to put it together. Like all the others, he had made dozens of flights in our dirigibles.

When I first decided to lead the venture, Alessandrini was one of those whom I intended to take with me. Even if he had refused, I would have, metaphorically, forced him to come. But there was no need, for when I asked him he at once said yes. And as I insisted on telling him to consider well the risks he would be running, and began to explain them to him, he broke in: "No need of all that! You are going—so I'm coming too."

But a few days before we left, Alessandrini fell seriously ill with double pneumonia, so that the *Norge* left Rome without him. I had resigned myself to losing him; but one day, after our arrival in Russia, I saw him enter the hangar at Gatschina, cheerful and smiling as usual.

From Leningrad to Teller, Alessandrini did not leave his post on board. He stayed beside me in the cabin, and often took over the rudder. From time to time I sent him into the interior of the ship to inspect it and see that all was in order, or to help Cecioni. With his good-humoured, rosy face he brought a note of gaiety to both the Polar expeditions in which he took part.

These were the five Italians who made the first crossing of the Arctic Ocean with me, and with me flew twice over the North Pole.

To find out exactly how much of the useful load could be taken up by petrol, we had to know the weight of each member of the crew. I had them weighed in their ordinary clothes, without their furs or overcoats, and this was the result:

		kg.	(approx. equivalent)
Alessandrini	..	67	10 stone
Arduino	.. ..	82	13 ,,
Caratti	.. ..	72	11 ,,
Cecioni	.. ..	97	15¼ ,,
Gottwaldt	..	89	14 ,,
Horgen	.. ..	82	13 ,,
Malmgren	..	69	10½ ,,
Nobile	.. ..	60	9½ ,,
Olomkin	.. ..	85	13½ ,,
Omdal	.. ..	73	11½ ,,
Pomella	.. ..	59	9¼ ,,
Riiser-Larsen	..	99	15½ ,,
Wisting	.. ..	76	12 ,,

and finally, the journalist Ramm, at 91 kg. (14¼ stone.)

The King at Ciampino

Now that the work was finished, on February 27th, with a flight over Naples I started a series of tests that were to last all through March. King Victor Emmanuel intended to take part in one of these flights, but on the day that had been arranged, weather conditions were so bad that I had to limit myself to making one or two low-altitude circuits of the field.

I was on quite friendly terms with the King. For years past he had been interested in the construction of our dirigibles, and had always seemed to be pleased when I invited him to visit our works and fly in the airships I had built. One of his latest flights had been on the *Roma*, before it was handed over to the American Army. On that occasion I had admired his calm when, by an error in pilotage, the ship tilted at a dangerous angle. The King, who was chatting as he looked out of a porthole, gave no sign that he had noticed anything wrong, although he had to cling on to the parapet to keep his balance, and quietly went on with the conversation.

He was very simple in his manners, and so was not surprised when I received him without any ceremony; in fact, judging from the way he looked at me, I think he liked it.

Once the Polar expedition had been decided upon, he wanted to know all about it. He had confidence in our airship, but he did not hide from me his anxiety about the meteorological conditions we might meet, more especially the risk that the ship might be weighed down by ice. I remembered his accurate observations a few weeks later, when, right in the midst of the Polar regions, I was surprised at the rapidity with which ice formed on the metal parts of the airship.

Mussolini and the Expedition

Often in these last years I have asked myself whether the *Norge* expedition would have taken place, even if Mussolini had not been in power.

That is a question which is not easily answered. Even without Mussolini the Aeroclub of Norway might have bought *N.1* from the Italian Government. This was not the first dirigible that had been sold abroad; others in previous years had been built by us for the American Army and Navy, the Spanish Navy; for the Argentine, England and Japan.

But it is very doubtful whether things would have gone as quickly as they did with Mussolini. When Air Ministry officials, who were airship experts, told him that it was impossible to reach the Pole with a ship as small as *N.1*, instead of being taken aback he reacted in his own fashion, sending General Bonzani (the Assistant Secretary for Aviation) to tell me to hurry up the start.

I saw Mussolini for the first time at the end of March, 1926, when I took Dr. Thommessen, President of the Aeroclub of Norway, to see him at Palazzo Chigi. He was in an excellent humour, affable and cordial—as he was whenever I saw him subsequently.

He asked questions about the preparations, fetched a map of

the Polar regions and indicated our proposed route. We discussed the various possibilities, and he said: "You will succeed—there is no doubt of that," in that quiet, sonorous voice that inspired confidence in those who listened to him. He asked what provisions we were taking: "Pemmican, biscuits, chocolate, tea." Suddenly he remarked: "But then—it's not necessary to eat." He seemed convinced of that—and almost succeeded in convincing me, who would willingly have left food behind in order to take on more fuel.

When we left, Mussolini said: "I shall come and say good-bye to you at Ciampino, and wish you good luck."

But before that I saw him on March 29th, the day when at Ciampino the dirigible was solemnly handed over to the expedition and christened the *Norge*.

The Italian flag which for 2 years had proudly flown from its stern was hauled down and replaced by that of Norway. Mussolini gave it to me, saying: "This is to be dropped on the ice of the Pole," and he ordered the officers who were standing by: "Prepare a fine casket to keep it in, on board."

He had said: "I will come to see you off," and kept his word. On April 3rd everything was ready at Ciampino. Mussolini arrived. It was the day after the Gibson woman had tried to assassinate him. His wound, which was probably still painful, had not prevented him from coming. He was pale, and there was a bandage over his nose.

He took up his position on the field to await the start, while I was busy with the preparations. But the weather, which since the early morning had been threatening, was rapidly getting worse.

I was in a quandary. Though I did not want to jeopardize the success of the expedition, right at the beginning, by a manœuvre which the high wind would render extremely hazardous, it was rather embarrassing to have to tell the Chief of Government: "I shall have to put off our departure," when he had arrived punctually, in spite of his physical condition.

Then I made up my mind and went to tell him: "The weather is too bad. I am putting off the start." "Good!" he said, "You are quite right. If the weather is unfavourable, it is better not to take the risk. You will start when it clears up."

He added that he would not be able to come back and see us off, because he had to journey to Tripoli. And he embraced me as he said good-bye: "You will succeed. Everything will go well. I am sure of it. You will go—and come back victorious."

The Load and the Crew at the Departure from Rome

Everything was in order a week before the *Norge* started: the equipment in place, the reservoirs full. Nothing was lacking except the personal luggage of the crew, and this was put aboard at the last moment.

The interior of the airship looked distinctly picturesque. We had distributed an enormous quantity of materials in the various sections of the hull, using the girders to support them. But the little control cabin was equally cluttered. When the kitbags and suitcases of some of the crew were added, there was hardly room to move. Among the many things on board I will mention, as a curiosity, 2 armchairs in steel tubing covered with velvet, intended for Amundsen and Ellsworth.

Twenty-one of us left Rome, including Major G. H. Scott, the English airship expert who had kindly put himself at our disposal to help prepare our landing at Pulham; and Lieutenant Mercier, of the French Air Ministry, who had asked to fly with us over France, in case we were forced to land there.

Besides these two officers, who left us when we reached England, we had on board as a passenger as far as Leningrad the journalist Quattrini—whom I liked at once because he struck up a great friendship with my little dog Titina; but in Russia he had to make way for Cesco Tomaselli of the *Corriere della Sera*.

The 21 people on board weighed altogether 3,600 lb., but allowing for each another 33 lb. for fur coats, changes of underwear, toilet articles, and provisions to be eaten during the flight, I arrived at a figure of 4,294 lb.

Besides the persons I have named we had on board, right from the start in Rome, a twenty-second who remained at her post all the way to Teller . . . someone who took up very little room and weighed practically nothing: Titina. Ten inches high and 12 lb. in weight—that was all.

Titina thoroughly disliked flying, but she would not let me go alone, and she was always under my feet on board. Though she was still very young, she had several hundreds of flying-hours to her credit when she took part in our expedition.

My Wife

A journey to the Pole was not something that was often undertaken in those days. As for flying there, no one had as yet done it at all. So it is not surprising that when I first mentioned it to my wife she did not believe me; then, when she realized that I was not joking, she raised a few objections, but she did not insist. She resigned herself.

That is not to say that she had any illusions about the risks I was running. She knew them all, because I had told her myself—and so had my brothers, who came to ask her to dissuade me from the undertaking. Her self-control was so great that she was able, without getting upset, to listen to the advice that I gave her about bringing up our daughter in case I did not come back.

But in the last days, when our parting was imminent, my wife began to show her distress. She could not sleep at night. Sometimes she could no longer restrain herself, and said: "I won't let you go!"

But she did.

On the morning of April 10th I thought that perhaps I would have to put off the start once again. But she, as she got out of bed, said to me: "I feel that you will start this morning. Go and get ready. I will come and say good-bye to you at Ciampino."

I waited for her. The airship was on the field. I trembled at the thought of seeing her arrive with her eyes swollen by weeping. It would be very difficult to take leave of her in those conditions. But instead, at the very last moment, she came forward to say good-bye—tranquil, serene, almost smiling. She kissed me gently, murmuring: "Go away happy!" And those fond, sweet words echoed in my mind at every moment during the flight.

When at the end of the expedition, after three days of silence, the wireless brought news that we had arrived safe and sound in Alaska, dissipating the anxiety of Italians throughout the world, since they could not get hold of me—up there in the peace of a tiny Eskimo village—many people made a great fuss of my wife.

It was the best way they could have found of thanking me. The telegram from the Queen of Italy to Maria, the roses Mussolini sent to my wife, were the most precious gifts I could have had.

Our little girl, Maria, was then eight and a half years old: the happy age of almost perfect ignorance. She hadn't the faintest idea what the Pole might be.

When she heard that "papa" was going to make this voyage, she made me show her the journey on a map, put one small finger on the Spitsbergen islands and said: "There—there's nothing in that! You'll get there in a moment."

Then even she, after she had heard the grown-ups talking, began to get worried. On the morning I left, when I hugged her to me, she was very quiet and pale.

THE FLIGHT FROM ROME TO THE
SVALBARD

The Start from Rome

WE started from Rome, then, on April 10th—a Saturday morning. I reached the Ciampino airfield about seven o'clock. Everything was ready. The latest weather reports, drawn up that morning, although not excellent were passable; but we would run into high winds over France. I decided to go.

Having tested the engines and loaded the provisions and luggage of the last arrivals, at nine o'clock I gave the order to bring the airship out of the hangar.

Nobody had been told about the start, except Thommessen and the Secretary of the Norwegian Legation, Vangensten: both were there. On the field there were engineers and workmen from the factory of Aeronautical Constructions—all those who had shared my years of work and struggle, and who had helped me to prepare the expedition.

I was waiting impatiently for my wife and child. At last they came.

At 9.30 a.m. I went on board. Two minutes later I gave the starting-signal: "Let go!" Freed from the pull of the men who were hanging on to the ropes, the airship rose slowly, solemnly, amid the clamour of farewells and good wishes. From the control cabin our tricolour flag fluttered bravely. I had the engines speeded up.

The spring sun was shining from a clear blue sky. After flying over the city I turned seawards.

At dusk we reached the coast of France.

I will not linger over the details of that marvellous flight along the Canal du Midi in the starlit darkness. A violent wind was blowing, sometimes reaching 36 m.p.h. It was in our favour; but later, over the north of France, it changed direction and became a head-wind, reducing our speed to a few miles an hour. So I had to force the engines, bringing our airspeed up to 58 m.p.h. Nevertheless, we took four hours and a half to cover the 102 miles between Angers and Rochefort.

At dawn, when the sun rose, the squalls increased to the point of producing a pitch and roll that became truly alarming each time when, in the hope of finding calmer weather, I tried to fly closer to the ground. We struggled on in these conditions for hours and hours—right up to Courcelles on the Channel coast, and across the Channel to England.

At last, NE. of London, the wind began to drop. At 3.20 in the afternoon, when we arrived at Pulham, conditions were much better. We landed at 5.50, after very difficult manœuvring.

On landing at Pulham we found the Crown Prince of Norway and Sir Samuel Hoare, the Minister for Air, waiting for us.

The only one who was not pleased about that stop in Pulham was my dog Titina—and with good reason, since she had no sooner arrived than the English shut her up in one of the store-houses of the hangar, requiring me to promise that no attempt would be made to set her free.

But next morning one of the Italians went to say "hello" to her and found that the poor animal, in her efforts to free herself, had torn her collar, and that she was so upset at being separated from us that she had not even touched her food. Moved to pity, he let her out and Titina, crazy with joy, came rushing up to me while I was giving orders in the hangar to prepare our departure. But her happiness was short-lived. She slipped away, out of the hangar into the field. We called to her and brought her back at once; but too late, she had already been seen. Shortly afterwards a gentleman in uniform called on me, tall and impressive; the Police Chief at Pulham: "Kindly keep the dog shut up! If she is found outside, we are entitled to kill her, and there is also a £200 fine." So Titina went back to prison; and although the English, to make her confinement more bearable, petted her, gave her sweets and a new collar, she cried all the time.

Having completed the various formalities, the Customs official stamped our log-book: "*Cleared inward. H.M. Airship Station, Pulham, Norfolk, April 11th, 1926.*"

Apart from their unkindness to Titina, the English treated us most courteously. I found several old acquaintances at Pulham: officers who had come to Rome a few years before, to take delivery of an airship that we had built for the English Air Force, Glad to see me, they put themselves at my disposal for anything we might need.

Meanwhile, on the morning after our arrival I had ordered Cecioni to fill up with petrol and gas and to check the engines. I wanted to be ready to leave next day, April 13th.

That afternoon I consulted the meteorologists: the prospects of continuing our voyage seemed fair, only one expert was doubtful, on account of a deep depression coming up from the Atlantic. It seemed to me that conditions might even justify trying to push on directly from Oslo to Spitsbergen, without stopping in Russia; therefore I telegraphed to our chief technician Rossi, who was at Vadsö, and to the Aeroclub of Norway, to know whether the two stations at Vadsö and King's Bay were ready to receive us. The reply was in the negative: work on the two mooring-masts and the hangar would not be finished before the end of April.

However, I decided to take advantage of the fine weather to go on at once to Russia, where we would wait until Vadsö and King's Bay were ready.

Our departure was fixed for the evening of the 13th. At ten o'clock, the last Customs formalities having been quickly completed, I gave the necessary orders. An hour later we cast off.

From Pulham to Gatschina

There were 20 men on board: all those who had started from Rome, except Scott, Mercier, the meteorologist Eredia, and Marconi's rigger Huggins, who had disembarked. In exchange we had taken on Captain Paonessa, Cesco Tomaselli, and the Norwegian Naval Attaché in London, who had asked me if he might fly with us as far as Oslo. So we had 4 passengers: this officer and the 3 journalists—Ramm, Quattrini and Tomaselli.

The route which I had arranged to follow: Pulham-Oslo-Stockholm—Helsinki—Leningrad—was not difficult, but I had not reckoned with the fog, which caused considerable deviations.

On the first leg, Pulham-Oslo, everything went well, although the fog below us cut off our view of the sea. We arrived in Oslo at 11.30 a.m. (Greenwich time), having covered 705 miles at an average speed of 57 m.p.h.

The Norwegians gave us a joyful welcome. Aeroplanes came to meet us. The whole city appeared *en fête*: thousands of people had gathered in the squares, in the streets, on the roofs of buildings. The King himself had come to the foot of the mooring-mast. Bright sunlight illuminated the magnificent spectacle.

In the afternoon, after the meteorological service had warned me that the weather was breaking up, I left the airship and went with Thommessen to the Grand Hotel, where I had a meeting with the meteorologists, who unanimously advised me to leave Oslo that very evening, as quickly as I could. The depression was advancing towards Norway, the weather was getting worse: already the sky was overcast.

I returned to the foot of the mast, and made arrangements to leave. Around midnight I started the manœuvre.

Below us, by the mast, the Italians carried out my orders in the darkness, broken only here and there by the scanty light of projectors. In the distance, around the fence that protected the mast, a crowd of spectators from time to time shouted joyful farewells, whilst I gave the last orders.

"*Unhook!*" and the Italian officer on the summit of the mast, obeying the order, set in motion the unhooking device. The airship was now only held by a solid hemp rope. "*Slip the rope!*" and the rope was slowly paid out, so that the nose of the ship very gradually slid away from the mast-head. I checked the equilibrium: everything was in order. As soon as the rope had been cut away, the airship would rise with no shock and at the right angle. "*Cut!*" The word rang into the darkness, and freed from the tie, the *Norge* rose, illuminated by the shafts of light, up into the darkness. A rapid turn to the pointers controlling the engine switchboards: the swish of the propellers told me that the order had been received and executed. Still climbing, the airship gathered speed.

Soon we found ourselves immersed in the thick fog which covered the hills of Oslo and the fjord. Rapidly we rose above it while I ordered Horgen, who was at the rudder, to steer southwards over the sea.

We had left Oslo at 1.08 on the morning of April 15th, in the dead of night. For many hours the fog was so thick that we crossed the Scandinavian peninsula and the Baltic without recognizing a single place. When at last, at dawn, the fog began to thin out, we found ourselves over land: countless small lakes, one beside another. This is a characteristic Finnish landscape; but there are also chains of little lakes in Esthonia and Latvia.

The radiogoniometer and a solar observation taken by Riiser-Larsen showed that we were in Finland; but we could not rely on our radiogoniometer, and as for the height of the sun, when Horgen repeated the measurement, it gave him a latitude half a degree further south.

I ordered Riiser-Larsen to scrutinize the ground and see if he could find any indication that would enable us to recognize where we were. Soon afterwards he said that, from the colour of a post-box and the direction in which a half-frozen stream was flowing, he was sure that we were in Finland. But it is easy to be mistaken. In fact, when I looked down I had the impression that the current was flowing in the opposite direction. To increase our doubts, Gottwaldt came to tell me that he was hearing the wireless station at Reval loud and clear, as if it were quite close.

So our uncertainty continued, until it became exasperating. To put an end to it, I gave orders to steer southwards. The reasoning which suggested this detour was simple: if it was true, as Riiser-Larsen maintained, that we were in Finland, by flying south we should soon come to the sea. If, on the other hand, after flying for an hour or two, we had not seen the sea, that would mean that we were on the other shore of the Baltic.

The sea did not appear. Now and again the great dark forests on the horizon gave us an illusion of it, but as we approached them we discovered our mistake. At last we found a farmstead, lost in the wide colourless plain. A group of peasants stared up at us. I had the idea of questioning them. I prepared a message: *"What country is this? Finland? If so, raise your arms in the air."* I had it translated into Swedish (which most Finns understand), Russian and German, and threw it down. The astonished peasants, gazing at the airship that was circling over their heads, did not notice the message and nobody picked it up. We went on flying south, following the railway which we had come across a while previously. At last we saw a town. I called the Russian, Olomkin. From the shape of a church he said that he was sure we were in Russia. But I wanted to know the name of the town: I decided to lose height and circle round the station until we could read its notice-board. The experiment succeeded: we were at Valga, on the railway line from Riga to Reval, on the borders of Esthonia and Lithuania. It was 3.27 p.m.

With the wind behind us we covered the 200 miles between Valga and Gatschina at an average speed of 70 m.p.h. This rapid flight over the snow-covered, wooded Russian plain . . . vast, empty, and so solemn in the sunset . . . and our arrival at Gatschina, are among my most vivid and beautiful memories of the journey. Dusk had already fallen when we arrived at the airfield, yet the whiteness of the snow illuminated it, throwing into strong relief the monk-like figures of the hooded Russian soldiers in their long, yellowish overcoats. As is customary, they were arranged in wedge formation—in two rows converging at the point—to receive us. It was 6.16 p.m. (Central European time). We had covered 738 miles in 17 hours.

I made a brief circuit of the field, and at 6.50 we came down on the snow. Old acquaintances and friends, who had been waiting there for us since the morning, greeted us with cries of joy: Bombieri, our Consul at Leningrad; our Naval Attaché; the Agent for Foreign Affairs, Weinstein; General Zinovieff, Professor Vorobieff, Professor Pouziecewsky, doyen of the Road and Railways Institute, and many others. The hangar was in darkness, on account of an unexpected breakdown, and the Russians carried out the manœuvre silently and efficiently, by the light of the snow and of a few portable lamps that we had on board. A few minutes later the *Norge* was safe in the hangar, after a flight lasting 43 hours.

I was exhausted. For 60 hours I had been awake, without closing my eyes for a moment: good training, indeed, for the Polar flight! Tired as I was, I was happy to have accomplished this second stage towards the North. We had arrived in Russia on April 15th—the exact date which I had given the Russian authorities 4 months earlier.

I could hardly stand. They put me into a sledge and took me to the Imperial Palace, where I was a guest of the Russian Government. An hour later, in one of the salons of the palace, I could barely summon up strength to murmur a few words of thanks in reply to the addresses of welcome from the Agent for Foreign Affairs and the doyen of the professors. Immediately afterwards I dropped into bed in the room they had assigned to me—the very room in which Kerensky had slept many years previously.

Our Welcome in Russia

In Russia we received a very friendly welcome.

The Soviet Government had kept its word, repairing the hangar at its own expense and equipping it with all the necessary services: supplies, workshops, ground crew and watchman. The organization had been carried out regardless of expense, with a lavish quantity of personnel and materials.

The sight of the people who every day hastened out to Salizy to visit the airship was very picturesque. Troops of schoolchildren accompanied by their teachers, pupils from the various military institutions, university students, officials, engineers, workmen, peasants, men and women of all ages and types, came daily in their thousands, crowding round the doors of the enclosure around the hangar. They were really interested: they asked questions, they wanted to see our flag. In many simple, affectionate ways they showed their admiration.

These demonstrations from total strangers moved me. In the train between Leningrad and Gatschina, in the street, in the hangar while we were working, everywhere people looked at us with a friendly respect. Especially around us Italians there had arisen an atmosphere of goodwill which warmed our hearts, making this long and nerve-racking wait in a foreign land far more bearable.

Flowers from the Imperial Park

One day, coming back from the hangar at Salizy, I found on the table of my splendid room in the Imperial Palace a tiny vase with some pretty little mauve flowers and a message: "Vera Makaroff offers you the first flowers from the Park."

I had no idea who Vera Makaroff might be, but later I learned that she was the wife of the director of the Imperial Palace, the superintendent of the Museum.

On my arrival at Gatschina, Makaroff had said to me: "Make yourself at home here. We want to do everything possible to make you comfortable." And in fact they spoiled me. As soon as the flowers faded, they were renewed, and I was surprised to find on my table a collection of Italian books, beautifully bound.

For hours and hours I remained alone, no one venturing to disturb me. Only from time to time an old servant entered, to ask if I wanted anything, if I would like some tea: a little woman with a wrinkled face, but with such sweet eyes and affectionate, almost maternal, manners. She took care of Titina, chatting away to her at length in her incomprehensible language.

Towards the end I fell ill and had to stay in bed for a day or two. How wretched it was to be so far from home, without any of my dear ones near me! The good woman understood and came to my room, trying to guess my needs, find out in advance what I wanted, since we could not understand each other. One evening when I was more than ever depressed by my solitude, she guessed how far my thoughts had strayed, and with a gesture full of kindness she took up my little girl's photo from the chest of drawers and looked at it affectionately. To be so moved by the kind action of an old Russian peasant-woman, one must know— as I did—that I should not see my dear ones for months, perhaps for years, perhaps never again.

As our departure approached, these good people did even more for me. With a piece of old carpet from the palace they made me a pair of warm boots that I used from Leningrad all the way to Teller; they packed food for the journey—not only essentials, but a number of delicacies which my companions consumed with great relish during our flight across the Barents Sea.

The night before we left, I think the Makaroffs hardly slept. Next morning, there they were at Salizy to say good-bye—and with them came the old servant, to caress Titina for the last time.

At the Academy of Sciences

My life was passed between Leningrad and Gatschina: at Gatschina to work, and at Leningrad for the various ceremonies at which I had to be present, or the lectures that I gave.

From the time of our arrival, a solemn reception had been in preparation for us at the Academy of Sciences. They asked me to fix the date, and I suggested April 21st.

On that day, in fact, the reception was held, presided over by the venerable Professor Karpinsky. The most authoritative representatives of Russian science were present. One could not imagine a more impressive recognition of the scientific value of our expedition.

There were speeches from Vice-President Stekloff, from Professor Schokalsky, President of the Russian Geographical Society, and from Professor Rynin, of the Institute of Aerial Communications in Leningrad. From the discourse of the last-named it was evident that, on account of the meteorological conditions we might encounter, the Russians were pessimistic about the result of our expedition. Rynin seemed particularly worried about snow-squalls.

I had a long talk with him, and with the other technicians and pilots. All, some more some less, thought it probable that ice or snow would form on the envelope of the dirigible, in such quantities as to bring us down. They cited the case of a kite-balloon which, getting into a cloud, had been driven down rapidly under the weight of ice, over an inch thick, that had formed in a few minutes on the steel cable that moored the aerostat to the ground.

Amundsen wants to Postpone the Polar Flight until June

Meanwhile, the days passed without any good news coming from Spitsbergen about the progress of the work there.

I was getting impatient. A week after our arrival in Russia, the airship was ready to start. All the work that I had ordered to be done was finished: the engines carefully overhauled; the only remaining reversing mechanism removed; one ring of the framework, which had broken in North France under the stress of the violent squalls, repaired and strengthened; the refuelling completed. Everything was ready. Besides this, weather conditions seemed favourable for crossing the Barents Sea.

On my arrival in Russia I had got into touch with Vallini, who was in charge of the work at King's Bay, and Rossi at Vadsö.

The latter gave me good news. The work was finished, and the fuel ready: we could land at Vadsö without anxiety. Meanwhile, Rossi, at my request, was sending me daily a report on the local wind conditions.

At Spitsbergen, however, the work had been delayed because the main group of Italians, with Vallini at their head, had only arrived on April 25th. I urged them on, telegraphing to Vallini not to trouble about the mooring-mast, but to concentrate on getting the hangar ready to receive us: I warned him that I intended to start at the earliest possible moment, not later than April 30th—so they must be ready for the dirigible.

But on April 22nd Vallini cabled me that a heavy blizzard had brought the work at King's Bay to a standstill. Probably it was due to the impression made by this blizzard, which had lasted for 2 whole days, that Amundsen telegraphed me, suggesting that we should put off the Polar flight until the early summer; when, according to him, there would be less danger of ice-formation on the airship.

I was completely taken aback by this telegram. The opinion that Amundsen was now, at the last moment, expressing about the advisability of attempting the flight in June instead of May, was altogether opposed to the convictions of the experts on Arctic weather conditions; and even to his own previous declarations. In fact, if we were to postpone the flight by a whole month it would, in my opinion, be equivalent to giving it up.

On the evening of April 29th I replied to Amundsen that, in in order to cross the Arctic from King's Bay to Point Barrow, we positively must have at least 286 cwt. of petrol; and that if we delayed the start until June, the higher temperature would make it impossible to load this amount.

In consequence, Amundsen changed his mind again, deciding to start early in May. Vallini had telegraphed that the hangar and mast would be ready from May 4th onwards.

Our Departure from Russia

We left on the morning of May 5th.

I had had 220 cwt. of petrol taken on board, with a proportionate quantity of oil, and about 300 gallons of water with glycerine. The crew was the same as on our arrival, with the addition of Alessandrini, who, cured of his pneumonia, had come by rail to Leningrad, and the replacement of Quattrini by the Russian journalist Lebedenko, who had asked to come with us as far as Spitsbergen.

At ground-level, when we were due to start, there was a rather strong north wind blowing, which higher up, at a thousand feet or over, reached from 30 to 36 ft. a second. This wind would delay our arrival at Vadsö by several hours. But weather conditions over the Barents Sea and Spitsbergen were fairly good; so I did not hesitate.

Around nine o'clock the ship was brought out of the hangar. Everything was ready. I said good-bye to the Russian authorities, and to the Italians who were on the field. At 9.30 I ordered the ropes to be let go. A cry broke out: *"Viva l'Italia!"* and the Russian soldiers cheered in their powerful voices, while their band struck up our national anthem.

The Last Sunset

Right from the beginning it was a difficult flight: sudden and violent changes of altitude, accompanied by pitching and rolling, which at times became really severe.

At 10.07 we saw the frozen sea, broken here and there by deep blue stretches of open water; at 10.22 we were above the port, and the ships gave us a friendly greeting with their sirens. Travelling up the Neva—blue, with white flecks of ice—in a few minutes we reached the city. At about 700 ft. we flew over the Winter Palace and along the Nevsky Prospect. In that shining May morning Leningrad, seen from above in the sunlight, through the clean cold air, looked very beautiful. All the more splendid by contrast with the wide, colourless, monotonous plain that followed, covered with snow. From time to time its whiteness was broken by dark blotches of forest.

At 11.45 we reached the ice-bound shore of Lake Ladoga: a vast, sunlit whiteness that quickly tired the eyes. At last, at 1.30 we saw ahead in the distance a long, blue curved streak, showing that the farther bank was in sight. Soon we passed over the azure band of water, pleasant to see after the continual dazzle of the ice. At 2.43 we had left the lake behind and were flying over an immense wooded plain, with stagnant water and snow: a desolate, infinitely sad landscape.

Over the lake the air had been calmer, but as soon as we left it the disturbances began again. Under the impulse of the violent squalls the airship proceeded by fits and starts; at times it seemed almost stationary, then it would go on with a sudden leap. At 4.45 we came to Petrosavodsk.

That night the sun set about ten o'clock, but between sunset and dawn the light never really failed. Inside the ship it was dark, but outside, in the glimmer coming from the north, one could see quite well. We were flying towards the light, turning our backs on the darkness. To us coming from the sunny South, it was a curious sensation to find the source of light in the North.

By one o'clock we saw the first signs of dawn, and at 2.26 the sun rose; nor did it set again for several days. Only when we reached Teller did we at last see it drop below the horizon: but the white nights—which in the long run tired us—lasted for us right up to June 21st, when we reached the Aleutian Islands. That day (we were at sea, between Nome and Seattle) I noted in my pocket diary: "At last, the first dark night!"

Despite the sun, it was cold on board. At an altitude of 2,200 ft., the outside temperature was 14° F., inside the ship it was 21·2° F. The Norwegians seemed to be suffering from it quite as much as we were, perhaps more. Some of them were stamping their feet to warm themselves.

At 4.40 a.m. the left-hand engine, which had been giving trouble for some minutes broke down. The crankshaft had snapped—damage too serious to be repaired in flight. I had the right-hand engine started up. At Vadsö there were reserve motors, but we would have wasted too much time in changing over; so I decided to push on, with one engine out of action, to Spitsbergen.

Soon afterwards, at five o'clock, we were passing over Kirkenes, where a factory siren hailed us, and at 5.30 we arrived at Vadsö. After the desolate Russian countryside, the prettily situated little village seemed much more attractive than it really was. I made a circuit up to the mooring-mast, built in the centre of a little island. The sirens of the ships in the port were blowing merrily. By 6.40 the *Norge* was hooked up to the mast. On top of the platform, in charge of the manœuvre, was Rossi: I waved to him. He was one of my trustiest collaborators. He had had the masts built in Italy, had then left for Norway and, in 20 days, with 3 Italian workmen, had set up the station at Vadsö.

Having given the orders for refuelling with petrol and gas, about 9.30 a.m. (Norwegian time), I went down to speak to the Governor, who was waiting at the foot of the mast and who took me back to his house, gay with Italian flags. They gave us lunch and we exchanged toasts. With this early morning meal we began to lose our sense of time, which afterwards deserted us altogether at King's Bay.

Across the Barents Sea

From Gatschina to Vadsö we had covered about 840 miles at an average speed of 40 m.p.h. There were still 780 miles to go— 410 to Bear Island, and about 370 from Bear Island to King's Bay.

At 3 p.m. (Central European time) I gave orders to cut the rope, and we left the mooring-mast, while Rossi called from the ground: "Good luck! *Arrivederci!*"

But we never did see each other again. A sad fate was in store for him: he was to die on board one of the airships which came out from Rome, 3 months later, to meet us in the Gulf of Naples.

From Vadsö we followed the coast as far as Vardö, which we reached at 4.12 p.m.; thence we struck out direct for Bear Island.

The crossing of the Barents Sea was much quieter than I had expected . . . almost disappointing.

Hardly had we left Vardö behind, when the sky began to cloud over: white horses tipped the grey sea, and we were immersed in rain. Then the rain changed to snow. Remembering the fears of the Russian aeronauts about damp snow, I sent Alessandrini to inspect the top of the ship. Everything was all right—the snow was not sticking. Later on we flew through snow two or three times more, but by now I was sure that there was nothing to fear from it.

Near the 74th parallel, at 9.15 p.m., we met the first mass of floating ice—a huge iceberg. Shortly afterwards, at 9.45, we passed to the right of Bear Island, noticing on our compass the magnetic disturbances that are characteristic of this locality.

About 2 hours later, at 11.58, another engine stopped: a cross-head had broken. For nearly 2 hours we had to fly with only one engine, until it had been repaired. Meanwhile the wind had dropped; the flight had become quiet and monotonous. After being on foot for 40 hours continuously, I felt the need of rest. My fatigue made the cold seem even worse. I tried to slip into the fur sleeping-bag that the officers of the Norwegian Navy had given me at Vadsö. It was warm, but shut up in it I seemed to be suffocating. Still, I managed to sleep for half an hour, until Lippi, who was at the helm, shouted: "Land ahoy!" I got up. Ahead, on the starboard bow, we could glimpse the mountains of Spitsbergen. Soon afterwards, at 2.20 a.m., we crossed over Sörkap.

Then the fog came down.

Fog had been one of the things that I most feared for our arrival at Spitsbergen, because it might have made it difficult to reconnoitre the ground, and perhaps impossible to land. Foreseeing this, I had had a number of little signal balloons prepared at King's Bay.

We all felt happy now that the goal was near: now we could not fail to reach King's Bay—or even the Pole. I forced the engines a little, to speed up the flight.

At 3.40 we passed Dunder Bay, at the tip of Torell Land; 50 minutes later we left to port Cape Linneus, at the mouth of the Icefjord. We had covered 120 miles at a speed of 54 m.p.h.

At this point the fog grew thicker. I gave orders to turn along the west coast of Prince Charles Land, avoiding the channel, so that we could circle over open sea if the fog swamped us; and while Riiser-Larsen, helped by Horgen, continued to attend to the route, I began to prepare for the landing.

For several hours I had been in communication with King's Bay. Vallini warned me that, as visibility was very bad, he had sent up the signal balloon. From time to time my brother transmitted weather reports.

Then the fog at King's Bay began to thin out.

At 5.51 we doubled Vogel Hoek, then flew over Quale Hoek, and finally, at quarter past six, we entered King's Bay. At the foot of the bay, on the white background of snow, there appeared a dark patch: the hangar. My heart gave a joyous leap.

At 6.40, after a brief circuit to reconnoitre the field, I threw down the rope. Amundsen, Ellsworth, the captain and sailors of the ship *Heimdal*, my brother and all the other Italians were there to receive us. A clamorous greeting rose from the ground. Then they pulled us down, and the *Norge* came gently to rest on the soft carpet of snow.

A few minutes later the airship was in the hangar, which had been decked out with the colours of Norway, Italy, and America. We disembarked, while the sailors from the *Heimdal* intoned their national anthem. An unforgettable moment: at last we had arrived at the gates of the Pole.

FROM KING'S BAY TO THE POLE

Life at King's Bay

WE had reached King's Bay on the morning of May 7th, a Friday; we left it at 9.50 a.m. on May 11th. Four days' halt in that great desert island, inhabited only by about 100 coal-miners and the staff of the Green Harbour weather station.

It was a strange life we led during this brief stay: with the cessation of all difference between day and night we had completely lost our sense of time; and the stimulation caused by the continual sunlight prevented us from sleeping regularly.

The group of little wooden huts where we Italians were lodging was a few hundred yards away from the hangar, near the frozen shore. The scenery was very attractive: around the small plain, with its covering of snow, rose a circle of beautiful mountains, their glaciers shining in the sunlight. Here and there one saw great bluish patches.

We found 14 Italians at King's Bay. Four of them—chosen from our cleverest experts among the workmen—had arrived on April 22nd. The others came 3 days later in the Norwegian navy ship *Heimdal*. Counting my brother Amedeo and the 9 who came in the *Norge*, we had a colony of 24 Italians altogether.

Our Meeting with Byrd

At King's Bay we met Byrd, who was then a lieutenant in the American Navy. When we arrived, Richard Evelyn Byrd had already been there for some time, with the American ship *Chantier* and his Fokker, preparing to fly to the Pole. Amundsen was not worried about it, thinking that the thick snow would delay him for quite a while. The same opinion was expressed by Riiser-Larsen, who said that with the skis he was using the machine would never take off. But in fact—contrary to these predictions—during the night of May 8th-9th, Byrd and his co-pilot Bennett unexpectedly started, returning in the afternoon of the same day after a flight of 15½ hours. He was warmly welcomed by the Italians and Norwegians, but as he had come back earlier than was expected, the photographers missed his arrival. Next day they made up for it, repeating the scene of his landing with an exchange of embraces between Byrd, Amundsen and Ellsworth—to the amusement of the watching Italians.

I myself met Byrd the day after, when he invited me—with Amundsen, Ellsworth and Riiser-Larsen—to dine on board his ship. I liked him very much: a pleasant, intelligent young man. He presented our expedition with a little compass, which he had had with him during his own flight.

He was very friendly. He told me that he had left before us, so that if he had had a forced landing we would be able to search for him. There was no doubt of that: if it had been necessary, we would have gone to his help. In exchange, the gallant American—who stayed on at King's Bay after we left—generously offered to go and look for us, in the days when the world was without news of us.

Byrd and Bennett's flight raised the question whether they really had reached the Pole. From a recent study published by Professor G. H. Liljequist, of the University of Uppsala,[1] it appears that, given the performance figures of the aeroplane and the prevalent weather conditions, they could not have travelled so far in the time.

This was Byrd's first and last flight in the Arctic regions. A year or two later he left for the Antarctic.

The Fuel Problem

There was a good deal of work to be done, in order to prepare the airship for the Polar flight. The port engine, as I have said, had been damaged beyond repair when the crankshaft broke as we were approaching Vadsö. It had to be dismounted, a new one put in its place and tested. Then we had to carry out a careful

[1] *Interavia*, Vol. XV, No. 5/1960, p. 589.

overhaul of the stabilizing surfaces, which had suffered considerably in our flights over Russia, particularly between Lake Ladoga and Lake Onega. There was a certain amount of damage to the lower keel which had to be repaired, and the torn rudder must be replaced. And since we had decided to make the crossing without ballast, the 4 water tanks mounted on the framework had to be substituted by an equivalent quantity of petrol. Besides this, it was important to make a careful examination of the ship and eliminate everything that was not absolutely necessary. We also had to inspect the structure minutely, load up with petrol and oil, prepare the anti-freeze mixture for the engine-cooling system, and complete our equipment with the materials that I had reckoned necessary only for the Polar crossing; besides, of course, the gear and provisions needed in case of a forced landing on the ice, which the Norwegians had prepared.

Finally, it was essential to procure a very high lift at the moment of take-off, so that we might have the maximum possible supply of petrol.

For months past petrol had been my major preoccupation: I was reckoning on a minimum of 65 hours' flying time, but secretly I aspired to more. With 130 cwt. of petrol we would be able to hold our own against a head-wind of 18 to 24 m.p.h.; but what guarantee was there that we would not meet a still stronger wind, or that fog would not make us stray off course, as had happened already in Europe? Nor could we exclude the possibility of finding extensive chains of mountains in the unexplored regions, which would force us to make a lengthy detour.

Atmospheric conditions (high pressure with a relatively low temperature) were favourable for obtaining a good lift. In addition, I had decided to start at the coldest hour of night. As for the hydrogen in the airship, it was quite pure; so that, all things considered, it was reasonable to hope that, at the moment of taking off, we would attain and possibly even surpass 210 cwt. of useful load.

On the basis of these calculations I had 140 cwt. of petrol and $7\frac{1}{2}$ cwt. of oil on board.

The Provisions

The reserve provisions, which we were to use in case of a forced landing, had been provided by the Aeroclub of Norway. They consisted of pemmican, chocolate, biscuits, dried milk, and malted milk tablets. In all, 834 lb. Allowing a daily ration of 1 lb. 10 oz. per man, they would have lasted about a month.

Those were, so to speak, our *actual* provisions. But in case we had had to remain several months in the Polar regions, our principal resource would have been two rifles and a liberal supply of cartridges. For that, however, Providence would have had to be sufficiently merciful to bring us down somewhere where Wisting, who was the hunter of the expedition, would have been able to use his skill.

Of course I had also thought of drinking water, but at the last moment—I don't know how—it was forgotten. I realized it when we were already several hours out from Spitsbergen. It was an unpleasant discovery, but I comforted myself with the thought that we had plenty of coffee and tea—and that in any case the Norwegians were not used to drinking water. I jealously guarded the gallon or so that Cecioni had brought—but this water froze and could not be used, except for a small quantity that I had put in a thermos flask. Cecioni and the engine mechanics quenched their thirst with oranges and lemons, although these too were half frozen.

We had on board several pounds of ground coffee, which we used at Teller, making it in a little "Neapolitan" percolator—the only kitchen utensil which had the honour of crossing the Arctic Ocean.

Behounek

I was in the hangar the day before we left, when I saw coming towards me a good-looking fair young man, tall and stout, with a well-rounded face and body. My brother, who was with him, explained that Dr. Behounek, who had come to King's Bay to make some studies of atmospheric electricity on his own account, wanted to install in the control cabin of the *Norge* an apparatus to measure the electrical conductivity of the atmosphere.

"But who would take the measurements during the flight?" I asked.

"I have made arrangements with Dr. Malmgren," replied Behounek.

I willingly agreed, called some workmen, and told them what had to be done.

Whilst they were carrying out the work, I noticed that Behounek did not leave the hangar for a single moment. That same night, when everything was ready for the start and other people had all gone to sleep, he was still there, walking up and down the hangar, to keep a loving eye on his measuring apparatus. At the end of the expedition he published, jointly with Malmgren, a note giving the results of the measurements taken during the Polar flight.

The Passengers and Crew

In our agreement with the Aeroclub of Norway it had been stipulated, at my request, that not more than 16 people should take part in the Polar flight. This was a maximum, but I reserved to myself the right to reduce the number to 15, eliminating one of the Norwegians, if at the moment of take-off I found it necessary. In this case, if I had had a free choice, I would have done without the journalist Ramm, who was no use whatever on board; but the Aeroclub declared that his participation was absolutely necessary, so as to fulfil their contracts with the Press. Therefore, I had selected first Omdal, who could easily be replaced by one of the Italian engine mechanics, and then the meteorologist Malmgren.

Nineteen of us had flown to King's Bay; but in order to take Amundsen and Ellsworth on board, 5 would have to be eliminated, to bring the number down to 16. These were: Gustave Amundsen, the explorer's nephew; the chief helmsman Lippi, the workman Bellocchi, and, as had already been settled, the journalists Tomaselli and Lebedenko. But besides the 5 I have mentioned, there was a sixth man out of the 19 who arrived at

King's Bay, who did not take part in the Polar flight: the wireless operator Olomkin. His place was taken by a Norwegian called Storm-Johnsen.

Here is the list of the men aboard the *Norge* during the crossing of the Arctic Ocean:

Roald AMUNDSEN.
Lincoln ELLSWORTH.
Umberto NOBILE, Commander of the Airship.
Hjalmar RIISER-LARSEN, First Navigating Officer.
Emil HORGEN, Second Navigating Officer.
Birger GOTTWALDT, in charge of the wireless.
Oscar WISTING, helmsman at the elevator wheel.
Finn MALMGREN, meteorologist.
Natale CECIONI, Chief engine mechanic.
Ettore ARDUINO, Assistant Chief engine mechanic.
Attilio CARATTI, engine mechanic.
Vincenzo POMELLA, engine mechanic.
Oscar OMDAL, engine mechanic.
Renato ALESSANDRINI, rigger and helmsman.
Frithjof STORM-JOHNSEN, wireless operator.
Fredrik RAMM, journalist.

Amundsen himself describes his position on board the *Norge*, in his book of memoirs, as follows: "On board, naturally, I had the easiest task of all. The others were busy keeping the airship going, and guiding it to its goal. My function was simply that of an explorer, who was looking at the ground below, studying its geographical character, and watching, particularly, to see if there appeared any signs of a possible Arctic continent."

Apart from Amundsen, Ellsworth and the journalist, who had nothing to do with running the airship, the flight was carried through by 12 men (6 Italians, 5 Norwegians, and 1 Swede), not counting the wireless operator, who remained unoccupied once we had crossed the Pole, owing to the impossibility of receiving or sending any signals.

The Start for the Pole

On the evening of Monday, May 10th, after the Italian workmen had been hard at it all day, the *Norge* was ready to leave. The equipment, the petrol, oil and provisions—everything was on board. The only thing lacking was the anti-freeze mixture in the engine radiators. I decided to start at one or two in the morning.

However, when I left the hangar about 10 p.m. to go to my lodgings and pack up my things, I found that a rather strong, squally wind had arisen, blowing diagonally across the mouth of the hangar. Later on it grew even stronger, so that towards eleven o'clock I decided to put off the start for several hours, in the hope that the wind would drop. I told Amundsen about it, and sent our men off to sleep. An hour or two later, about one o'clock, Malmgren came to tell me that the wind was less fierce. I went out into the cold night: in fact, it was much calmer. So I returned to the hangar to give orders and have the engine mechanics roused. Around three o'clock they came along, and as the weather was steadily improving, I ordered Cecioni to pour the anti-freeze mixture of water and glycerine into the radiators, and to test the engines; and sent Omdal to tell Amundsen that we would be ready to leave at five, so we should need the ground crew by four o'clock.

But four and five went by without anyone turning up. Meanwhile, the temperature went on rising, and with it the pressure in the gas-chambers, so that three times I had to open the valves. Since the loss of gas diminished our lift, I had reluctantly to unload 4 cwt. of petrol.

I was tired. It had been a busy day: the sleepless night in the cold hangar and the impatient waiting had worn me out. Towards six o'clock I could stand it no longer. I threw myself down on the floor of the control cabin. Someone passing by covered me with a rug, so that I should not feel the cold. . . . Later, about seven, when I woke up and went out to have a look, I found that the wind had risen again and was still blowing across the hangar.

Soon after seven the ground crew began to arrive but it was considerably later when Amundsen, Ellsworth, Riiser-Larsen and the other Norwegians turned up with their luggage and climbed on board. I pointed out to them that now the manœuvre of bringing the ship out of the hangar had become risky, but that I would try to do it between one gust and another. At last there came a moment when the wind shifted its direction, blowing more or less along the axis of the hangar. Taking advantage of a momentary lull, I ordered the manœuvre. There were minutes of suspense, especially when the fins almost grazed the hangar walls—a shock then would have ruined the whole expedition. At last I breathed again. The *Norge* was in the open: now our take-off was assured.

I had the ship brought out on to the snowfield and "weighed" it. To obtain the correct balance I had some tins of petrol and 2 bags of sand (altogether, less than 1½ cwt.) put aboard—and that was all the ballast I dared take, for a journey that was to last 3 days. I had now 137 cwt. of petrol. The engines were started up. I embraced my brother, said good-bye to Tomaselli and all the Italian officers and workmen who had helped so enthusiastically to prepare this final flight. Then, climbing on board, I gave the order to let go the ropes. It was 9.50 a.m.

The ship rose slowly, while they cheered us from the ground. When we were at 100 ft., I had the two engines speeded up to 1,000 r.p.m. and we climbed rapidly to 1,200 ft. I had told the navigating officers to keep as far as possible from the mountains as we left the bay. The weather was magnificent, the sky cloudless. The impressive Spitsbergen peaks glittered snow-white in the sunshine. I felt deeply happy: the malaise and weariness that had oppressed me on the previous evening and during the night had vanished as if by magic. How light I felt! A few hours previously I had been shivering with cold; now I would have liked to take off my furs.

We flew towards the mouth of the bay. The last stage of our journey had finally started. Our lovely ship was sailing along at nearly 50 miles an hour towards the Pole—and beyond the Pole, into the Unknown.

Every Man at his Post

On board, each of the 12 men responsible for running the ship had taken up the post assigned to him: Riiser-Larsen navigating, Wisting at the elevator, Horgen at the rudder; inside the keel Cecioni was supervising the engines and, helped by Arduino, regulating the distribution of fuel; Caratti was in the left-hand engine-boat, Pomella in the centre, Arduino and Omdal taking turns in the right. The wireless operator Johnsen had installed himself in the cabin, assisted and directed by Gottwaldt, who was himself concentrating on the radiogoniometry. Malmgren was attending to the plotting of the meteorological data which came in over the wireless from time to time; Alessandrini was doing a bit of everything: after having pulled in the mooring-ropes and made his usual careful inspection of the interior of the airship from bow to stern, he alternated between the control cabin—where he often relieved Horgen at the helm—and the inside of the hull, to check up and do any work that I asked him. Now and again he made a trip to ascertain that ice was not forming on the outside of the ship, and that the valves were properly closed. This was not a pleasant task, as he had to go through a small window in the bow of the ship, climb up a steep steel ladder on the outside, and, in an icy wind blowing nearly 50 miles an hour, crawl along the top of the ship, from bow to stern, for a length of 70 to 80 yds., clinging with one hand to the guide-rope that had been fixed there. But Alessandrini never refused, and each time he came back calm and satisfied, to tell me the result: "All's well!" Just once he reported that it had been impossible to check the valves, because the layer of ice that had formed on the top of the dirigible was too slippery.

During the flight between Spitsbergen and Point Barrow, Riiser-Larsen was indefatigable, spending his time between plotting the speed and drift, measuring the height of the sun and checking the compasses, allowing himself only a few hours of sleep. It was certainly largely owing to him that we were able to keep so closely to our chosen route.

The magnetic compasses, as we had expected, worked well all

the time. The solar compass was a good check, enabling us to ascertain that the others were in order; so that, during the long periods when the sun was invisible, and when between the Pole and Alaska the solar compass froze up, we could continue to fly, without difficulty, by the magnetic compass alone.

On board, of course, we were well stocked with navigational charts for all the lands and seas surrounding the Arctic ice-cap; it had been quite easy to obtain these. But for Alaska I had only been able to get, through the Geodetic Institute for the Coasts of the United States, a map of the northern coasts with a scale of 1:1,600,000—the only one existing, but unfortunately incomplete, especially in the orographic part that interested me most.

This inadequacy of the Alaska chart—and especially the scanty information about the heights of the mountains between Point Barrow and Nome—had its consequences when we were caught by fog in the Bering Straits.

There were not enough of us to draw up a regular rota of duties. The rudder was manned alternately by Horgen, Alessandrini, and—during the second day—Malmgren, whose meteorological work had been interrupted by the silence of the radio. Wisting, at the elevator, was tireless; and when the wireless packed up, Gottwaldt was often able to replace him, allowing him at last to rest a little. At critical moments, I stood beside them, and more than once my timely intervention served to prevent a catastrophe. During the third day, when wind, fog and the uneven ground made flying very dangerous, I had to take over the elevator wheel for long spells.

Except for the wireless operator Johnsen, who, after leaving the Pole, was able to rest to his heart's content, the other members of the expedition had very little sleep. In the last day, fatigue was at its height, and it was very difficult to keep alert: I remember several times catching the man at the elevator wheel with his eyes closed. Riiser-Larsen later described how he thought he saw a squadron of cavalry, where there was nothing but the empty ice. It was a dramatic situation indeed to find ourselves tired out, on the very day when we needed all our wits about us to bring the airship safely through the storm.

Whenever sleep was possible, any spot would suffice for it. If I went into the hull, I was often faced by the problem of having to climb over a sleeping man. Amundsen's favourite place was the end of the control cabin, near where Ramm had installed himself.

The inside of the ship was truly picturesque: kitbags, outer clothes, gear, spare parts for the engines, provisions, tents, skis, a spare propeller, a sledge: an enormous conglomeration of materials dispersed here and there in apparent disorder on the various metallic sections, from stem to stern. But the air was clean, cool and fresh, by contrast with the control cabin, where ten people living on top of one another had produced an atmosphere of littered stuffiness.

The Pack-ice

When we left King's Bay we were sure that we should easily reach the Pole.

We had 770 miles to travel, and the weather conditions were such that it seemed improbable they would suddenly change during the 16 hours that it would take us to cover this distance at our normal cruising speed.

But what would happen beyond the Pole, in the unexplored zone, nobody could say. What the weather would be like, whether or no we should find the mountain range which Peary thought he had glimpsed, where, when and how we should land, and what would happen to us after the landing: all these were questions which could only be answered by guesswork. At bottom, this very challenge to the unknown constituted the fascination of our enterprise.

We had left King's Bay at 8.50 a.m. (G.M.T.). In a few minutes we had reached a height of 1,350 ft. and stabilized our speed at 48 m.p.h., travelling with the port and centre engines running at 1,200 r.p.m. As the wind created by our own thrust began to chill the gas, the ship rather suddenly became heavy, so that to maintain altitude I had to give it dynamic lift, raising the nose by 3 to 6 degrees.

We cleared the ice-strewn bay, and half an hour later, when we had crossed Cape Mitre, we turned northwards, flying along the

coast of Haakon VII Land, over a sea sprinkled rather sparsely
with small ice-floes. The sky was still blue, but ahead of us cloud
was forming. In the distance, on the horizon, there appeared a
vague, whitish streak—the margin of the pack-ice.

Shortly afterwards, towards ten o'clock, the sky became
covered by a thin veil of cloud, through which we dimly
glimpsed the sun. The sea was still open, but in front of us the
line of the pack-ice grew steadily clearer. The white crests
of Spitsbergen lay behind us to starboard. We were passing
over Dane Island, whence Andrée had started out 29 years
before, on the flight from which he did not return.

Here the sky cleared again to blue. At 10.35 we crossed
Amsterdam Island. Leaving behind us Haakon VII Land, a few
minutes later we came to the edge of the pack. It was 10.44.

Before us the sunlit icy plain stretched as far as eye could see,
under a pure blue sky. Measuring with a stop-watch the speed of
our shadow upon the ice, I obtained a result of $6\frac{1}{2}$ seconds,
corresponding to a ground-speed of $33\frac{1}{2}$ m.p.h. That meant a
fairly strong head-wind, characteristic of the margin of the pack.
I decided to come lower, in the hope of making more headway,
and as the airship was still heavy, it sufficed to bring it on to a
level keel, for us to lose height at the rate of nearly 4 ft. to the
second. At 600 ft., a new speed-measurement showed that we had
gained $9\frac{1}{2}$ m.p.h. We continued for about an hour at this height.

At this low altitude we could see many details of the frozen sea.
We caught sight of a white fox. A little farther on there were the
first traces of bears: two lines drawn close together—the imprints
of their paws. We saw the first channel, then occasional irregularly
shaped pools, in which glimmered some "white fish"—the last
living creatures we met on our journey. Beyond this the pools
disappeared and the ice once more became compact.

At 11.52 our speed at 600 ft. was still 43 m.p.h. It was possible
that the wind higher up had changed direction, so I climbed to
3,650 ft., at which height the Goertz apparatus indicated a
ground-speed of $51\frac{1}{2}$ m.p.h. With minor variations we maintained this altitude for about 8 hours.

The Lifeless Desert

At 3.30 p.m. we once more saw traces of Polar bears on the pack, and these were the last. We were just beyond the 83rd parallel, and at this point the Arctic desert appeared in all its desolation. Every living shape, every trace of life, was entirely absent.

From time to time the monotony of the icy plain was broken by little serpentine channels, in which, as we drew nearer to the Pole, the water more often than not was frozen: thin ice, revealed by its grey, slightly bluish colour.

The flight went on monotonously, calmly, without anything particular happening. The ship was still from 800 to 1,000 lb. heavy, but everything in it was working smoothly. Our morale on board was excellent. Everyone was excited at the thought that in a few hours we would reach the Pole. The sunlight on the vast ice-field gave it a semblance of life, so that no one on board felt that we were flying over a desert, no one was oppressed by that enormous desolation. Why, then—was it as simple and easy as this to go to the Pole?

Cecioni, when he came to the cabin to tell me that his engines were running well, remarked jubilantly: "So this is the terrible Pole!" "Just wait!" I replied, "perhaps you are crowing too early!"

The Ice-formation

And in fact it was too early, for just about that time our troubles began.

At 6.45 p.m. the port engine suddenly stopped. When we investigated, we found that the fuel lead of the carburettor had been blocked by a piece of ice about 8 in. long, which had formed in a bend. This curious phenomenon, probably due to water-vapour in the jackets, happened once again shortly before we reached the Pole.

The weather was changing. At 9.42 p.m. the sky was almost entirely covered. Half an hour later, at 88° of latitude, it cleared, but only for a while. Here the channels in the pack, more and more numerous, struck me by their regularity. At 10.15 we encountered snow, and a few minutes later a thick fog.

This fog caused the first ice-formation. In a few minutes all the outside metal parts of the ship were covered. Ice also formed on the celluloid windows, blocking our vision, and on the exterior of the control cabin. I rose at once to 2,000 ft., but this did not suffice to avert the peril. Ice continued to form, forcing us to climb to nearly 3,000 ft., above the fog, where the phenomenon ceased.

Meanwhile, we were steadily approaching the Pole. At 10.15 p.m. (G.M.T.)—midnight on the meridian where we were flying—we measured the height of the sun to determine our latitude: we were approximately at 88° 30'. In an hour or two we would reach our goal.

The Flags over the Pole

Towards 10.30 the snow, which had been very thick for an hour and ten minutes, grew somewhat thinner, so that we caught glimpses of the pack. Soon afterwards it ceased altogether.

The sky had again clouded over, and the landscape all of a sudden looked sad and solemn. There is nothing better than sunshine to give life and sparkle even to inanimate things, but its absence made us realize the mortal stillness that brooded over all. Upon the immense frozen plain scattered patches of fog showed up as drab spots. The whole atmosphere had acquired a pearly grey shade. Our measurements at 11.45 gave the following results: drift, 0; speed, $42\frac{1}{2}$ m.p.h.; outside temperature 14·00° F., inside temperature, 24·8° F.; altitude, 2,350 ft. We were gradually losing height, almost without realizing it, as if the ground were slowly drawing us down. We were at 89 degrees. An hour later, at 50 minutes past midnight on May 12th, I definitely started to descend. By one o'clock we were at 1,000 ft., and a few minutes later at 750. Now we were very near the Pole. Riiser-Larsen at a porthole, bent over the sextant in his hands, was ready to snatch any instant when the sun peeped out from the clouds.

As we approached, the excitement on board went on growing. Nobody spoke, but one could read the happy impatience in their

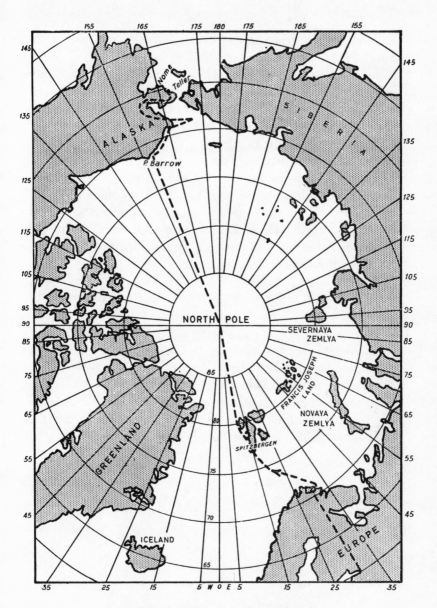

The *Norge*'s Flight across the North Pole

faces. I called Alessandrini: "Get the flag ready!" The little Norwegian and American flags, fixed like pennants to their staves, had been kept ready in the control cabin since the beginning of the flight; but ours was too big for that. We had to take it out of its casket, unfold it, and fasten it to the staff which my officers had prepared at King's Bay. Alessandrini went, and as he took a long time fixing it with loving care, I urged him impatiently: "Hurry up!" We were almost there.

At last he brought it to my side.

At 1.30 a.m. the height of the sun, shining from time to time among the clouds, told us that we were at the Pole. We came down lower still, to something like 600 ft.: wishing to get as close as possible to the surface of the limitless frozen sea, I had the engines slowed down. Their rhythm died away, so that the silence of the desert became more apparent. In that silence we solemnly dropped the flags.

The log-book notes only: "May 12, 1926, 1.30 a.m."—and then, in large, firm handwriting: "PLANTED THE ITALIAN FLAG AT THE POLE."

My comrades watched the stirring scene. One of them, Alessandrini, came to me a few minutes later in the cabin, radiant, saying: "Ours was the most beautiful!"

When the rite was finished, with my heart full of joy and pride I ordered the engine mechanic to speed up again, while we headed the ship towards the coast of Alaska. So we passed on into the unknown region beyond the Pole.

IN THE UNEXPLORED ZONE

The Fog, and the First Damage by Icing

AT the Pole the landscape had taken on a characteristic aspect. Not that there was any change in the icy plain, which was still monotonously the same; but the grey sky, broken here and there on the horizon by yellowish gleams, accentuated its desolation, while the wan light showed up the irregularities of the pack.

In this atmosphere we went on flying for several hours, maintaining an altitude of between 1,800 and 2,400 ft. Towards 8 a.m. we went lower. At 8.30 the altimeter indicated 780 ft., and I noted in the log: "The sky has been blue for some hours. The airship is almost in equilibrium." But half an hour later, at nine o'clock, when we were approximately at 85° of latitude, the fog returned, and this time it remained thick until we reached 82° 40'. In this fog, ice projectiles began to be flung against the sides of the ship.

The first damage caused by them took place at 1.40 p.m., when we were approximately on the 82nd parallel, about 540 miles from the Pole. Suddenly we heard a sinister noise, like an explosion. Suspecting that one of the blades of the wireless rotor had snapped, I had it stopped. In any case, it was revolving quite uselessly, since the wireless had not worked for several hours. But the rotor was intact. Soon they came to tell me that the covering of the metal framework of the ship had been holed by a piece of ice flung from a propeller—that of the starboard engine, which was being run by Arduino. I had this stopped, to make sure that ice had not formed on the airscrew . . . there was some, but not much.

At 2.10 p.m. I wrote in the log: "Gottwaldt came to show me the sleeve of ice that has formed round the radio antenna."

My subsequent notes seem to have been made in a great hurry. Preoccupied as I was with making arrangements to reduce the peril to a minimum, I barely had time to scribble in haste: "I have sent Alessandrini to repair the rent. Ice has formed on all the metal parts, chiefly on the front surfaces which are the most exposed to the wind. About 3 mm. on the solar compass."

A little later, at 3.37 p.m. I noted: "The airship seems to be in static equilibrium. We have been flying for 30 hours and have consumed about $2\frac{1}{2}$ tons of petrol and oil; yet I have not once drawn off gas!"

That meant that we were very heavy, and no doubt the weight was largely due to the ice that had formed; but now that we were clear of the fog, there was no fear that it might increase to the point of forcing us down. On the other hand, I was really worried by the pieces of ice which, flung off from the airscrews as if from a sling, kept violently striking against the hull of the ship. One of them might pierce the walls of the gas-chamber and cause an irreparable loss of hydrogen. But luckily up till now it had only been the air-chamber that was holed. In fact, the log continued: "Alessandrini reported that the ice has torn the air-chamber in several places, on the starboard side, corresponding with the engine-boat. I told him to go and see if it could be mended."

But Alessandrini came back and told me that he had not been able to carry out the repairs.

A Few Hours of Truce

There followed a few hours of relative calm. From time to time that sinister crack which had accompanied the lacerations was repeated, but without any consequences. By this time, I had a fairly clear idea of what caused it: under the pressure of the wind, the ice that had been forming on various parts of the ship was breaking away in pieces, and some of these struck the moving airscrews, producing this very characteristic sound. My greatest fear was that the airscrews might splinter, and that the splinters might strike the envelope and seriously damage it. This danger applied more particularly to the two lateral propellers, since the centre one was better sheltered from the falling ice. That was why, later on, I decided to keep all three engines running, the central one at the normal number of revolutions, the two side ones at reduced speed, so as to diminish the violence of the projectiles.

Between the 80th and 79th degrees, the fog opened out, giving us a glimpse of the frozen sea. We were flying at 2,400 ft. Taking advantage of the break in the fog, we measured the drift: 13° to the left. It seemed that the wind had changed direction and freshened.

In this brief respite I had time to look around. We had been in the air for $32\frac{1}{2}$ hours. The cabin was horribly dirty. The dozens of thermos flasks heaped on the floor, near the little cupboard where we kept the charts and navigation books, presented a particularly sad spectacle: some of them empty, others overturned, others broken. Coffee and tea had been spilt everywhere, and all over the place were the remains of food. In the midst of all this mess there stuck out picturesquely Amundsen's enormous feet, with his grass-stuffed shoes, his diver's gaiters and red and white gloves.

At 6.30 p.m. we had reached the 79th parallel, and I wrote in the log: "Across the rare gaps in the fog we can glimpse the sea-ice."

Therefore there was still frozen sea below us. Even if we could not say definitely that there were no islands between 85° 5′ and 82° 40′, when we had quite lost sight of the ground; still, we could conclude that between the Pole and the northern coast of Alaska there was no such extensive land or archipelago as Harris had declared probably existed. We had seen not a trace of land along our course, lying between the meridians 166° and 157° 30′ W. of Greenwich. We could therefore definitely affirm that a sea occupies these regions—a sea which we were the first men in the world to cross: the Arctic Ocean.

Scenery of the Arctic Ocean: New Anxieties

At 9.15 p.m. the rising fog compelled us to climb to 3,500 ft., and we maintained this height, or slightly less, for an hour, when the fog lowered and we were able to descend to 2,000 ft. But at 15 minutes past midnight on May 13, all of a sudden it rose and swamped us—thick fog mingled with snow. We again climbed rapidly to something over 3,000 ft., remaining at this altitude until after nearly an hour the fog seemed to be growing thinner. At 1.45 a.m., when we were approximately at 74° 16', I noted in the log: "We have come down to 900 ft. and can see the frozen ocean: it looks much rougher than what we have seen between Spitsbergen and the Pole. I can now understand why no one has been able to travel over it with sledges."

Meanwhile, ice was forming again. It was continually striking the sides of the ship, and now and then we heard the noises like little explosions caused by the ice that, detaching itself from the various parts of the airship, fell into the propellers. Each time it gave us a moment of acute suspense: had any fresh damage been done? And if so, where? At this time, 2.35, I find the note: "*Gualdrappa!*" (This is our name for the material covering the metal framework of the airship, which until now had been the principal target for the projectiles.) But this time it was unharmed.

Later, two words have been written: "*Sirena*" and "*Trombe.*" The wind, in fact, was whistling through the joints of the cabin portholes, against every projecting part of the ship and against its covering, producing a noise that at times was like a trumpet, at others like a factory siren. The illusion was so perfect that Alessandrini, forgetting in what part of the world we were, exclaimed: "Commander, there's a factory below us!"

Once more I quote, literally, from the log my impressions, just as they were hurriedly and concisely scribbled down, at the moment I experienced them:

"Magnificent scenery—the Polar regions, just as I imagined them. The surface of the limitless sea of ice—all white—seems veiled in a transparent whitish mist. Here and there the whiteness is streaked with blue—that tenuous shade of blue, so characteristic of the ice."

The vast expanse of frozen sea, with its shadows, dark patches, embroidery of blue, was truly fascinating. From time to time there appeared long serpentine channels, dark grey in colour; and once, what looked like a wide black river, its banks formed by layer on layer of blue-sprinkled ice.

The airship itself had toned into the Polar landscape, now that ice had formed on almost all its metal parts—sometimes half an inch thick or more. The duralumin engine-boats looked lovely picked out with white along the radiator connections, the gangways, the suspension cables. The solar compass, the drift-meter, the tachometer, the metal rings of the mooring-ropes—all were adorned with ice. It was as though the ship had been festively decorated, now that the Polar crossing was on the point of being successfully achieved.

My musings were brusquely interrupted by a sharp noise coming from inside the ship. I went to look. A piece of ice flung off the starboard airscrew had ripped the covering for over a yard. Cecioni started to mend it. "The emaillite is almost finished," he told me. Emaillite was the liquid we used to stick the stuff which covered the hull. We had taken a good supply of it, but there had been so many gashes to repair! If this went on, we would be in serious trouble.

Land

The next entry in the log reads: "4.30 a.m. Height, 240;[1] outside temperature, −10·5° C.[2] The airship seems heavy. We must be near land by now."

All of us were eagerly hoping to catch sight of the coast. When at last, at 6.45 a.m., the navigating officer who was scanning the horizon cried: "Land ahead to starboard!" it was a moment of joyful excitement.

I leaned out of the cabin. The keen, cold wind that whipped my face was refreshing. Looking ahead, I saw in the distance on the right a line of pearl-grey hills. Half an hour later, at 7.15 we were crossing the strip of open water that divides the pack from the land-ice; and at last, at 7.35, we reached the flat, uniform coast. The only thing that showed us we were now over land was the different look of the ice—smooth and compact, so unlike the sea-ice. From it there emerged bands of rock, with a curious black and white effect. To my excited imagination they looked like dark sphinxes, separated one from another by short tracts of snow.

[1] 750 ft. (approx.).   [2] 13° F.

I gave orders to turn right and follow the coast, to make sure where we were; but the icy, desert shore, with no outstanding characteristics, was not recognizable. Therefore we would have to fly along it until we came to one of the tiny villages scattered along the coast between the river Colville and Cape Lisburne, which at that time housed altogether a population of 640 Eskimos and 15 or 20 white men.

At 8.20 we came across the first Eskimos. We were flying low, between 600 and 750 ft. from the ground, and could see them distinctly. There were 5 or 6 of them. Clothed in their *parkas*, with arms dangling and heads in air, they were gaping up at us in evident astonishment. I wonder what they thought of us, what idea they had of the flying monster, with its humming engines, that passed over their heads, coming from the hostile and in-accessible North? A member of Wilkins' expedition, with whom I travelled some weeks later from Nome to Seattle, told me that the old Eskimos of Point Barrow, who saw us passing in the distance, thought we were the Devil. An idea not very flattering for us—but certainly less dangerous than that of an Eskimo child next day at Teller—the son of a seal-hunter—who, when he saw us arrive, ran to his father, calling him to shoot us down. And as the man hesitated to take his rifle, he insisted impatiently: "Daddy, why don't you shoot?" The good lad was convinced that our ship was a gigantic flying seal!

Other people thought that we were a large whale.

A few minutes later, at 8.40, we identified Wainwright. A reindeer farm, a group of huts, a little red-roofed building which was the State school, a few Eskimos. We had therefore struck the Alaskan coast about 6 miles S. of the 71st parallel.

OVER THE BERING STRAITS

The Last Notes in the Log

HAVING left behind us Wainwright, a village of a hundred Eskimos, we continued along the coast towards Icy Cape, to find Hope Point and thence strike direct towards Nome, crossing Kotzbue Bay and the hills of the Seward Peninsula.

The landscape was changing. It had lost the magnificence and grandiose scale of the Polar scenery, and looked merely colourless and desolate. The log at 10.15 a.m. notes: "Height 300 metres.[1] It has been raining for some time, and the dirigible has got heavier. Flying calmly over a dull region: the sky is grey, the sea white with ice, not a single channel breaking it up." And a little later, with a note of disquiet: "I have been thinking for a long time about the fate of our beautiful airship! What shall we do with it at Nome?" An anguished inquiry to which I did not yet know the answer.

The log continues: "11 o'clock. The airship is rather light. Up till now all three engines have been running. I shall remember this last part of the journey—these strange, flat, white Alaskan coasts, with their black rocks. An odd contrast of black and white."

As a matter of fact, though they looked to me like rocks, they were probably small sandbanks running parallel to the ice-bound coast, enclosing a series of long, narrow lagoons, also frozen.

We were flying quickly, for a strong NE. wind had arisen. The weather was rapidly becoming bad; without being aware of it, we were approaching the centre of a deep depression over the Bering Straits.

Towards 12.30 we were probably about 35 miles east of Cape

[1] 900 ft. (approx.).

Lisburne. The log reads: "Since 1.15 p.m., thick fog. I have slowed down the engines and climbed to 1,200 metres.[1] We are flying with one engine at 1,000 r.p.m., the other two throttled to their minimum. Visibility very bad. I slow down again. Soon afterwards——"

Here my notes abruptly stop.

I don't remember what incident compelled me to break off the sentence I had begun; but certainly from that moment there began for me hours of spasmodic attention. Having several times to take over the elevator wheel myself, I had no longer a moment for writing notes.

The emergencies of this last day of flight found the crew already tired from their hard work and lack of sleep during the two previous days. In the last 76 hours I had had no more than an hour or two of rest; and during the Polar crossing, the fog, the ice projectiles and the damage they caused, had made my long vigil even more trying.

Having now reached the coast of Alaska, and being less worried about the dangers we might meet, my nervous tension had relaxed. I was thinking, it is true, about the difficulties and unknown factors of our landing; but since, according to my calculations, this would not take place for about 12 hours, I thought I would allow myself a bit of rest. On the contrary, these last hours—and they lengthened to 24—were the worst of all, especially for me.

The Nightmare of Fog

In default of the log-book, I am continuing my story on the basis of the notes I wrote at Teller a day or two after our arrival, when the memory and impressions of this terrible last day were still fresh in my mind. Here and there my recollections are helped by a few remarks scribbled on the navigation charts, and above all by the altimeter cards, whose zigzag diagrams are in themselves a vivid picture of our ups-and-downs.

The fog probably began soon after 12 noon, making us lose sight of the coast. When it thinned out I found that we were still

[2] 3,600 ft. (approx.).

over land, but it was impossible to say where. As we continued to fly WNW., we at last caught sight of a frozen river, probably the Kukpuk. The ground was rough and hilly; in front and to the right of us were mountains that appeared to be about 3,000 ft. high. I decided to follow the river, flying low; this seemed the best means of getting back to the coast.

Suddenly, almost unexpectedly, towards 2 p.m., a new fog-bank rolled up and completely submerged us. There was the risk of crashing into the mountains—very close to us now—between which we were flying. I at once had the speed reduced, and quickly rose to the height of full expansion;[1] but I could not escape from the fog. I dared not go higher, for if I did it would mean opening the valves to draw gas, and I feared that in the fog, ice might form on the valve seats. So we went on flying blindly in the midst of the hills. Our altitude was about 3,500 ft.—probably higher than the peaks around, but I could not be sure of this, as our charts gave no specific information. We continued thus for a very long hour, flying through the fog. Then at last it lowered to 2,700 or 3,000 ft., and once more we saw the sun. I breathed again. Later, the fog rose once more, but this time I found no difficulty in bringing the airship up to nearly 4,000 ft. It was not necessary to maintain this altitude for long, however, as towards 4.40 the fog once again dropped lower. An hour later it began to clear: we went on descending, until at 600 ft. we saw the frozen sea. It was 6.30 p.m.

Our Return to the Coast

We were, then, over the sea, but just where, nobody could tell—certainly nearer the coast of Asia than America. Now we had to turn back until we again struck the shore-line of Alaska, which I intended not to leave again, until we reached Nome. So I ordered the helmsman to steer eastwards, and had the engines speeded up.

We had to keep low, so as not to lose sight of the sea. But the

[1] *Height of full expansion:* the height at which the gas contained in the envelope of an airship, expanding with the lessening of atmospheric pressure, completely fills it.

air was rough and there was a strong cross-wind. At times we were suddenly tossed up or down, 150 ft. or more. To keep the ship in control became very difficult; consequently I myself had to stay almost continually at the elevator wheel. In these unnerving conditions we went on flying under the whitish fog for what seemed an interminable time.

But suddenly, after half an hour, the pack stopped—and there was the open sea: a wild, foam-crested sea, raised by the strong NE. wind. We still did not know our position: only, vaguely, that we were near the Bering Straits.

With the strong wind that was blowing, this stormy open sea worried me. If the engines broke down or the fuel ran out, we would be driven helplessly before the wind, right out into the ocean towards the Aleutian Islands, or perhaps even towards Japan. It is a curious thing that only now, when the sea was no longer icebound, did I realize that we were on the threshold of the Pacific, so many thousands of miles from Italy; and I must confess that even in the midst of my anxieties I felt a thrill of pride at the feat achieved by the little airship that I myself had built and piloted.

After perhaps an hour and a half we again saw compact ice— a sign that the coast was not far away. Above the pack we continued for some time in exhausting conditions: all this whiteness dazzled us and was terribly tiring. Feeling hot, I took off my fur coat, although the temperature in the front part of the cabin was several degrees below freezing: the effort of handling the elevator wheel had warmed me up.

At last once more the anxiously awaited cry rang out on board: "Land ahoy!" The coast appeared ahead on the horizon, amidst the pale fog. It was nearly 9.30 p.m. when we reached it.

In Kotzbue Bay

The worst part of our flight was now beginning: four hours and a half of torment, from 9.30 p.m. on May 13th till 2 a.m. on the 14th, without a moment of truce. Our tired nerves had to rally with a supreme effort to stand up to the strain.

I cannot attempt to give any details of this breathless race under the implacable fog, among the hills, over the ice of Kotzbue Bay, over the frozen lagoons. Who can tell what route we followed, or how we wound in and out through the fog? Even today I can still live through the emotions of this wild flight under the fog, without knowing where we were or where we were going; but the recollection is confused, as in a nightmare. I vividly remember only the most dramatic moments when a catastrophe seemed imminent.

So, at 9.30 we reached the coast. We saw some huts near which human figures were moving about—certainly Eskimos. I noticed the dogs, which seemed terrified as we passed: one of them, tied to a post, was running madly round it in circles. We made a turn over the little village. Amundsen thought he recognized it as Kivalina. Riiser-Larsen suggested that we should land there, but I rejected the idea. We had still plenty of fuel, and with the NE. wind helping us there was no reason to stop: we might go on to Nome, where they were expecting us. It would now be easy to get there, flying low along the coast.

It was at this point that Riiser-Larsen proposed that we should ascertain our position by taking the height of the sun. For that we needed to climb above the fog; but as there were hills around, I reduced the engine revolutions to a minimum.

By this time the ship was light, and it climbed rapidly through the fog, which went on thinning out and becoming luminous, until at last we saw the sun. Riiser-Larsen took an altitude with his sextant. Meanwhile, we had reached the height of full expansion, and the sun had warmed the gas which quickly expanded: I saw the pressure in the manometers rapidly rising. I opened all the valves, but this did not check our ascent: the pressure went on mounting. Nothing remained for it but to descend dynamically, accelerating the engines; but as we were down by the stern, the first effect of this was inevitably to increase the speed of the climb. Therefore we had to bring the ship on to a level keel—or, better still, point the nose downwards. So I ordered two of the Norwegians who were in the control cabin to climb up inside the ship and go at once to the extreme tip of the bow; but they did not understand the order, given in English. I can still see Gottwaldt, poised on the ladder on to which he had climbed, looking at me in bewilderment, uncertain what I wanted him to do—while the pressure in the gauges went on rising: 60, 70, 80 mm. A really critical situation. The elevator fins were hard down, in the position for a descent—but still we rose. If this went on, in a few moments the valves would open automatically, causing a disastrous loss of hydrogen. *"Subito a prua!"* I shouted, this time in Italian, accompanying the words with a gesture. At last the Norwegians understood and carried out the order. The nose came down and we began to descend: the pressure dropped. I drew a long breath of relief.

In a few minutes we had risen to 5,400 ft.: now we were coming down just as quickly, completely immersed in fog. I ordered Riiser-Larsen to turn seawards to lessen the risk of crashing into the hills. But at 600 ft. there was still land below us. It was 10.20.

The height of the sun just taken had given us a latitude of 67° 5′, confirming that we were near Kivalina. Now we had to reach the coast again, but in order not to lose our way once more, we were forced to fly very low under the fog. In such circumstances the navigation became extremely dangerous owing to the uneven nature of the ground. So once again I had to take over the elevator wheel, replacing Wisting, who was so tired that at times I saw him unconsciously closing his eyes.

This part of our flight was for me a continuous nervous tension, a spasmodic strain of concentration. One had to handle the wheel and at the same time look out of the window to see, before it was too late, the peaks that surged up unexpectedly through the fog. Sometimes we were so near the ground that once or twice the trailing wireless antenna caught against some obstacle and broke. I was very tired: I had not had a single moment to sit down and rest; there were times when I felt I could bear it no longer. I realized that my instinct of self-preservation had vanished; if my own life had been the only one at stake, I would have let my eyes close in irresistible sleep. But the sense of responsibility was strong, and I could still find—I don't know how—strength to resist my physical exhaustion and stay glued to my post, with my eyes open and my mind alert, in a supreme effort of will-power.

At last, after four hours and a half of this nightmarish flying in fog, we came across an extremely sinuous frozen river. I looked at the chart with Riiser-Larsen: we identified it easily, for its winding course suggested its name: Serpentine River. Soon afterwards we came to the mouth of the little Shishmaref Bay. It was two o'clock in the early morning of the 14th. At last we were back on the route to Nome. Half an hour later we emerged from the Shishmaref inlet, leaving to port the small island of Sarichef.

It is difficult to say precisely where we had been since Kivalina. Probably we had passed to the north of Kotzebue, and then across Eschscholtz Bay; thence between Kivalik and Candle in the direction of Goodhope Bay as far as the Serpentine River.

Now that we knew where we were, it would have been easy to reach Nome along the coast, maintaining a constant height and speed over the sea. Leaving Riiser-Larsen to do this, I sat down, utterly exhausted.

My notes had broken off about 2 p.m. on May 13th; so I had undergone 12 hours of uninterrupted strain—not easy to endure after 3 days and nights almost without sleep. I sat down in Amundsen's armchair and slipped my legs into the fur bag in which Titina had been sleeping almost solidly for three days.

At 3.30 a.m. the airship was over Prince of Wales Cape, having covered the 70 miles which separated this point from the Shishmaref inlet in 56 minutes. The wind was right behind us.

THE END OF THE FLIGHT

Our Arrival at Port Clarence

AFTER cat-napping painfully for a while, still anxious to keep an eye on what was happening, I had at last drowsed off, when Riiser-Larsen came to wake me: "We're getting near," he said, "in half an hour we shall be at Nome."

It was about 6.30 a.m. I got up from the armchair with that peculiar sick feeling that comes from insufficient rest. It was cold. I went to the front of the cabin and glanced at the instruments, to get an idea of how the ship was trimmed; then I leaned out to have a look. Below us the dark, stormy sea was flecked with foam. The wan grey sky was streaked by black clouds, bearing down upon us from the north. From time to time there were flurries of snow. The ship, shaken by the squally wind, was pitching and rolling.

I called Alessandrini: "Hang out the mooring-ropes and prepare to drop down the landing-rope." While he was doing this, I thought over the difficulties of landing. At Nome they were waiting for us: I myself had telegraphed from King's Bay, telling them to prepare the ground-crew. Even so, with such a strong wind and inexperienced men, the manœuvre was not without its dangers. It would be necessary to give clear and precise instructions. I called Riiser-Larsen and got him to prepare a message. Then I went on turning over in my own mind the orders I should have to give, once we had landed, to have the airship deflated as quickly and safely as possible.

Meanwhile, we were approaching the coast. Pack-ice had replaced the open sea. We were flying along a desolate grey shore, with hills that were even more dreary. Here was a pale, frozen river: a little farther along, some dark masses that were apparently huts; and finally, to complete the miserable picture, a three-masted barque, abandoned, lying on its side amid the ice. We went on. I was surprised not to see any large group of houses, such as I imagined Nome to be. Wisting was at the helm with Amundsen standing beside him. Both of them knew the locality well, having visited it several times. "Where is the place?" I asked. "Down there," replied Riiser-Larsen, pointing in the general direction of the river.

We turned back, once more seeing the abandoned boat, and again approached the edge of the ice. In order to reach the river, I tried to cross the frozen lagoon, separated from the sea by a narrow tongue of land, but realised that in such rough air it would have been dangerous to follow the river between the hills. Again we flew to the right. Down there, a few miles away, we could see habitations. I tried to reach them, speeding up all three engines to 1,200 r.p.m. Notwithstanding this, we were making very little headway against the wind.

In the meantime a new decision was forming in my mind. I would give up Nome, which obviously was still a long way off, and come to land as soon as possible. The weather was getting even worse. The sky above us was black. At one moment, as we were crossing the coast near a hill, the ship pitched dangerously, assuming an angle of 30 degrees. To go on flying in these conditions, with the persistent gale and a crew exhausted with their efforts, would have been madness. The Italians on board had been working incessantly for 4 days—it was a miracle that they were still able to stand.

It was a dramatic moment. I felt the full weight of the responsibility on my shoulders: on my decision depended the fate of the crew: half an hour of delay in carrying it out might mean a catastrophe, a tragic conclusion to our enterprise. We had to land before the storm made it impossible for me to control the airship.

Quickly, I reviewed in my mind all the difficulties and dangers of landing in a gale, with no help from the ground, and considered the various solutions. My first idea was to descend in the open sea, by the edge of the ice. We had all the necessary equipment for this, including inflatable dinghies. But, although we could have saved the crew, this would have meant losing the airship, left to drift at the mercy of the waves. So it was better to come down on the coastal ice, as near as possible to the tiny village we had seen, where, even if I could not bring the ship to a dead stop, we could let the wind drive her along on her belly without undue risk. There would then be time to send down the men and deflate the envelope.

I told Riiser-Larsen of my decision. He, however, suggested that we should cut out the canvas covering the cabin walls, collect the crew together, and tell them to hang on outside until the moment of impact, and then at a given signal all drop off together, letting the ship fly away. This was a desperate solution, which showed how serious our position was; but it would have exposed the crew to a very great risk. Besides, I did not want to lose the ship. So I kept to my former plan: a static landing on the ice.

The Landing

I called Cecioni and ordered him to prepare the landing-sack,[1] filling it with all the heavy materials at our disposal, including the tins of pemmican. Meanwhile, I had the engines slowed down, to check the trim of the ship. We were a trifle heavy: the *Norge* was descending slowly, while the wind and our own headway were carrying us towards the village. But we could not yet land, as the sack was not ready. It was a long job: a mooring-rope had to be fixed to the top end, and an anchor to the bottom. So I had to get the engines going again. Suddenly, thick fog covered us, giving me hardly time to order Riiser-Larsen, who was at the rudder, to turn to port and avoid the hills. As the fog spread out the little village reappeared—a row of grey huts amid the ice.

At last the sack was ready. I told Cecioni to put it outside the control cabin. Too heavy for him, it slipped through his hands and fell out. Now it was hanging from the hull of the airship, at the bow.

We came down again. I brought the ship up-wind, over the frozen sea, a mile or two from the village, and again slowed down the engines. We continued to descend slowly. "Pay out

[1] See Appendix.

the sack!" And it came down, stopping about 100 ft. below the airship. On the ground I saw a group of 7 or 8 men. A slight burst of engine-power carried us towards them. We came lower: I saw the sack touch ground, its anchor sliding over the ice. The men grabbed the rope. I gave orders to release gas; this made the airship heavier and brought it down. "Look out for the shock!" But the impact, taken up by the rubber shock-absorbers underneath the cabin, was slight. We bounced several feet into the air. "Draw gas again!" I cried. A few moments later we touched the ice—and this time we stayed down.

We had arrived!

I thought of the danger that might arise if my men, in their anxiety to set foot on the ground, left the cabin too hurriedly. The airship, unexpectedly lightened by several hundredweight, might have been whipped out of the hands of the inexperienced people who were holding the mooring-ropes. *"Nessuno si muova!"* I shouted at the top of my voice. For the second time during this last day of flight I experienced the efficacy of my own language—for the order, given in Italian, was understood by everybody. In addition, I stationed myself in the doorway of the cabin, barring the exit.

I sent Cecioni down to help the men on the ground, and continued to draw off gas. Then, one by one, I sent down Riiser-Larsen, Amundsen, Ellsworth, and the rest. It was 7.30 on the morning of May 14th (G.M.T.); or 8.30 p.m. on the 13th by Alaskan time.

The wind at ground-level was not very strong, though the weather was still threatening. We had to deflate the airship quickly, if we did not want to lose it. I tried to reduce the damage to a minimum, and so, guessing that the ship would settle down on the port side, I ordered Cecioni, on the ground, to smash with his hatchet the companionway that linked the left engine-boat with the hull. He did so. Meanwhile, I sent Alessandrini aloft to cut the rip-panels[1] as soon as I gave him the order. When I

---

[1] These, in our technical jargon, are the bands let into the walls of the gas-chambers on the top of the airship, which can easily be torn out by a single pull, letting the gas escape freely.

thought that everything was ready, I turned round to see that everyone was out of the ship. I found good old Wisting standing beside me: "Thanks for the journey!" he said. These simple words pleased me, and I still remember them. When he too was down, I shouted to Alessandrini to rip the panels. A minute or two passed: I was anxious about Alessandrini, who took some time to descend, but at last he reappeared.

The body of the airship began to sway: then it dropped on its left side, so suddenly that I had hardly time to avoid being hit by the metal framework as it came down. The control cabin was overturned: the engine-boats disappeared under the envelope.

Our great adventure was finished.

I turned round to look. Beside me were standing Cecioni, Arduino, Caratti, Pomella, and Alessandrini—tired and dishevelled, but with joy in their eyes. Amundsen, Ellsworth, and some of the others had gone off towards the village. Then our own men too went in search of a bed, where they could at last sleep after three long days of fatigue and emotions.

They went away: I stayed for some time with Alessandrini, looking at our ship. We were all unhurt—but the *Norge* was lying lifeless, destroyed, on the white snowfield. She had brought us safe and sound, for thousands of miles, to our goal, always obedient to commands, untiring, almost as if she realized the magnitude of the task I had set her; she had docilely allowed herself to be tied up to mooring-masts—she, who so loved the freedom of the skies; she had bravely faced up to gales, in France, in Russia, over the Bering Straits, without her strong, elastic framework giving way; she had withstood wind, snow, frost, rain and fog.

Now she was lying on her side, mortally wounded—and it was I who had dealt her the deathblow!

At Teller

I could not bring myself to leave the place where we had landed. My mind was in tumult. Now my thoughts flew to Italy—to the dear country we had left more than a month before, and the beloved ones who were anxiously waiting there.

Where were we? Someone had answered: "At Teller, a hundred miles from Nome." Then Gottwaldt came to tell me: "There is a wireless station here, but there aren't any operators." So we would be able to tell the world of the successful outcome of our flight, telegraph to Italy that our marvellous adventure was at an end, and that we were all safe and well. Thoughts went whirling through my brain. All traces of the deadly fatigue that had threatened to overwhelm me during the last few hours had disappeared. Every faculty of spirit and body was overexcited, every sense sharpened.

But, as if by contrast, nature around was quiet and still. A solemn peace hung over the little village. The quiet, surprised Eskimos stood around, staring at the flying monster which sprawled helplessly on the frozen lagoon. They showed no sign of being upset by our unexpected arrival out of the sky.

The cold night and grey sky struck a note of sadness.

I went to join my companions, who had by this time gathered around an improvised table, where, for the first time in three days, some hot food was being served out to them. Everyone was in high spirits. Sitting next to me, Amundsen and Ellsworth repeatedly and effusively expressed their gratitude. Ellsworth, particularly, was quite emotional, making me the most cordial offers of friendship: "My house in New York is always open to you—so is my villa at Florence."

So our expedition had come to its victorious end. With a small airship, meant for flying over the Tyrrhenian Sea, we had reached the Pacific Ocean from Rome, across the Pole, in a flight that had lasted altogether 171 hours. We had covered 7,800 miles, braving countless risks and adversities, and the unknown conditions of the unexplored zone stretching from the Pole to the American continent. Through the large black patch which indicated these regions on the Arctic charts, showing them as inaccessible, we had drawn a line of light, approximately following the 159th meridian west of Greenwich, 1,200 miles long and about 48 to 54 miles wide. We had proved that there is no continent in these parts, but a frozen sea—the Arctic Ocean—and we had been the first to cross that sea. A geographical question that had been argued for years had finally been settled. Following our route in the opposite direction, it would one day be possible to reach the Pole from the Bering Straits by submarine.

While I was walking away from the spot where we had landed, a white man had stepped out from among the group of Eskimos, saying: "Commander, you need rest. When you are ready, come up to my house, over there. I have a nice room for you." In these words I was offered hospitality by a short, broad, powerfully-built man, with a resolute and energetic expression and grey eyes twinkling with humour. In due course I heard his name: Petersen—Captain Petersen, who during the summer season, when the sea was open, sent out some little boats along the coast, carrying passengers and goods. I turned to look at the wooden house that he pointed out to me. A huge notice-board with the inscription "GENERAL MERCHANDISE" showed that it was a shop. The board and the ambitious title were a relic of the ancient splendours of Teller, when during the "gold rush" 10,000 miners camped there in the summer months. Now the inhabitants were reduced to 55—only about 10 of them white men, the others being Eskimos.

The first night at Teller was sleepless for me, in addition to the three previous ones: I was too excited and over-tired to sleep.

As dozens of thoughts and recollections went whirling through my brain, I remembered how well and enthusiastically my Italian companions had performed their duties. I decided to call them together next morning and express my gratitude. But when the time came, I did not make any speeches—simply said: "We'll start right away to dismount the airship; and before anything else, let us measure the amount of petrol and oil that is left."

They set to work at once with their usual calm, although an icy wind was blowing, which at times lashed our faces and hands almost unbearably. Later, they told me that we still had $26\frac{1}{2}$ cwt. of petrol, and $4\frac{1}{2}$ of oil.

Our crossing of the Arctic from Spitsbergen to Alaska, over the Pole, had lasted 70 hours and 40 minutes, and we had travelled

3,180 miles at an average speed of 45 m.p.h. For each mile we had consumed about 2·25 lb. of petrol and 27·4 gm. of oil.

We remained 18 days at Teller—the time necessary to finish dismounting the airship and to sort out the materials, so that they could be taken back to Europe with as little damage as possible. This stay in the tiny Eskimo village, whose perfect quiet was only broken now and again by the barking of dogs, tied up to their posts, and the whistling of the wind, was just what I needed after so much strain and anxiety.

RETURNING HOME

At Nome

I LEFT Teller with my Italian comrades on the morning of May 31st.

I had got up early to help prepare the sledges. The dogs, as always when a journey was in sight, were rushing round the posts, barking furiously. All of them wanted to come and were quivering with impatience, but very few were chosen.

When the sledges were ready we left.

This 2 hours' run over the icy sea was intoxicating. The air was cold and keen, the dogs ran swiftly. From time to time the driver gave a shout, and the leading dog, understanding it, carried out his order: "right", "left", "slower", "straight ahead". It was a spectacle that never ceased to fascinate me. Especially moving was the expression in the fine eyes of the "leader", when now and again it turned back to look at its owner, as if to ask him dumbly whether all was well.

In 2 hours we arrived at the edge of the pack, where an American coastguard vessel was waiting for us. It was commanded by Captain Ross, chief of the station at Nome, who, as soon as he heard of our arrival at Teller, had kindly put himself at my disposal. We disembarked at two o'clock in the morning.

Waiting for us were Father La Fortune and Father Post, two Jesuits from the Mission at Nome; the woman secretary of the "welcome committee" that the citizens of Nome had formed to greet and fête the Italian members of the expedition; and Polet, one of our two compatriots who were living in that town.

The whole population greeted us very cordially. The two missionaries, delighted by a message that I had brought from Rome, from the General of the Jesuits, Father Vladimir Ledochovski, and all the more so because it was the first and only letter that had come from Europe to America by such an unusual route, could not do enough for me.

They were my favourite company during the fortnight I stayed at Nome, especially Father La Fortune, a Canadian who had dedicated 25 years to educating the Eskimos. He knew their minds, their habits, their needs, and their language, better than any other man.

By comparison with Teller, Nome, with its 1,000 inhabitants, was a "city". We were lodged in the Main Street—a long, narrow street edged by two rows of small houses, most of them wooden, and a pavement, also made of wood. There were even a cinema and a ballroom, where a large reception was held in honour of us Italians. On this occasion a long banner had been slung across the street, inscribed: "FROM ROME TO NOME." The assonance had pleased the Americans. In any case, they pretended at Nome never to have heard of Teller.

I passed my time between visiting the Jesuits and sitting in my own room, busy with the articles that Ugo Ojetti had urgently asked me to cable to the *Corriere della Sera*. (Which did not prevent him from hauling me over the coals when, after the first cable, he realized that I was transmitting them textually, complete with all the articles and prepositions . . . and there were plenty of these!) Also, I had to reply to the avalanche of telegrams received from Italy and America. Some of these latter contained the oddest proposals—a testimony to the enterprising and utilitarian spirit of the Americans, to whom our Polar adventure, with its world-wide repercussions, suggested the idea of the most extravagant speculations.

Despite these minor diversions, I was soon regretting my quiet life at Teller, and I was really getting rather bored with Nome, when the arrival of the *Victoria* was announced.

The news aroused great excitement everywhere. It was important not only for us but for the whole population: this ship was making its first voyage of the year. To realize the importance of this event, one must bear in mind that for three-quarters of the year the life of the little community practically came to a standstill. Nome lived in a lethargy from autumn till spring. In the summer it woke up, into feverish life and activity.

So great preparations were being made for the arrival of the *Victoria*. Shopkeepers were making out their orders, families spring-cleaning their houses to welcome back their young folk. And then the whole community, according to their long-established custom, were preparing a grand ball for those whom they expected.

On June 17th, on board the *Victoria*, we finally left for Seattle. It was not a very pleasant voyage. Ice held up the ship for 2 days, and when it disappeared a strong wind arose, making us pitch most disagreeably. At last, after a brief halt at Falsepasse in the Aleutian Islands, on June 27th, the eleventh day of the voyage, we came in sight of Seattle. When we had passed through Admiralty Strait, we saw coming to meet us a boat with a large Italian flag, crowded with a joyful throng of singing men and women. Even Nature seemed to be taking part in our happiness, for a glorious sun was shining in the blue sky, while through the warm air there rang the notes of an old Neapolitan song: "*O sole mio.*"

Returning Home

At Seattle the expedition broke up. Amundsen, who declared that with this crossing of the Arctic Ocean he had closed his career as an explorer, was going back to Norway; Ellsworth was staying in America, and perhaps already thinking of the Antarctic; I was returning to Italy.

Our names were henceforward linked together in the history of Polar exploration. Together we had crossed the Arctic, together our flags had dropped upon the Pole. Each of us had contributed his own share to the success of the enterprise. Amundsen, who had first thought of it, had brought to it the prestige of his past exploits; Ellsworth had made it a practical possibility by putting up his share of the expenses; I had borne the responsibility of preparing the ship and superintending the flight from Rome to America. Our widely divergent life-paths had run together for a while; but now at Seattle they branched off again, each following its own course. I was never to see Amundsen again, though once more his name was to be linked with mine; 5 years later I met Ellsworth for the second time in the Arctic, in an island of Franz Josef Land.

So we Italians went back home. As a matter of fact, I would have liked to go at once to Japan, to equip and get ready an airship built for the Japanese Navy, a task I had undertaken some time previously. From Nome I had already cabled my wife to join me in San Francisco with the child, before I embarked for Yokohama. But while I was still in Nome, Mussolini had ordered me to put off that journey for several months and come back to Italy, after having made a tour of the Italian colonies in the United States.

So at Seattle, having parted from Amundsen, Ellsworth and the others, I and my Italians started on a memorable journey which brought us into contact with crowds of our emigrants: Seattle, San Francisco, Santa Barbara, Los Angeles, Chicago, Cleveland, Akron, Rochester, Philadelphia, Pittsburgh, Boston, Providence, Washington, New York, were the successive stages of this return home.

The Italians in America were proud that an airship from their own country had been the first to cross the Arctic Ocean, and they showed their feelings in many ways. Enthusiastic crowds swarmed in the streets when we arrived, and seized upon us. Thousands and thousands of workmen, with their hard, calloused hands, shook mine, until it became swollen and painful. Wherever we went, we heard over and over again: "We prayed for you!" Old peasant-women, probably from the South of Italy, pushed through the crowd to exclaim with deep feeling: "Blessed be the mothers that bore you!" Young boys whom we did not know embraced us, weeping.

To these spontaneous popular demonstrations were added the rather wearisome official receptions.

Nor was there lacking a visit to the President of the United States in Washington—a visit which, from the way it turned out, I shall never forget.

The President at that time was Coolidge. I was accompanied on my visit by De Martino, our Ambassador in America, and Captain Scaroni, our Air Attaché. On the way to the White House, De Martino said more than once: "Don't be surprised if you find the President rather cold. He is a taciturn and very severe man."

Titina had come with us. She had always followed us everywhere, and she did not like to be left alone in the hotel, even on such an occasion. But when we were in the antechamber, Scaroni said to me: "I'll stay outside with Titina." I was preparing to go in alone with De Martino, when an usher came to say: "You can bring the little dog in too. The President will be pleased." So Titina came in.

It was a large room with a daïs. Along one side, on the right as one entered, wide windows opened upon the park. Coolidge— tall, thin, clean-cut, serious—invited us to sit down around him, and the Ambassador began to make the usual conventional remarks. Suddenly I noticed that Scaroni had become scarlet in the face. I did not at first realize why; then, following his glance, I saw Titina, right in the middle of the carpet, calmly fulfilling one of her minor needs. Embarrassed, I got up and took her in my arms to put her outside, on the greensward; but the President, laughing, stopped me: "Let her stay!" And from that moment his tongue was loosened, and he became cordial and expansive.

When we left the Ambassador was still amazed, and said to me: "I've never seen the President so good-humoured and chatty."

Needless to say that, as we were in America, the newspapers got hold of the story, and next day headlined it on the front page.

Towards the end of July we embarked at New York on board the *Biancamano*, to return to Italy. We arrived at Naples on August 2nd. It was sunset. The gulf was sprinkled with hundreds of white sails coming to meet us; flights of aeroplanes were whirling about the sky; farther off, in the direction of Rome, we saw the well-known silhouettes of two of our airships: a solemn moment which will remain for ever engraved on my mind.

In Italy we were received triumphantly: honours, rewards,

receptions awaited us; but at the very moment when I set foot again in the little house where my wife was eagerly awaiting me, my thoughts were already leaping forward to a new enterprise. We had opened the way to the Pole. We must go back there to complete the work that we had begun.

It had to happen.

The Polar sky had to see an Italian-born airship once again.

My Dispute with Amundsen

This ends the story of the first crossing made by man of the Arctic Ocean.

There would be nothing to add, were it not for the necessity of mentioning the dispute that arose between Amundsen and myself at the end of the expedition. It is not the first time in the history of Polar exploration that this has happened. But the quarrel between the two of us developed a particularly keen intensity—probably because, being of different languages and nationalities, we had not been able to get to know and appreciate each other in the short time that we were in contact, before and during the flight. The main cause, however, was that the expedition, as it took shape, was essentially an aeronautical enterprise.

Trouble broke out quite unexpectedly, with an article published by Amundsen in an American magazine, containing the most incredible accusations, insults, trivial and impertinent complaints of all kinds. This article was brought to my notice by King Victor Emmanuel, who requested me to answer it at once. I did so, and imagined that this had closed the unfortunate dispute; in fact, I did not even mention it in the book that I published in 1928. But, alas! Amundsen's attack was renewed in an even more violent form in his book of memoirs: *My Life as an Explorer*, which I read only after the *Italia* expedition.

The unhappy circumstance that he had died when flying to the help of the castaways of that expedition obliged me to keep silent—as I have done for a third of a century. And I would have maintained this silence, had I not recently seen reprinted in English the old calumnies which I hoped had long since been forgotten. In justice to myself, and out of respect to the readers of this book, I am obliged now to recapitulate these charges and to defend myself.

My relations with Amundsen had been unhappy from the start. The trouble originated when the Aeroclub of Norway induced him to agree reluctantly that the expedition should be officially entitled: AMUNDSEN-ELLSWORTH-NOBILE TRANSPOLAR FLIGHT. Later, he admitted that this had been done solely "*to gratify the local pride while we were taking the ship over*", and added: "*. . . no publicity would be given to Nobile after we got the* N.1 *out of Italy.*" Consciously or subconsciously, therefore, Amundsen, while signing this agreement, already had it in mind not to respect it, wishing to treat me as a "*hired pilot*" (his own expression), rather than a joint leader of the expedition who had built the ship and fitted it out for the Polar flight.

On this point it is worth remarking that, by our contract with the Aeroclub, the Norwegians (including Amundsen) were to be paid a salary, whereas we Italians were to receive graded bonuses at various stages of the flight: had it ended in disaster, we would have got little except the discredit.

This attitude led to a series of pinpricks, some of which I noticed at the time, while others escaped me until my attention was called to them. Outwardly, however, we were on the normal friendly terms of those who are sharing in a hazardous enterprise; at least, until I joined Amundsen and Ellsworth at Nome. Here we had several clashes because I was anxious to write my account of the aeronautical side of the flight (as I had contracted to do), and the other two seemed determined to exclude my collaboration in their articles, and later in their book. I should specify that I had agreed to make over to the Aeroclub of Norway any money that I might receive from writing or lecturing about the expedition, so no personal gain was involved.

When Amundsen and Ellsworth's book *The First Crossing of the Polar Sea* appeared, I noticed that the official name of the expedition was nowhere mentioned. But I did not mind this until I read the article published by Amundsen in America, and later his book of memoirs, where I was astonished and distressed to find a very scathing criticism of myself. With the personal side of this I do not intend to deal. Clearly, no man enjoys being held up to ridicule as a compound of vanity, egotism and self-seeking; but this kind of mud dries off in the course of years and can be brushed away—if not with a smile at least with a shrug. Where my technical competence is concerned, it is another matter; not only my own credit is involved, but that of my country. So I will briefly outline these charges, and answer them as fairly and dispassionately as I can.

It should be borne in mind that Amundsen knew absolutely nothing about the construction and handling of airships—so little that he describes the *Norge* as "*a soft-nosed gas bag*". It was in fact a semi-rigid, with a nose-cap of steel tubing.

(1) *He states that Riiser-Larsen brought the ship out of the hangar at King's Bay, whilst I stood around doing nothing.* Certainly he did— at my request and briefed by me—because orders to the ground-crew of Norwegian miners and sailors obviously had to be given in their own language. The Italians, under my supervision, were helping.

(2) He gives a highly picturesque, if somewhat inaccurate, account of the incident over Kivalina which I have already described: "*Nobile now made an effort to get the nose of the* Norge *pointed downwards. The ship did not respond to the rudder.*" (It is, of course, the *elevator* which controls the upward or downward movement of an airship.) "*Then Nobile lost his head completely. With tears streaming down his face, and wringing his hands, he stood screaming: 'Run to the bow! Run to the bow!' Three of our Norwegians dashed forward on the runway under the bag and by their weight forced the* Norge *downward.*"

I did not see Amundsen in the front part of the pilot cabin where I was standing at the moment of this incident; certainly, my face might have been strained by the mental tension and the physical effort, but I can assure the reader that I was not in tears. This stupid lie has been denied also by Gottwaldt, one of the Norwegians whom I ordered to move towards the bow. Gottwaldt, standing on the ladder which led to the interior of the hull, was looking me right in the face, puzzled by my order given in English—a language foreign to both of us. Therefore I flung out my hand, pointing the way I wanted him to go. My resolute gesture becomes in Amundsen's words "a wringing of the hands", as in despair.

But the oddest thing is the phrase: "*Nobile lost his head completely.*" One might expect that, having lost my head, I would have given a wrong order: on the contrary, it was the right one. Amundsen himself tacitly admits this when he declares that as soon as the Norwegians obeyed me the nose of the ship came down.

(3) Continuing his account of the flight through the fog between Kivalina and Teller, Amundsen writes: "*The ship was speeding towards the rough ice below us. Another moment, and we should be dashed to pieces. Riiser-Larsen sensed the danger. Nobile seemed insensible of it: he stood like a man in a trance. Riiser-Larsen sprang to the wheel himself, thrust Nobile roughly to one side, and himself spun the wheel round.*"

Here once more he has failed to realize that Riiser-Larsen and I were acting in concert. We were flying almost at ground-level under thick fog over a very hilly country. In such conditions the handling of the elevator had become very difficult, and as no Norwegian was sufficiently expert I had to take the wheel myself, watching the ground and quickly manœuvring in order to avoid collisions. But from where I stood the vision of the ground was not clear enough; therefore I stationed Riiser-Larsen at a porthole to warn me of obstacles. Each time he saw the ground rising through the fog, he was to shout "Up!", reinforcing the warning when necessary with a gesture of his hand towards the elevator.

By this stage of the flight, having slept only 3 hours out of the preceding 97, I was thoroughly exhausted; yet from somewhere I drew sufficient reserve of strength to make a landing which aroused the admiration of the Zeppelin Goodyear Corporation pilots—and of Amundsen himself. "*The landing was one of the achievements one will always remember,*" he records in his book. "*It was splendidly done and we take off our hats to the skipper of the ship for the quiet, neat manner in which he accomplished it."*

(4) Amundsen accuses me of wasting useful load by *"secreting in the Norge . . . the bulk and weight of heavy uniforms"*, for myself and two of my men, so that we should make a good show on arrival in America.

These were the uniforms—not "resplendent", as Amundsen asserts, but rather shabby from much use—which Arduino, Caratti and I had worn all through the flight under our heavy jerseys and furs . . . just as the others were wearing their civilian suits. Any of the Norwegians, who had seen us on the earlier stages, could have told Amundsen this; but he himself, who only joined us at King's Bay, did not notice our uniforms until we discarded our Arctic clothing in the warmer air of Seattle. For some reason this old tunic of mine infuriated Amundsen; especially when, as we disembarked, a pretty Italian girl came forward and presented me with a bunch of flowers: *"Here in miniature, Nobile had the triumph for which his uniform was a part of the planning."*

While on this subject I might point out that I had been obliged to unload fuel equivalent to the weight of two heavy men, because the Norwegians came on board late, so that we lost the benefit of the additional lift we should have obtained from the cold early morning air, before the sun had expanded the gas and forced me to open the valves.

After all I have revealed, the reader can draw his own conclusions, taking into consideration that Tryggve Gran, the Antarctic explorer; Captain Nielsen, who commanded the ship *Heimdal*; Professor A. Hoel, the eminent expert upon Arctic expeditions; and Dr. Thommessen, President of the Aeroclub of Norway—who might have been expected to support their fellow-countryman—in fact defended me against his charges. The accusations in themselves are self-contradictory and absurd, but on account of the name of their author they might be perpetuated. To avert that risk I have thought it necessary to tell the facts exactly as they happened. This is all the more painful to me, since I had hoped that the whole trivial, bitter wrangle would have been washed from the world's memory, as it had been from mine, when the waters of the Barents Sea closed over Amundsen, as with a generous impulse he himself put it all behind him and flew to the help of the *Italia* castaways.

PART TWO

THE TRAGEDY OF THE *ITALIA*

ORIGIN AND PREPARATION OF THE EXPEDITION

The First Idea

AT Teller, three days after landing there with the *Norge*, I was already thinking of a new expedition.

One day (I don't know how) I discovered in an out-of-the-way corner of the little wooden house where I was staying, a small cardboard terrestrial globe. I took it and carried it into the front room where, when I was not outside superintending the dismantling of the airship, I spent most of my time reading or dreaming.

I was meditating in front of this globe when Riiser-Larsen, the second-in-command of the *Norge*, who was also a guest of Captain Petersen, came in to say good morning, taking the little pipe from his mouth. He sat down opposite me and cast a look of curiosity at the globe, perhaps surprised to find such a thing on this desolate icebound coast.

"I was thinking," I said, "that with that strong wind astern the *Norge* might have gone much farther south, as far as Seattle perhaps."

In fact, it would have been possible, because on our arrival at Teller we still had a good stock of petrol on board.

So we went on to discuss the possibility of flying to Tokio and San Francisco across the Arctic Ocean, starting from Scandinavia.

Suddenly I said: "I think we ought to make a new expedition. After all, our journey has been practical proof that the airship is the best means of exploring unknown country from above. There is still so much to be done."

"That's true," replied Riiser-Larsen, "But with this enterprise Amundsen has closed his career as an explorer. He has finished—he's going to retire."

"Very well," I said, "Then we will go on. It would be a pity not to make use of the hangar at King's Bay, and the mooring-masts set up at Oslo and Vadsö."

Then I outlined my idea to him. In two years' time, in 1928, we would be able to make the new expedition. We would have raised the necessary money in Italy. The dirigible was there: a sister-ship of the *Norge*, then under construction. The expedition would be called Nobile—Riiser-Larsen, and would fly the Italian flag.

We promised each other that we would discuss it further. But we never did, because of the misunderstandings that I have just described.

On my return to Italy in August, 1926, I met Dr. Thommessen, President of the Aeroclub of Norway, and discussed with him the possibility of using the King's Bay hangar and the mooring-mast at Vadsö for the new expedition. He willingly agreed, promising that he would get the Aeroclub to grant me the rights to use these constructions for a period of 3 years.

So my idea was beginning to take concrete shape, when in September, 1926, Mussolini ordered me to finish as quickly as possible the construction of a new dirigible I had designed, three times larger than the *Norge*, to make a non-stop flight from Rome to Buenos Aires; so that for the moment I was obliged to lay aside my plan for an Arctic venture.

A few months later, while I was in Japan, getting ready the airship built for the Japanese Navy, Balbo—whom Mussolini had created Under-Secretary for Aviation—cabled to tell me that the Italian Government had given up the idea of this flight from Italy to the Argentine. It seemed a good opportunity to ask that the new airship, by this time well on the way to completion, should be allocated to the Polar flight that I was planning. With this ship we could have expanded the programme of the expedition; among other things we might have started out from Leningrad and flown across the Pole to Tokio. By doing this, in all probability, when we arrived in Japan the dirigible would have been bought by the Japanese Navy, who were keenly interested in my new construction.

I cabled to Rome. But the Italian Government had decided to stop building the new airship, and however much I insisted, I could not shake their decision. In fact, to avoid any possibility of the airship being completed at some future time, Balbo ordered that the part already made should be broken up and sold for scrap!

But all this, however trying it was, could not deter me from carrying out my project of an Arctic expedition, using the sister-ship of the *Norge* which I have already mentioned. It was to be finished in the spring of 1927, and the first test flights were planned for the summer of that year.

Planning the Expedition

Our venture in the *Norge*—the pioneer Arctic expedition with a dirigible—had led to important geographical results. We had explored over 50,000 square miles of the unknown region between the Pole and the northern coasts of Alaska, and had proved the existence there of a frozen sea; but there were still approximately 1,500,000 square miles of unexplored territory within the Arctic Circle. The most interesting points to explore would be along the coasts of Greenland, Siberia and Canada, where the shallowness of the sea made it probable that lands of greater or less extent might emerge above its surface. So we gradually drew up the programme of the new expedition: a voyage of exploration in the region of Severnaya Zemlya (origin-ally called Nicholas II Land), of which only a part of the eastern coast was then known; a second towards the coasts of Greenland and Canada; a third in the regions immediately round the Pole, with the intention of making a descent there.

Besides these geographical problems—in themselves so interest-ing and attractive—the expedition would also undertake an ambitious programme of scientific research in the fields of oceanography, terrestrial magnetism, gravity, atmospheric elec-tricity and radioactivity, and Polar biology. To tell the truth, so far as scientific observations were concerned, the *Norge* expedition had not done much. The hazardous nature of the crossing from Spitsbergen to the American coast, starting from Rome with such a small airship, had obliged us to concentrate our attention on the aeronautical problem, at the expense of the purely scientific side. The new expedition, on the other hand, would be able to boast of being the first scientific aerial exploration of the Arctic.

As soon as I came back to Italy from Japan in the summer of 1927, I outlined to Mussolini, in an interview at which Balbo was also present, the programme of the expedition. He listened attentively and then said: "Perhaps it would be better not to tempt Fate a second time. Still, I recognize the scientific importance of the idea. We will talk about it again next week." But we did not speak of it again until the eve of the departure.

Balbo had suggested that I should interest the Italian Royal Geographical Society in my plan, and ask it to sponsor the enterprise. Acting on this advice, on July 12th I explained my plans to the governing Council of the Society, which greeted them with enthusiasm and agreed that the expedition should be under the aegis of the Italian Geographical Society.

A few days later (July 21st), the Mayor of Milan in his turn wrote to me, confirming the offer made by the City of Milan to raise by private subscription the cost of the undertaking. According to a rough estimate I had made, this amounted to $3\frac{1}{2}$ million lire.

Several months passed before any definite decision was taken, but at last, in October, 1927, Balbo summoned me to his office at the Viminale, and announced, smiling, that Mussolini had given his consent to the enterprise, provided that it took place under the auspices of the Geographical Society, and that the expenses were borne by the Milanese Committee. It was understood that the Air Ministry should supply the dirigible and its crew at its own charge, and that the preparations should be made in the Government workshops of which I was the Chief, and with Government personnel—on condition, however, that all expenses entailed should be reimbursed by the same Committee. These agreements took definite shape in December, 1927, in a written agreement between the Italian Royal Geographical Society and the Under-Secretary for Air.

Meanwhile, I had had various conversations with Admiral

Sirianni, Under-Secretary for the Navy, who had most enthusi-astically promised the enterprise his full support. He would send the ship *Città di Milano* to King's Bay on a training cruise, and at the same time it could be used to transport materials for the expedition and lend its sailors as a ground-crew for handling the dirigible.

The Choice of the Crew

When it was known that I was preparing a new Arctic expedi-tion applications to join it poured in by hundreds from all parts of Italy, from men of every class, every grade of ability, every profession; and not from Italy alone, but several from Germany, France, and even Norway.

I had only too many to choose from. But when it came to the point the selection was enormously simplified by the fact that before all others, I gave preference to my well-tried companions of the *Norge*.

I asked Arduino, Caratti, Pomella, and Alessandrini—all veterans of that expedition—if they intended to come with me, pointing out to them the risks of this new venture, which in many respects I considered greater than those of the former one. All four accepted enthusiastically, without discussion, without making stipulations or conditions of any kind.

With Arduino, a chief motor engineer of great merit, and Caratti and Pomella, exceptionally able mechanics, the engines would undoubtedly be looked after in the best possible manner. It was only necessary to add a fourth man to allow adequate rest during our flights to this very important part of the crew. My choice fell on Ciocca, one of my good veteran workmen and a first-class mechanic, who had worked with me for years and was devoted to me.

I have already introduced the first four of these companions. It is sufficient to add here that during the second enterprise they confirmed those exceptional technical and moral qualities which had made them, on that memorable occasion, such incomparable colleagues—intelligent, loyal, ready for anything, even to give their lives for me.

The group of engine mechanics as I said above was completed by Ciocca. Slender and lean, he also had a great power of endurance, combined with the advantage of lightness. He had been in my employ for years, and I had come to have a high opinion not only of his skill as a workman but of his character. Already, on the *Norge* expedition, he had gone as far as King's Bay. He was cheerful and good company, and showed in private a delightfully individual sense of humour, which, out of respect, he concealed in my presence.

Having thus chosen the chief engineer and the motor mechanics, I felt that Cecioni's presence on board was no longer necessary. Still, he might be valuable at King's Bay, on account of his rare mechanical ability, and during our flights also he could help steer the ship, especially at the elevator-wheel. So after a little hesitation, it was finally decided that he should come too. And so the group of Italians who had been with me on the *Norge* took part, one and all, in the *Italia* expedition.

To complete the crew we needed 2 officers, who would take charge of the navigation and the astronomical observations, a helmsman for the steering-wheel, another for the elevator, and 2 wireless operators.

For the two navigating officers I applied to the Admiralty who particularly recommended Commanders Mariano and Zappi. Both of them, but more especially Zappi, had some experience of airships. When they were introduced, they made an excellent impression on me. I did not regret my choice, for from the very first flights they carried out their job in the most satisfactory way. Later on, during the vicissitudes of the voyages from Milan to Stolp and from Stolp to King's Bay, I had occasion to admire their calm and disciplined bearing.

At the same time the Admiralty sent me two other officers to choose from, and one of them—Viglieri—particularly pleased me. After I had inquired into his previous record I asked to have him too, meaning to use him either to man the steering-wheel or to help with the navigation. He appeared delighted at the choice. How well founded the instinctive liking that had attracted me to him had been, the tragic events of our expedition were to show.

Finally I chose Trojani, to take turns with Cecioni at the elevator-wheel. This young engineer, whom I had known for over 12 years, had collaborated with me not only in the designing and construction of various dirigibles, but also in the preparation of the *Norge* expedition. He was a clever and conscientious technician, scrupulous in the accomplishment of his duties, calm and reflective. Besides being useful to steer the ship in flight he would, I knew, be a valuable assistant in preparing the expedition. And certainly, when it came to the final preparations not one of the crew was better acquainted with every part of the ship and its equipment.

Our wireless operators were Pedretti and Biagi. These two petty officers were well worthy to join the elect group of the veterans of the *Norge*. If there was nothing to choose between the two in the matter of skill they were very different in physical appearance: the one fair, blue-eyed, with clean-cut features; the other dark, massive and robust. Two different types of the Italian race—physically so dissimilar, and yet so alike in their simple and ingenuous good nature, their steadiness and resistance to fatigue.

And so the crew was complete. But it is not to be imagined that the choice had been as rapid and easy as might appear from this brief description. They were not definitely chosen until I had seen how they behaved on the trial flights, and until they had all been thoroughly examined by three Air Ministry doctors, with the most up-to-date tests of nerves and constitution, to make certain that each one, besides being fit for the strain of the flights, was tough enough to stand the hardships of camping or marching on the ice.

My Scientific Collaborators

Pontremoli, Malmgren, Behounek: three young and valiant scientists—an Italian, a Swede, and a Czechoslovak. Of these, alas! only one has returned, to collect and publish the results of their joint work, in which the other two are more than ever living. It is due to these savants that the expedition has, in a large measure, achieved the aims which it set out to accomplish.

The scientific report of the expedition has dealt with them all, and more especially with the work of Malmgren, who died so stoically, and Pontremoli, who was lost with the airship. Here I will confine myself to telling how it was decided that they should join the expedition.

Pontremoli, an intrepid young man, not new to aeronautical ventures, a lecturer in science at the University of Milan, took the initiative of asking to share in the expedition. He was a pupil of Rutherford and Corbino, and was introduced to me by eminent Italian men of science, who praised him most warmly. When I got to know him personally, his enthusiasm and his scientific attainments conquered me, and I did not hesitate an instant to accept his collaboration. My choice met with the unanimous approval of all scientific circles in Italy that were interested in the expedition.

In fact, no choice could have been happier. Pontremoli combined in himself all the necessary qualities: a vast scientific learning, an ardent zest for experiment, and a genius for assimilation, in addition to great physical strength and a stout heart, that did not flinch at any responsibility or risk.

Finn Malmgren, a professor of the University of Uppsala, had already taken part as meteorologist in the *Norge* expedition.

I had met him for the first time at Oslo in January 1926. At that time he was collaborating with the Norwegian meteorologists at Bergen, and, hearing that I was at Oslo, he came to see me.

I found myself faced by an attractive young man, about thirty—rather short, fair, with blue eyes and a keen glance. We spoke of the expedition, the meteorological service, and the difficulties which we should probably encounter during the flight. Suddenly he remarked: "For my part I think the probability of success is about 50 per cent., but our chances of saving ourselves are, of course, greater."

This level-headed attitude pleased me—all the more so since, in spite of his pessimistic forecast, the young Swede showed not the slightest hesitation to make himself responsible for the meteorological service of the enterprise.

There is no doubt that Malmgren was an ideal meteorologist for a Polar expedition, but I must state that this was not the only motive that induced me to ask for his co-operation: as he had great experience of oceanographical work, I wished to entrust him with this research, which was such an important part of my programme.

A group of scientific researches of great importance were those referring to the electricity and radioactivity of the atmosphere in the Arctic Circle. For these I invited the co-operation of Dr. Francis Behounek, of the Wireless Institute at Prague, the same young scientist whom I had met at King's Bay in May, 1926, and who had already initiated similar experiments during the *Norge* expedition.

In December, 1927, Behounek wrote to me from Prague, accepting my proposal with evident pleasure: "*Je trouve très méritoire votre intention de faire de l'expédition prochaine une œuvre purement scientifique.*"

In the tale which follows it will be seen what Olympian serenity, what supreme indifference to life, what moral rectitude —and at a given moment what an amount of energy—he showed in the most tragic moments that we experienced.

This is how the expedition was finally constituted:
1. Dr. ALDO PONTREMOLI, Professor of Physics at the University of Milan. Age 31. Of Milan.
2. Dr. FINN MALMGREN, Professor of the University of Uppsala. Age 33. Of Uppsala.
3. Dr. FRANCIS BEHOUNEK, Director of the Prague Wireless Institute, Professor of the University of Prague. Age 31.
4. ADALBERTO MARIANO, Commander. First Officer. Age 30. Of Rivarolo Canavese. (Torino.)
5. FILIPPO ZAPPI, Commander. Age 31. Of Mercato Saraceno. (Forli.)
6. ALFREDO VIGLIERI, Lieut.-Commander. Age 28. Of Sarzana.
7. FELICE TROJANI. Engineer. Age 31. Of Rome.
8. NATALE CECIONI, Chief Technician. Age 41. Of Fiesole. (Florence.)
9. ETTORE ARDUINO, Sub-Lieutenant. Chief Motor Engineer. Age 38. Of Verona.

10. ATTILIO CARATTI, Petty Officer. Motor mechanic. Age 33. Of Rovato.
11. VINCENZO POMELLA. Foreman motor mechanic. Age 30. Of St. Elia, Fiumerapido. (Cassino.)
12. RENATO ALESSANDRINI, Foreman rigger. Age 38. Of Rome.
13. CALISTO CIOCCA. Motor mechanic. Age 31. Of Turin.
14. ETTORE PEDRETTI, Petty Officer. Wireless Operator. Age 34. Of Ravarino. (Modena.)
15. GUISEPPE BIAGI, Petty Officer, 2nd class. Wireless Operator. Age 31. Of Medicina. (Bologna.)
16. FRANCESCO TOMASELLI, *Dottore in Lettere*, Captain of the Alpini. Journalist. Age 34. Of Venice.
17. UGO LAGO, *Dottore in Lettere*, Journalist. Age 28. Of Noto. (Syracuse.)

Eighteen people with myself—without counting Titina, the faithful companion of so many flights.

Equipment for the Arctic

To equip the airship for the Polar expedition, to prepare the special equipment that was necessary, and to choose the instruments on board, certainly required several months of intense work; but it did not present any special difficulties, given the experience we had acquired during the *Norge* expedition.

On the other hand, there were many new problems in preparing the Polar equipment, which I wanted to be as complete as possible. We had not only to foresee the case that, after an accident, the whole crew would have to come down upon the ice and march over it; but also that 2 or 3 men might be put down and left alone somewhere to set up a station for scientific observations. They must be equipped for a long stay, at least until the following spring, in the place where they had been disembarked.

Naturally I took into account the experience of all preceding expeditions. The type of sledge, tent, sleeping-bag, and the rest was not decided upon before finding out what Nansen, Scott, Peary, the Duke of the Abruzzi, Amundsen and Sverdrup had used, and noting the results obtained by them.

Having made my choice, I went to ask Nansen's approval.

The illustrious scientist received me in his little villa at Oslo and kept me in conversation for fully 3 hours. After hearing every detail of our preparations he gave me valuable advice—which I naturally followed to the letter—on the construction of sledges, the provision of fur suits, etc. He even carried his courtesy and interest so far as to promise me that he would ask Otto Sverdrup, his old comrade of the *Fram* expedition, to look after the preparation of sledges, fur clothing, and sleeping-bags.

And this was arranged. Captain Sverdrup and Professor Hoel very kindly undertook to supervise on my behalf the construction of sledges, sleeping-bags, caïques, and reindeer-skin suits.

I will not go into minute details of the equipment, the choice and preparation of which was made with great care and required months of work. It was as complete as possible: sledges of different sizes, skis, snowshoes, clothes, a light canvas boat built under Sverdrup's supervision, rubber dinghies, footgear of various types, reserve provisions, and the rest. These materials were almost all kept inside the airship, distributed evenly among the sections of metallic framework from bow to stern. They could have been used by the men who disappeared on board the airship after the catastrophe.

Here I will briefly mention those things which were very important while we were marooned on the pack, especially the type of tent used, chosen after long and patient search. The experience of Scott's expedition suggested that we should have a double tent, made of silk, with an airspace of about 3 in. between the two layers. The floor was of waterproof material. The tent was square, with an outside measurement of 9 ft. Its walls rose vertically for about a yard, then sloped inwards, pyramid-wise, to a central peak 7 ft. high, supported by a tent-pole. Its circular entrance hole was lined with a cylindrical sleeve, and when this was tied up the tent was hermetically closed. In practice this type proved almost perfect. The "red tent" protected us very well against wind and cold, although the waterproof flooring was not so effective against the damp arising from the ice as it dissolved from the contact with our bodies.

The individual sleeping-bags were of reindeer-skin with the hair on the outside. They had been made under the care of

Sverdrup, Isachsen and Tryggve Gran—one of the survivors of
Scott's expedition.

Each man was provided with a reindeer-skin coat of the kind
used by the Eskimos in Alaska, called *parka*, and besides this with
a lambswool flying-suit, with the fur inside and an outer covering
of windproof and waterproof cloth. This suit was in three parts—
jacket, trousers and hood, and could easily be hermetically closed,
without needing buttons, of course. It weighed about 7½ lb. This
was what all the men were wearing at the moment when we crashed.
It proved sufficient protection against the cold, even for the three
who undertook to march to the coast. There were shoes of all kinds;
besides the ordinary leather and rubber pairs, on the advice of
Nansen and Hoel we added *finsko* and *komager*, which are excellent
against the bitter cold of an Arctic winter, when they are filled with
carex-grass. But during our stay on the pack, as the snow dissolved
with the rising temperature, they became practically useless.

The reserve provisions consisted of chocolate, biscuits, malted
milk tablets, and butter; but the most valuable proved to be
pemmican—that classic of all Polar expeditions, which is a concentrated and compressed mixture of meat, fat and vegetables,
prepared in half-pound packs wrapped in tinfoil. The pemmican
was an essential part of our reserve supplies. To appreciate its
usefulness, one must have eaten it in the conditions in which we
found ourselves after the crash. Even the most fastidious found
pemmican soup delicious.

I will not give particulars of the rest of the equipment; but
I must not forget to mention that the choice of firearms, and even
of the pickaxes and ice-axes, was made on the advice of experts;
and that every man of the crew had a pocket-knife with several
blades, a small magnetic pocket-compass, a good watch, two pairs
of dark glasses as protection against snow-glare, and even a
veil, in case we landed near the Mackenzie or in any other
mosquito-infested country.

Foreseeing the possibility of a catastrophe on our return to the
Svalbard, a couple of hundred miles short of King's Bay, I

urged that one or two seaplanes should be allotted to the expedition. These would have been valuable for carrying prompt
help to men stranded by this or any similar misfortune, once
they had succeeded in signalling their whereabouts. In one of
the meetings held in the Viminale Palace I presented my ideas on
this subject, pointing out that—in this unfortunate eventuality—
the pilot could bring us help even without descending on the
pack, simply by throwing down provisions, sledges, or any other
requisite. But Balbo refused to allot us the seaplanes.

I even went further, and thought it wise to ask for several
Alpini soldiers, chosen amongst the most expert skiers, to be sent
to King's Bay, in readiness for any emergency. So a band of
8 Alpini was formed under Captain Sora—nearly all of them born
and bred among the snow and ice of the Alps, steeled to the
hardest exertions, and first-class skiers. How useful these Alpini
proved, while the airship was at King's Bay, and later on after the
catastrophe, is common knowledge.

Captain Sora was selected from three of the best ski-ing
instructors in the Italian Army. The frank, open face of this young
officer pleased me, and the gallant march which he made with the
Dutchman Van Dongen to reach Foyn Island proved that I had
not been mistaken in my choice.

I was glad to have at King's Bay also some members of the
Italian University Students Alpine Association (S.U.C.A.I.),
amongst them Albertini and Matteoda, who, in their march along
the coast of North-East Land in search of Mariano's party,
magnificently justified the hopes that had been set on them.

THE FLIGHT FROM MILAN TO
KING'S BAY

The Flight to Stolp

DURING the second half of March the organization was completed and the expedition set in motion: on March 19th the *Città di Milano* weighed anchor from Spezia, bound for King's Bay, while at the same time the *Italia* was transferred from Rome to Milan, ready to fly across Europe. In the early hours of the 24th the *Hobby* in its turn left Tromsö for King's Bay, bringing the new canvas covering of the hangar and about 300 tons of materials, with which the dirigible could be refuelled and repaired if by any chance the *Città di Milano* should arrive too late. The master builder Arild and some Norwegian workmen went with these materials. A group of Italians, including Captain Sora and the designer De Martino, was headed by my brother Amedeo, who, as in 1926, was going to set up a weather station in Spitsbergen. Two other groups of Italian workmen left at the same time for Vadsö and Stolp, where, as I have said, I meant to halt during the voyage of the *Italia* to the Svalbard to refuel with petrol and hydrogen.

On March 31st the crew of the *Italia* was received by Pope Pius XI who had already followed with close interest the fortunes of the *Norge* expedition. As a keen mountaineer he well knew the peril of the ice and snow, so I had not been at all surprised when he called my attention even then to the possibility of ice forming on the dirigible—as, in fact, occurred on several occasions.

Besides, his knowledge of Polar expeditions, as of so many other subjects, was exceptional. He was so well acquainted with the literature as to quote, in the various conversations I had with him, important details which had escaped me. But the Pope had

THE TRAGEDY OF THE ITALIA

taken even more interest in this new expedition than in the former one, asking me to keep him informed of the preparations, the scientific programme, and the difficulties we expected to encounter. His interest went so far that he personally hunted for a series of meteorological data collected during the Austrian expedition to Franz-Josef Land, which I myself had been unable to trace.

And so the Pope received us: an audience that was at the same time simple and solemn.

He addressed us as a father might his children who were setting out for a noble but dangerous venture. We were struck by his affectionately paternal manner, and by the gentle tone of voice in which he told us that in all human undertakings, at a given moment, a higher force intervenes, to turn the scale of human endeavour for good or for ill, and that therefore he would pray for us.

Then he announced the mission which he was confiding to us: to carry the emblem of Christ to the summit of the world—a beautiful oak cross which he himself had had prepared. Its upper part had been hollowed out, and in the cavity a parchment placed, on which the following words were written:

HOC SIGNUM JESU CHRISTI REGIS

IPSE EIUS VICARIUS

PIUS XI PONT. MAX.

HUMBERTO NOBILI SOCIISQUE

ITER AERIUM

AERE MEDIOLANENSI INSTITUENTIBUS

PRID. KAL. APR. A. MCMXXVIII

BENE PRECATUS TRADIDIT

DEMITTENDUM DUCI

POLUM ITERUM TRANSVOLANTI

AD ORBIS TERRAE VERTICEM

CONSECRANDUM

(This emblem of Our Lord Jesus Christ has today, the 31st of March, 1928, been entrusted with dedicatory prayers by His Vicar, Pius XI, Pontifex Maximus, to Umberto Nobile and his companions, on the eve of their aerial journey at the charges of the City of Milan, to be dropped by the leader of the expedition, flying for the second time over the Pole; thus to consecrate the summit of the world.)

"And like all crosses," he added with a smile, "this one will be heavy to carry."

Having finished his speech, he blessed us and went towards the door, but on the threshold he turned back. He had still something to add. It seemed as though he had not said enough. Perhaps he did not find it easy to separate from us.

We were moved by this. It seemed to us that no one understood or appreciated better than he the spirit which had animated us in preparing the enterprise. We left the Vatican deeply comforted and with our hearts at peace.

A few days later I had a farewell audience of the King, who, having personally experienced the difficulties of the climate in the Arctic, which he had twice visited in his youth, took particular interest in the account I gave him, and asked for information on many details. In the end he took leave of me cordially with fervent good wishes for the success of this new enterprise.

Then, on April 11th, I was received by Mussolini, who was affable and kind as ever. Map in hand, I explained the complete plan of our expedition, and summed up for him the main points of the preparation. He expressed himself delighted:

"Good!" he said. "You have foreseen everything. That's the best way to succeed. To provide for everything—one hundred per cent. That's my system, too!"

Then he remarked: "The enterprise is not one of those destined to strike the popular imagination, like your 1926 expedition. But it will attract the attention of the scientific world. I see already that there is a great deal of interest in it abroad." And he parted from me with the warmest phrases of good will.

We were now ready to start. . . .

We left Milan, with 20 people on board, on the night of April 14th-15th, at 1.55 a.m. I kept secret my decision, so as not to have a troublesome crowd on the airfield and in the hangar.

The meteorological situation was not altogether favourable. During that day there had been bad weather all over Germany, although according to the news from Lindenberg Observatory conditions had now improved. But all things considered, since Malmgren and our Italian meteorologist were both entirely in favour of it, I decided to start.

"We shall have some difficulties," said Malmgren. "But we cannot hope for anything better during the next few days."

From an aeronautical point of view this journey from the Valley of the Po to the Baltic was certainly one of the most interesting voyages recently undertaken by a small dirigible. During the whole 1,200 miles it seemed as though all atmospheric trials had conspired to put our ship and crew to a hard test: rain, fog, hail, lightning, ice, snow—nothing was spared us. So there is every reason to consider this flight of 30½ hours as the sternest proof of the pluck and skill of the crew and the worth of the airship.

Gusts of wind, rising to 24 m.p.h., buffeted us, especially as we crossed the Karst between Trieste and Sadobrava, where a squall more violent than usual broke the left horizontal fin.

At 8.10 a.m. we flew over Lubiana, continuing by way of Körmend and Sopron, two little Hungarian towns not far from the Austrian border. At 2.40 p.m., under a completely grey sky and in what the weather report called "a nasty drizzle", we passed over Vienna, and at 4.05 p.m. over Brünn (Brno) in Czechoslovakia, whence we went on northwards towards Kraliky. In the meantime, weather conditions were beginning to worry me very much.

Some hours before, while we were over Czechoslovakia, the Prague Meteorological Office had warned us that the whole of Moravia and Silesia was covered with storm-clouds accompanied by lightning flashes and strong winds. Not far from Brünn my anxiety was increased by another message, saying that Bohemia was at that moment being crossed by a storm-front, which was advancing ENE. at a speed of 40 m.p.h.

In fact, as we approached the Sudetes we found our way almost completely barred by thick masses of cloud, which here

and there assumed a menacing aspect. Only in the direction of
the valley for which we were steering was the sky a trifle clearer.

We continued cautiously on our way. By this time we were
close to the pass, and soon we should have crossed it, apparently
without difficulty. But quite unexpectedly a deluge of rain over-
took and surrounded us. We found ourselves wrapped in cloud,
and could hardly see the earth. A violent hailstorm lashed down,
and amongst the hailstones glimmered the first streaks of lightning.

It was a terrible moment. The storm was round us on all sides:
flashes followed hard on one another—lightning to right, to left,
in front of us, behind us, accompanied by deafening peals of
thunder. It seemed as if there were no way out. From one moment
to another a thunderbolt might strike the ship and set it on fire.

Yet everyone on board remained perfectly calm. I brought the
dirigible as low as possible (450 ft. from the ground) to reduce
the danger of being struck, and at the same time ordered the
helmsman to steer for a spot where the sky appeared less dark.
For half an hour we sailed on over the mountains through the
storm: now rising and descending to cross a peak, now swerving
right or left to avoid others too high. It was a wild course, and
needed continuous concentrated attention to avoid hitting the
mountains which suddenly surged out of the fog right in our path.
But at last, following the break in the clouds, we came out into
the plain. The sky in front was almost clear; we had left the
storm behind us in the mountains.

All the same, we no longer knew exactly where we were. In
that dizzy crossing of the mountains, skimming the ground
amidst clouds and hail, continual lightning, and shattering
thunder, my only thought had been to escape as quickly as
possible from the storm, without troubling where we went provided we got out into clearer weather. So that now we were
back in the plain we were not sure if we had crossed the mountains
in the direction of Glatz or had turned back towards Brünn.

Only one of the navigating officers was convinced that we were
on the north side of the Sudetes, whilst the others both maintained
that we were back in Czechoslovakia. This opinion, incidentally,
was confirmed by a radiogram from Prague, telling us that at

8.25 p.m. the *Italia* had been several miles south of Brünn. But this was a mistake. Very soon, by carefully observing the locality, we made up our minds that we were near Glatz in Silesia.

Meanwhile I had decided not to go on northwards without first receiving satisfactory news of the weather. So I gave orders to cruise up and down where we were, pending the information for which I had asked Lindenberg Observatory. I was even ready, if the meteorologists advised me, to turn back to Italy. We had been in such danger during the storm that I did not want to run the same risk again. I was so anxious to arrive at the Svalbard that I would not compromise the success of the voyage by insisting on continuing at all costs, even if the weather was definitely bad.

But fortunately at 9.55 p.m. Lindenberg Observatory telegraphed: "Meteorological conditions permit you to navigate as far as Stolp."

In fact, the northern sky in front of us was brightening up. The air had become clear and transparent, so that the countless lights of the cities below sparkled clearly as we passed them. I then decided to go on. At 0.35 on April 16th we were over Oppeln and at 1.58 over Breslau.

Beyond Breslau a thick bank of cloud forced us up to 7,500 ft. At 4.8 a.m. we sailed over Posen.

The last hours of our flight to Stolp were calm. Only from time to time we were overtaken by rain, and then ice showed signs of forming on the metal of the airship. The temperature was about 23° F., more than 30 degrees lower than when we left Milan, so that we suffered a bit from the cold, being unprepared for such a great difference.

At 7.50 on the morning of April 16th we landed successfully on the field at Jesseritz, being splendidly helped on our manœuvres by the Germans, who had fetched soldiers specially from the garrison at Stolp.

Upon our arrival we found that the upper fin had also been broken, while all three airscrews were eroded by the hailstones that had struck them.

From Germany to the Svalbard

The two fins could easily have been repaired on the spot with the means we had at our disposal, but to eliminate the possibility of a similar accident recurring I had decided to repair and strengthen the second lateral fin as well. There was a fair amount to be done, but I sent to Italy for some workmen and the necessary materials. In about 10 days everything was finished; the motors and other parts had been carefully overhauled and a few minor repairs executed, so that on April 28th we were ready to resume our flight.

The same day my brother Amedeo telegraphed from King's Bay that the mooring-mast and the hangar were ready. A few days before, a violent wind had damaged the canvas doors of the hangar, but they had now been repaired.

I was impatient to go on to the Svalbard, and Malmgren too urged me to start as soon as possible. However, the *Città di Milano*, with most of the men and materials necessary for the expedition, had been held up for some days at Tromsö. . . . They could not make up their minds to start for King's Bay, having received news that the Bay was largely frozen over.

Now if the *Città di Milano* intended to wait until the Bay was free from ice, another 2 or 3 weeks must pass before it arrived, whilst I had reckoned on its being there not later than April 25th. So long a delay endangered the success of the whole expedition.

I telegraphed to the *Città di Milano*, telling them that after all, it was not essential to come alongside the landing-stage, since they could unload the necessary men and materials on the ice, as the *Hobby* had already done. Meanwhile I reflected that if the weather turned favourable we must take advantage of it, even though the *Città di Milano* had not yet arrived at King's Bay; so I decided to get ready to start.

I foresaw great difficulties in this flight from Germany to the Svalbard; for I had no illusions that we should again be favoured with a meteorological situation like that on the voyage of the *Norge* from Leningrad to King's Bay in 1926. It was idle to hope that the same thing would happen again. We must accept any tolerable conditions.

On April 30th the Tromsö Geophysical Institute informed us that the meteorological situation led them to expect good weather in the Scandinavian Peninsula and a strong wind on the Barents Sea (Force 5, Beaufort Scale).[1] In sending me this forecast the Institute advised me to start, adding: "Such a situation is as good as one can hope for at this time of year. There are uncertainties and risks, but these are inevitable."

We could not leave that day, however, because the violent wind blowing at Stolp prevented us from coming out of the hangar, and it held us up for the two following days.

At last on the evening of May 2nd—with Malmgren's full approval—I decided to start, although in the whole region around Stolp, at less than 1,000 ft., a head-wind of 30 m.p.h. was blowing. I went to tell my wife, who had come with the child to Germany to see me once more before I went farther. She wanted to walk back with me. Passing a little church, she said to me, "Let's go in." We went in. The church was dark and empty. The dear little woman knelt down to pray. When we came out of the church she would not leave me until the moment of our departure.

We left Stolp at 3.28 a.m. on May 3rd, with a strong north wind blowing about 24 m.p.h.

There were 18 of us on board. The ship was in excellent trim, including the scientific instruments to be used on the journey. Our equipment comprised everything necessary for coping with the worst emergencies, including several boats in case we were forced down into the Barents Sea.

Although the wind was usually against us, we covered the 395 miles between Stolp and Stockholm in only $7\frac{1}{2}$ hours, having forced the engines from the start. At 11 a.m., escorted by several seaplanes that had come out to welcome us, we arrived over the beautiful Swedish capital, and we dropped a letter of greetings over the little house where Malmgren's mother was waiting.

We crossed Finland by night, with a strong, steady wind that considerably reduced our speed, but without hampering the

[1] 17 to 21 m.p.h.

navigation. The landscape, with its vast snow-covered plains, recalled northern Russia.

At 9.40 p.m. we were over Kalajoki, and half an hour after midnight we reached Kemi, the little Finnish town situated at the head of the Gulf of Bothnia. Thence we steered for Rovaniemi, which we flew over at 1.49. A few hours later our first troubles began.

The meteorological data pouring into our wireless cabin showed that a depression had formed over the Barents Sea. There would be strong northerly winds between Norway and Spitsbergen, and moderate east winds in the neighbourhood of Vadsö.

The last message received from the Tromsö Geophysical Institute was somewhat alarming: it warned us that the depression centred between Bear Island and Spitsbergen was moving eastwards, and it advised us to increase our speed.

In consequence of this warning I forced the speed, putting the third motor into action and accelerating the other two.

Beyond Pekkala, which we reached at 5.50, the visibility— already indifferent—became thoroughly bad. Very soon the fog swallowed us up, often cutting us from sight of the ground, although we were flying extremely low. For an hour we travelled thus over the hills in the fog, and navigation was very dangerous. We also had some traces of ice formation.

At last, thinking it too risky to go on over such uneven country in the fog, we climbed up and continued to sail above it, until we imagined that there must be sea below. And in fact, when we dived down, we could see Vadsö on the coast not far away, with the little island and the mooring-mast sticking up. It was 8.55 a.m.

Quarter of an hour later the *Italia* was attached to the mast, after a difficult manœuvre, during which—perhaps because it was impossible to use the lateral ground-ropes—a gust of wind forced the prow against the mast-head, doing some slight damage, which was quickly repaired.

As soon as we were moored we began to lay in a fresh stock of hydrogen, petrol, oil, and water.

Three or four hours later we had finished refuelling and were ready to go on, but weather conditions between the north coast of Norway and Spitsbergen made it out of the question to leave that day. There was nothing for it, then, but to wait patiently until the depression announced by the Geophysical Institute reached us, with its accompanying east wind.

The wind struck us early in the evening, but it was not strong. Tired as I was by my long watch, I went to sleep for a time in one of the rubber dinghies inside the hull, telling the officer on duty to wake me if anything happened.

During the night the wind freshened, so that they roused me after an hour or two. I went down at once to the control cabin, to give the necessary orders for dealing with the situation, if a squall should tear the airship from the mast. One could feel its steel framework quivering as the powerful wind sent it spinning now and again around the pylon. From time to time there were flurries of snow.

Later in the morning, things grew even worse. The wind increased to 40 m.p.h., and the gusts were so violent that they broke some steel tubing at the tip of the stern, which was repaired on the spot. From time to time dark clouds passed overhead and the snow fell thickly. My fear that it would settle on the envelope and weigh down the ship kept me in anxiety for some time, until Alessandrini—whom I had sent out to reconnoitre on the bow— came back to tell me that the stiff wind was sweeping away most of the snow. There was nothing to fear on that score, at least so long as the wind lasted.

After midday the wind began to drop, and as the temperature was steadily rising the snowstorms gave place to torrents of rain: this was still more trying, for the water ran down the sides of the ship, penetrated into the cabin and soaked everything. But at last even the rain stopped, and the weather seemed to be on the mend.

We left Vadsö at 8.34 p.m. on May 5th.

We had 19 on board (having embarked one of the Italians at the halt), and had 123½ cwt. of petrol, with which we could have covered the distance to King's Bay, even with a wind of 36 m.p.h. blowing steadily against us the whole time.

The first part of the journey, between the coast of Norway and Bear Island, passed off without any particular difficulty, although we very often ran into fogs, and from time to time were surrounded by snow-storms. But, as the Tromsö Bureau had predicted, the wind was not strong, so by 4.30 next morning we easily reached Bear Island, which was mantled in white. We flew over the little meteorological observatory, where the two physicists who had helped us so indefatigably with their information were waiting for us.

Between Bear Island and the Svalbard the weather grew worse. According to the Tromsö forecast we ought to have met with a strong north wind, but the event did not correspond with this. Suddenly we found ourselves in the head of a cyclone advancing from Iceland, which set up violent south-east winds (36 to 42 m.p.h.) on our course.

Along the west coast of Spitsbergen we were smothered in a thick snow-storm. The whole atmosphere was in tumult. We saw great masses of cloud scudding in various directions, mainly NW. It was a magnificent sight. "The situation is rather dangerous," remarked Malmgren, "the atmosphere is full of energy."

At this moment the tempest seemed to be getting the upper hand of us: we were advancing almost broadside-on and, without realizing it, were driven out of our course. Still, I was not worried. We could face the storm better in the air than tied to the mast at Vadsö. I felt far safer aloft, because, when all was said and done, we had enough petrol to go on sailing—if necessary—another 3 days. By making use of the south-east wind we could even have reached the Arctic Ocean at once.

This idea tempted me again, as in 1926, and I was going to put it into practice straight away, when, as on the *Norge* flight, a serious flaw developed and put one of our engines definitely out of use. In these circumstances, it would have been rash to lengthen the journey unnecessarily, so I decided to go straight on to King's Bay.

When we got clear of the blizzard we found ourselves in the strait between Prince Charles Island and the Great Svalbard, instead of to left of this island. Having checked our position with the help of the wireless reports, we crossed the strait and steered for the mouth of the Bay.

Better news now arrived from Ny Aalesund. The wind was still strong, but the barometer was going up. As it was now certain that we should have good visibility for landing, we entered the Bay. It was 11.22 a.m. Half an hour afterwards, tacking on account of the heavy wind, we were over Ny Aalesund. As before, the hangar and the mast were ready to receive us. There was also the *Città di Milano* decked in flags, and the little Norwegian whaler—the *Hobby*.

At 12.45 p.m. I gave orders to drop the mooring-cable, which was promptly grasped by the Alpine skiers and then held firmly by the sailors. The dirigible was dragged down to earth, but, as the gusts were so strong that they prevented its being pulled into the hangar, I was obliged to moor it to the mast.

Meanwhile, I had sent down most of the crew, keeping on board with me, besides the engine mechanics, only Trojani and one of the Naval officers; that is to say, the indispensable minimum for navigating the ship.

But fortunately, with the help of the Norwegian miners, who had hurried along as soon as I sent for them, to replace the Italian sailors whom the captain of the *Città di Milano* had not wanted to leave on the spot, all ended well. Three-quarters of an hour later, taking advantage of a momentary lull, I had the airship unmoored from the mast and put safely into the hangar.

And so at last, after 82 hours, I, too, was able to leave the ship and go to rest.

Altogether, we had flown 2,100 miles from Stolp.

AT KING'S BAY

A First Unsuccessful Flight of Exploration

TO change the damaged engine and overhaul the other two; examine point by point the structure and organs of the dirigible and replenish it with petrol, oil, and hydrogen; embark the equipment and provisions needed for coping with an emergency; put all the instruments in order for the scientific observations planned in our programme: all this had to be done, during the days that followed our arrival at King's Bay, before the *Italia* could start on her first flight of exploration.

Our task was complicated by the fact that most of the necessary materials were on the *Città di Milano*, and had to be laboriously dragged for over a mile in thick snow, from the spot amid the ice where the ship lay anchored, to the hangar. But after four days' hard work we were at last ready.

Meanwhile Malmgren and I had arranged with the Tromsö Geophysical Institute to supply the necessary information and weather forecasts for our explorations.

An integral part of our programme was a flight to Severnaya Zemlya, and one or two to the Pole during which—either going out or coming back—we intended to cross at least once the unexplored zone north of Greenland, and another between the 30th and 40th meridians E. of Greenwich. We also admitted the possibility of going on from the Pole to the mouth of the Mackenzie, on the north coast of America.

At bottom I did not mind the order in which these flights were undertaken, so I decided that it should depend solely upon weather conditions. I had numbered the 5 routes on my programme, and arranged with the Tromsö Institute to tell us at once whenever the weather was suitable for any of the flights indicated by these conventional numbers.

On May 10th Tromsö telegraphed that weather conditions favoured a flight to Nicholas II Land (or Severnaya Zemlya, as the Russians now call it). So I gave orders for the start, which took place at 7.55 a.m. next day.

The temperature during the preceding days had fluctuated round about 14° F., but that morning it shot up above zero, forcing me to unload several hundred tins of petrol, and also— to my great regret—leave Behounek behind. Complaisant as ever, he showed no signs of his disappointment, and immediately arranged with Pontremoli to carry out the measurements of atmospheric electricity in his stead.

The crew now consisted of 2 physicists—Malmgren and Pontremoli; 3 Naval officers—Mariano, Zappi and Viglieri; the engineer—Trojani; the chief technician—Cecioni; the chief motor engineer—Arduino; 3 motor-mechanics—Pomella, Caratti, and Ciocca; the rigger—Alessandrini; and the wireless operator—Biagi. Counting myself, we were 14.

We left the bay at Cape Mitre, flew northwards, and coasted along Haakon VII Land, over open sea.

At this point Alessandrini reported that a wire rope controlling the rudder was badly worn in one place and several strands were broken. I lost no time in sending someone to reinforce it. If by bad luck this rope had given way unexpectedly it might have had very serious consequences, in the bad weather that developed subsequently.

At Barren Cape, where we found patches of floating ice, we turned eastwards, steering for Moffen Island.

Here the weather suddenly grew worse. The atmospheric pressure fell, and we were enveloped by a violent gale, with snow and fog, lasting over 2 hours. Ice began to form all over the ship, and the snow sticking to it accumulated in considerable quantities, chiefly on the canvas walls of the pilot-cabin.

As we approached Cape North the pressure went on falling and the weather grew steadily worse. In fact, the latest wireless bulletins indicated that the general state of the weather all along our course had unexpectedly changed. I then decided to steer northwards, hoping to find better conditions, but soon I was convinced that the situation was just as bad in the North.

This being the case, the only thing to do was to return to our base, which we did.

At 4.10 p.m. we landed and had the dirigible put back into its hangar.

Malmgren at once sent the following message to the Tromsö Geophysical Institute:

Happy home after unsuccessful flight in heavy wind with snow and ice-crust (*sic*). We are ready for a new trial.

MALMGREN.

Netherthcless, from a scientific point of view this flight had not been wasted, for even in these 8 hours Pontremoli had been able to make 10 observations of penetrating radiation, 5 of the gradient of electric potential, 2 of atmospheric conductibility, and 4 of radioactivity. We had also made four series of measurements with the Bidlingmayer double compass; but only one was any good, as the others had been disturbed by the continual pitching and tossing of the airship.

Two Days of Anxiety at King's Bay

Our hangar consisted merely of two canvas-covered wooden walls, between which the dirigible was moored, as in a corridor. Its ends were closed by canvas curtains, which could be lifted or dropped. So the ship was fairly well protected against side winds, but less so against winds blowing straight down the hangar, which often made the canvas flap so violently that it seemed like giving way. Further, with no roof whatever, snow, rain, and sun could strike freely on the ship.

From this arose a serious danger, which I had foreseen ever since the *Norge* expedition: the possibility of snow piling up on the ship so heavily as to break its back. This danger materialized on May 12th and 13th, when it snowed without stopping. Such a heavy and prolonged snowfall was quite exceptional at King's Bay at that time of year.

It began on the morning of the 12th, while preparations for the next flight—which I had planned for the following day—were being eagerly pushed forward.

At first we had wind and snow together, so that it was very trying to move about in the thick of the blizzard, which made it difficult even to find the hangar. The dirigible, however, was in no danger, for the wind swept away the snow as it fell, just as when we were moored to the mast at Vadsö.

But later, when the wind dropped, the snow went on falling thickly and accumulated on the ship in layers that deepened visibly from hour to hour: half an inch, one inch . . . ! The airship was being loaded so quickly that at one moment, in spite of all we could do, whether to increase its upward lift or to lighten it of as much snow as possible, besides petrol and equipment, I doubted if we could stop its steady increase in weight.

By this time the pilot-cabin and the stern engine-boat were dragging heavily on the floor of the hangar. The stern, with the two great lateral fins, was so heavily loaded that the metal plating underneath began to buckle, as if about to give way under the strain of supporting the snow; this was clear from the many creases in its outer covering of varnished cloth.

There was serious cause for worry. But my anxiety was increased by weighing the snow which had fallen during 1 hour on a flat surface a yard square—over a pound! Remember that at least 2,000 sq. yds. of the ship's horizontal surface were exposed to the snow; that meant that every hour it was burdened by more than a ton!

To free the dirigible from the snow which had already collected and was still piling up was the preoccupation which harried me for 2 days and nights; and the thought of the damage the men might accidentally do to the envelope, either by walking over it or in the act of sweeping, increased my anxiety. But at last the indefatigable efforts of our workmen and sailors defeated the snowfall, and the peril of an excessive increase in weight was definitely avoided. The temperature, too, was gradually rising, and the snow began to melt.

Even this welcome thaw, however, gave rise to worry, for fear the temperature might drop again and freeze the water dripping

down the sides and the residue of the unmelted snow, caking the
ship with a tenacious layer of ice.

But fortunately, once the snow had stopped, the sky cleared
and a radiant sun shone out to dry the water that was spouting
from all parts of the ship, as if from gutters. I immediately sent a
few expert workmen to overhaul the envelope, and they found a
few insignificant tears, which were carefully mended. The stuff
was rather worn in the centre, towards the bow, where the
sweepers had been working most; so I had it strengthened with a
long strip of rubberized fabric.

Umberto Nobile before the *Norge* expedition.

(*Above*) The *Norge* flying over Leningrad.

(*Below*) The pilot's cabin in the *Italia*.

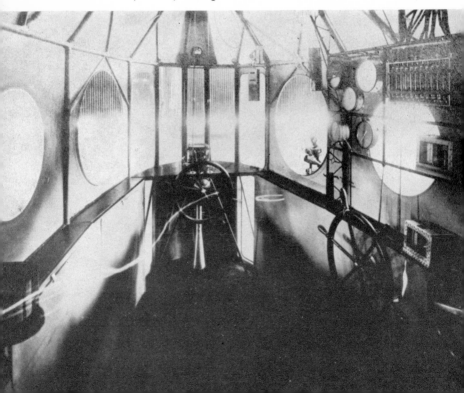

(Left) The *Italia* starts her flight to King's Bay from Stolp, on the Baltic Sea.

(Below) The *Italia* inside the hangar at King's Bay (the chain-ballast can be seen).

(Above) On board the *Italia* at the mooring mast at Vardsö: *(l. to r.)* a Norwegian Navy officer, Malmgren, Mariano, another Norwegian Navy officer, Nobile.

(Below) Navy officers at King's Bay: *(center)* Zappi, with Mariano at his right and Viglieri at his left.

(Above) The Polar Ocean as it looked near the North Pole.

(Below) Dropping the flag at the Pole.

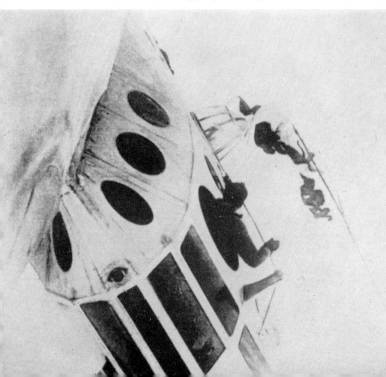

(Above) The Red Tent.

(Below) The seaplane S.55 lands near the *Citta di Milano* at Virigo Bay, after an unsuccessful attempt to reach the Red Tent (18th June 1928).

On the pack, near the Red Tent, at the arrival of Lundborg. With the help of Viglieri (hidden behind him) and Behounek, Nobile gets up to greet the aviator.

(Above) Zappi climbs on board the *Krassin*.
(Below) The *Krassin* beside the Red Tent.

THE FLIGHT TO SEVERNAYA ZEMLYA[1]

ON the morning of May 14th, as the weather was rapidly improving at King's Bay and I had received good news of meteorological conditions in the eastern sector of the Polar basin, I resolved at once to prepare for a fresh start to explore the two unknown zones between Spitsbergen and Franz Josef Land and between the latter and Severnaya Zemlya.

I was chiefly concerned about the petrol. The main difficulty of the project was not, in fact, the 2,100 miles to be travelled, but rather the necessity of returning to our starting-point. Fuel must therefore be sufficient to enable us to reach our base without fail, even if we met with strong head-winds. I decided to take no less than 140 cwt. of petrol—sufficient for about 85 hours of flight at our normal speed of 48 m.p.h.

But this large quantity of petrol could only be had by giving up ballast altogether; so I unhesitatingly suppressed the last of the 4 water-tanks we had had on board when we left Milan, replacing the 66 gallons of water and glycerine by petrol. This was a serious sacrifice, which can only be fully appreciated by experts, and I tried to compensate for it by taking 550 lb. of petrol in tins, that could at need be thrown out as ballast.

Loading the petrol and oil was simple and rapid, compared with the far more complicated process of embarking equipment, stores, clothing, etc., which weighed in all several tons. It was no light matter, especially in our case, to choose and prepare these materials, and arrange them where they were ready to hand and at the same time properly distributed as regards weight. Great care was necessary in choosing the instruments for the scientific observations in the programme. This was done, under my supervision, by Pontremoli, Behounek and Malmgren.

[1] This country was originally called Nicholas II Land; later Lenin Land; finally Severnaya Zemlya (Northern Land).

Altogether, counting spare parts, repairing materials, tools, provisions, and the equipment I have mentioned, our cargo weighed 58 cwt. Adding to this figure 140 cwt. of petrol, over 9 cwt. of oil, and 28 cwt. represented by the crew, we get a total load of 236 cwt. at starting—a really remarkable load for an airship of only 24,000 cubic yards, especially as the temperature—round about freezing-point—was very much higher than I had hoped after my experience in 1926.

An hour after midnight everything was ready for the start. But on being tested the oil circulation of one of the 3 engines proved defective. We tried repeatedly, but unsuccessfully, to eliminate the trouble, and finally decided to alter the tubing. And so we hung about for 12 hours in the hangar, in a suspense that tired mind and body far more than a day's flight. But in the end, at 1 p.m. on the 15th, we were ready, and at 1.20 we set off.

There were 16 men on board: Malmgren and Pontremoli; the three navigating officers—Mariano, Zappi, and Viglieri, Trojani and Cecioni, for the elevator; Arduino, the chief motor engineer; three motor mechanics—Caratti, Ciocca, and the indefatigable Pomella; two wireless operators—Pedretti and Biagi; and lastly Alessandrini—cheerful and serene as ever—and Tomaselli.

Cesco Tomaselli represented the Press; but I must admit that during this flight he did his best to make up for it by acting as steward into the bargain.

My first intention had been to exclude the journalists from these exploring flights, and in fact there had been none on our journey to Cape North. But Tomaselli and Lago had been so chagrined at this decision that I felt bound to go back on it; so in the end I decided to take them in turn. The difficulty was to decide which should come first. Each wished to be the first to face the hazards of a Polar flight. To put an end to the dispute they decided to trust to luck. . . . The toss of a coin—heads or tails? Lago got it. The expressive eyes of the young Sicilian lit up with joy. . . . But then I intervened to give priority to the elder. And so their fate was settled.

At the beginning of the voyage there was nothing remarkable.

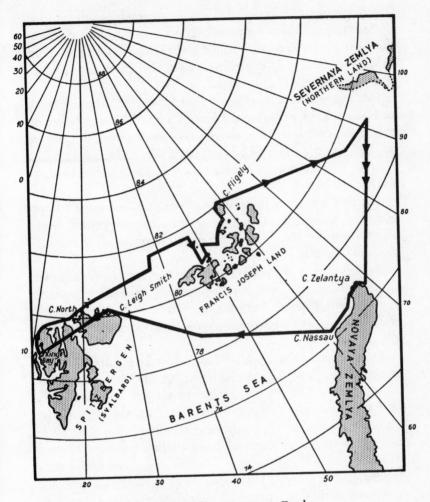

The *Italia*'s Flight to Severnaya Zemlya

The sailing was absolutely calm and the weather splendid. So we decided to profit by the unusually good light for photographing that part of the west coast which had remained indefinite, even in the latest maps. At one point we left the sea for a while and flew over the hills of Dane Island.

Nothing particularly struck my attention along the east coast of Haakon VII Land as far as Barren Cape, which we reached at 2.45 p.m., except that the sea was completely open, in contrast to 1926, when we had found it covered here and there with ice.

From Barren Cape we went on towards Cape North, heading for Moffen Island.

The first ice worth mentioning appeared as we crossed Cape Hansteen, though on our left the sea to the north was still open. But there was a white line on the distant horizon, which marked the southern limit of the pack.

At 5.25 p.m. we passed over Cape North, so near that we could clearly distinguish a pillar, probably erected to mark a trigonometrical point. Here the sea was quite frozen over, and from this moment the ice was almost continuous for the rest of the journey.

At first, along the coast of North-East Land, the pack was frequently broken by pools and leads, but later they ceased.

Beyond Cape North the weather—fine until now—suddenly changed. At 5.50 p.m. we were overtaken for the first time by snow, and after this it snowed frequently during the whole voyage. We were not surprised, being accustomed to meet it even in zones of high barometrical pressure, like that in which we were travelling. But we had learnt that when pressure was high the snow was never thick enough to reduce the visibility excessively. In fact, even now, when we were fully surrounded, we could still see clearly up to about 6 miles.

I looked out of the porthole to see the pack, and once more I was struck by the glorious harmony between the pure white of the snow and the delicate, cloudy pearl-grey of the freshly frozen pools, bordered with blue. The blending of tints was thrown into even greater relief by the uniform grey sky overhead.

We were travelling towards the unexplored region that

extends north of Spitsbergen and Franz Josef Land, between the 25th and 45th meridian E. of Greenwich and the parallels 81° and 85° N. In the heart of this our maps indicated the probable existence of a tract called Gillis Land.

Shortly before we reached this region the fog came down. Once again ice formed more or less everywhere, especially on the outer covering of the cabin and the keel, and even on the envelope. The quantity was much greater than on previous occasions, so that the weight of the airship was noticeably increased. This disquieting phenomenon only stopped when we dived under the fog, to about 500 ft. above the pack.

Later on these incrustations formed more than once during the journey, and we even had splinters of ice striking the envelope in the way that had made us so anxious during the crossing from the Pole to Alaska in 1926; but this time they were much less noticeable and did not do any damage. I was surprised to see, however, that a considerable quantity of ice had formed on the wooden bars of the screw that acted as a fan to start the dynamo of the wireless. Often the centrifugal force loosened pieces of it and flung them violently against the side of the commander's cabin, producing a characteristic noise like a pistol-shot.

At 10.30 p.m. I gave orders to steer northwards, so as to penetrate deeper into that unexplored region. And so at 11.15 we reached latitude 81° 47′ and longitude 37° 21′ E., without finding any vestige of coast. Then we went on south-east towards Franz Josef Land.

The only signs of life in this frozen wilderness were a few black birds, which we saw flying towards us from the north (about 36° 35′ longitude and 81° 18′ latitude), but as soon as they noticed us they swerved away and disappeared eastwards. Later, near Alexandra Land, we caught sight of a bear, which was startled to see us and scuttled off towards the south.

At 2.20 a.m. on May 16th, flying under low clouds and in the fog, we sighted one of the islands of Franz Josef Land. The sky was still grey all over and the visibility much reduced—certainly the worst during the whole voyage. As we approached land we found a vast stretch of open water, but

10 minutes later we were again over ice, though on our left the
sea was open.

When we reached Albert Armitage Island visibility was so
bad that we decided to coast along the archipelago, so as not to
lose the way. We touched in succession Arthur Island, Alfred
Harmsworth, Salisbury, and Frederick Jackson Islands, Charles
Alexander Land, Austria Strait, Prince Rudolph Island; and at
9.5 a.m. on the 16th we reached Cape Fligely.

Thence we steered eastwards into the heart of the great unexplored region between the 75th meridian E. of Greenwich and
the east coast of Severnaya Zemlya (78°-84° of latitude N.).
Before entering it we explored the northern part of the small area
(80°-82° of latitude N. and 72°-70° of longitude E.), without
noticing anything special.

Beyond Cape Fligely the sky cleared again, and visibility
became so good that we could see distinctly for at least 30 miles
all round us; this went on for about 4 hours, from nine to one
o'clock.

About an hour after leaving Rudolph Island behind we found
the pack frequently broken by large pools; farther on still it
changed again, the zones of open water disappeared, and we
noticed masses of old ice lightly covered with snow—a sign that
violent winds had blown in all directions across this region.

At 11.15 a strange optical illusion attracted my attention:
in the sky on the horizon there appeared a vague outline,
like some fantastic city of white and blue crystal rising from
the ice.

As we advanced towards Severnaya Zemlya the pack changed
afresh: it was broken by great pools of open sea. In some places
the water evaporating from them rose in mist and still further
shortened the range of visibility.

At 5.10 p.m. we crossed the first large patch of water. The
sky cleared at this moment and the sun shone out. A few minutes
later we returned to the frozen sea. A flight of birds appeared on
the wing.

At 6.5 we found a great stretch of open water, some 6 miles
wide, running for about 25 miles SE. and NW. (80° latitude N.

and 84° longitude E. of Greenwich). South of it was observed a long bank of cumulus, which Malmgren judged to be clouds over land.

All these indications taken together led our meteorologist to consider that land might lie to the north of this wide expanse of water. So I gave orders to deviate a few degrees northwards from our course, in the hope of finding the coast; but soon afterwards the characteristic sea-ice began once more.

Of course, it is by no means certain to infer the existence of land from seeing open water and observing the shape of clouds; but, if any weight at all is to be attached to observations of this nature, one must conclude that land really exists somewhere near the point mentioned (80° latitude N. and 84½° longitude E.).

But unfortunately we found no trace of it on the route we followed. In fact, without any success, we turned eastwards as far as 79° 16' latitude N. and 91° 40' longitude E. of Greenwich.

It was now 11.15 p.m. on the 16th, and we had been flying for 34 hours.

In the meantime weather conditions had changed for the worse, owing to a cyclone which had broken out over Taymir Island and set up strong northerly winds in the region we were crossing.

Between Cape North and Franz Josef Land this side wind had interfered with our navigation, though not seriously. But beyond Franz Josef Land, as we approached Severnaya Zemlya, it had grown stronger, until it reached and even passed 24 m.p.h., making it difficult to keep the ship on course. For hours on end we had advanced with a drift of 30 or 40 degrees. What was worse, the squalls produced violent swerves of 10 or 20 degrees and more, which made our direction uncertain.

With such weather I began to think about returning. Our outward voyage had already lasted ten hours longer than I had reckoned, and we had consumed a large part of the petrol intended as a reserve. It would have been rash to use any more, because with such changeable conditions our return might quite well be hindered by strong head-winds.

So I gave orders to stop travelling eastwards and to turn round.

To retrace our outward journey seemed risky, as it would have entailed another struggle with that brutal north wind. I decided to steer for Cape Zelantya—the extreme northern point of Novaya Zemlya—and thence to Spitsbergen. And so we did.

During the night we crossed in good visibility another 240 miles of unknown territory, without finding anything specially remarkable.

At 4.20 a.m. on the 16th we reached Cape Vissinger Hoft, on the east coast, which we followed up against the wind as far as Cape Zhelanaya, in some places flying over hilly ground. Thence we redescended in a fog along the west coast to Cape Nassau, reaching it at 8.35 a.m. From this point we steered for Abel Island, the most easterly of the Spitsbergen group; but at 8 p.m. (42° 10′ of longitude E. and 78° 40′ of latitude N.) we turned a trifle northwards, steering for Cape Leigh Smith.

These 480 miles across the pack on the Barents Sea were un-eventful. The monotony of the navigation was hardly inter-rupted by a few slight snow-storms and a low bank of fog, which we flew above at 1,800 feet.

We arrived at Cape Leigh Smith at 3.55 a.m. on the 18th, after passing Great Island—which appeared to us several miles farther from the coast than it was marked on the map. Beyond Cape Leigh Smith we flew overland, leaving on our left the series of small islands which flank the coast in one part, and at 5.40 we reached Cape Brunn, where we found a small patch of open water.

At Cape Brunn the sky—which until then had remained grey—suddenly cleared up, and a dazzling sun shone out to illumine the vast frozen wastes of North-East Land.

I decided to take advantage of the exceptional visibility to cross North-East Land and the northern part of the main island of Spitsbergen, flying in a straight line over the mountains from Cape Brunn to King's Bay. This flight presented a special interest, as the interior of North-East Land (like that of the main island) was for the greater part unknown.

This crossing made at a height varying between 7,500 and 8,500 ft., was not fruitless, for it enabled us to ascertain that the interior of North-East Land is not an area of continental ice, as is shown in many maps. During our flight, in fact, we found that the covering of ice on that land is very thin. At every moment we saw bare rocks emerging, swept clear of snow by the wind. Between them were places covered with soft snow, under which there may have been ice. But we found no sign of thick and extensive ice-formations, except in one spot, where we recognized a genuine glacier moving northwards; but even this seemed rather small.

The last part of the journey was a splendid finish to our rapid flight of exploration.

This flight under a blue sky, above the marvellous Spitsbergen mountains, so fantastically shaped and all gleaming with ice and snow, raised our spirits and magically chased away our fatigue, so that, after three days of sleepless exertion, we felt as fresh as if we had just started.

At 9.15 a.m., after crossing North-East Land, Hinlopen Strait, New Friesland, and Andrée Land, the *Italia* returned for a third time, by a most original route, to King's Bay. At 10.20 we landed.

The first flight of exploration, lasting exactly 69 hours, had been brought to a successful close, after we had travelled about 2,400 miles and explored some 17,250 square miles of unknown territory. We had proved that the land shown in English maps as Gillis Land, part of which other expeditions had already found not to be there, did not in fact exist at all.[1] Our exploration in the region of Severnaya Zemlya had enabled us to indicate the extreme eastern limits to which this could extend, and also the probable existence of land near 80° of latitude N. and 84° 30′ of longitude E. of Greenwich. Finally, we had made the first crossing of North-East Land, ascertaining that it is not thickly covered with ice, as had been supposed.

As to the purely scientific work, Malmgren collected a series of meteorological data, and some important observations on the

[1] The existence of this land had been affirmed by the Dutch captain Cornelius Giles, who thought he had glimpsed it during a voyage in 1707.

state of the ice, while Pontremoli made numerous observations of the horizontal component of the terrestrial magnetic field and a series of measurements of the electrical conductibility of the atmosphere, besides 59 measurements of penetrating radiations and 31 of atmospheric radioactivity.

THE VOYAGE TO THE POLE

Preparations

AFTER giving the crew a short rest, on the morning of May 21st we began to put the *Italia* in order for the next flight. I was only waiting until the Geophysical Institute at Tromsö signalled favourable weather conditions for the start.

In agreement with Malmgren I had drawn up the plan of the next two flights: first of all we would go to the Pole across the north of Greenland; then we would leave on a fourth and last flight, without any prearranged route or goal, but simply with the idea of taking the best possible advantage of the wind to carry us over unexplored territory. By this means the crew would not be exhausted by a long struggle with the wind, and we would have been able to fly on a single engine, reducing not only our petrol consumption but also the number of mechanics. I proposed to have only 12 men on board, choosing those who were the most eager to brave the risks and discomforts of a long and adventurous voyage. My idea was to remain at least a week in the air. Whether we would travel towards Severnaya Zemlya or towards the American coast was something we would decide *en route*, taking into account the meteorological situation. A bold plan, no doubt, but studied in every detail: I was sure that it would succeed. Malmgren was enthusiastic about this flight, which was to conclude our expedition. Meanwhile, we decided to push on with the flight to the Pole.

This time too I provided for about 140 cwt. of petrol. To be exact, there were $135\frac{1}{2}$ cwt. in tanks and $4\frac{1}{2}$ cwt. in tins, some of them in the cabin and the rest inside the framework. The oil was in proportion.

The crew were to be the same as before, with one wireless

operator instead of two, the previous flights having shown that one was enough. As for the Naval officers, I could at need have reduced the number by leaving out Viglieri, whose presence on board, though extremely useful, was not indispensable. But I reserved my decision until the last moment, making it conditional upon the available lift. Including Viglieri (who did in fact come) the part of the crew who were to work and navigate the ship remained the same as on the flight to Severnaya Zemlya. As wireless operator I chose Biagi, who had proved physically fitter than Pedretti to stand the fatigues of the voyage.

This time, all three scientists came: Pontremoli, Malmgren and Behounek. As we had previously settled, I took the journalist Lago instead of Tomaselli.

I again provided against the possibility of a forced landing on the ice of the Polar sea, and embarked all the materials that might have helped to save the whole expedition if this happened. Altogether they weighed 9½ cwt., and were placed inside the hull, distributed along the various metallic sections.

The reserve provisions, consisting mainly of pemmican and chocolate, weighed about as much and were sufficient for at least three months. Besides these, having arranged that if weather conditions permitted, two or three of us would descend at the Pole to carry out the scientific research planned in our programme, I also had 2 waterproof sacks filled with everything necessary to keep three men alive on the pack for three weeks. In them were put 2 sleeping-bags, a tent, 3 pairs of *finsko*, a Colt revolver with 100 cartridges, a pickaxe, 4 lb. of colouring powder, some smoke-signals, a megaphone, a Nansen type stove, a tin of match-boxes, some solid fuel, a tin of pemmican, one of malted milk, and one of biscuits. This decision was really providential, because one of these sacks was picked up on the ice when we crashed. Without it, we should all have perished.

Nor was it less providential that, on this flight too, we took a small emergency wireless set in the control-cabin. The day before leaving, I ordered the wireless operators to test it, adjusting it to a wave-length of 32 metres. It was this very set which, found by chance on the ice after the crash, enabled us to get in touch with the civilized world.

All these preparations took two days of hard work. Meanwhile, Malmgren was keeping watch on the weather situation. On May 20th the Geophysical Institute at Tromsö had told us that the centre of the depression over Bear Island now lay at 75° of latitude N. and 25° of longitude E. of Greenwich, and was moving steadily north-eastwards. But by the morning of the 22nd the situation had changed: the centre of the depression had moved SE. of Spitsbergen, while an anticyclone was covering Greenland, and a centre of low pressure lay to the SW. of Iceland.

At noon on the same day the Tromsö Institute telegraphed, advising me to leave by routes 2 and 5. Route 2 was that from Greenland to the Pole, and route 5 from the Pole to the mouth of the Mackenzie River. I took this advice and ordered the members of the crew to get ready. Meanwhile, I sent them to sleep, telling them to be in the hangar by eleven that night.

During the night Tromsö telegraphed several times, saying that the meteorological situation was unchanged. At Ny Aalesund, local weather conditions were excellent, although the temperature was relatively high. The sky was blue and the air calm.

Towards 2.30 a.m. I had the ship filled with gas. When the envelope was full and the pressure began to rise I had an inspection made, to see that all was in order. Suddenly I heard a little hissing sound. I at once sent someone out on to the top of the dirigible to find out what had happened, and he discovered a small slit, due to a flaw in the material. This was promptly repaired.

I then proceeded to have a thorough investigation made by a technician and two workmen to see that there were no other defects, and to this end I made a further test, with as high a pressure of gas as possible. Shortly after four o'clock I gave the order to bring the ship out of the hangar.

On the field, when the engines were already running, I had one final weighing-up, and found that it was possible to take Viglieri. I signed him to get in. Now that everyone was at his post, Father Gianfranceschi—the chaplain of the expedition—

recited a short prayer, to which we listened bare-headed. Then, with no more delay, I gave the order: "Let go!" The men loosed the ropes with which they were holding down the nose of the ship. We rose slowly, whilst a terrific "Hurrah!" rang out from the 150 persons present. I accelerated all three engines, keeping the nose on the entrance of the bay.

And so the *Italia* left for the Pole, on her third and last voyage of exploration, from which she was fated never to return.

It was 4.28 a.m. on May 23rd.

Towards the Pole

At 4.51 a.m., leaving Cape Mitre on our left, we began to coast along Haakon VII Land, as far as the northern point of Amsterdam Island, which we reached at 5.41. Hardly had we passed the island when a strong north wind bore down on us and considerably reduced our speed.

For about an hour we continued along the 11th meridian E. of Greenwich, then at 6.40 turned 20 degrees to the left, steering for Cape Bridgmann, on the north coast of Greenland.

Until now we had been sailing over open sea, but a few minutes later—at 6.50 (about $80\frac{1}{2}°$ of latitude and 10° of longitude E.)—we came across the pack, all smothered in fog. From that moment until 1.15 p.m.—about $6\frac{1}{2}$ hours—the fog continued, dense and unbroken. At first we flew low underneath it; then from 10.40 to 12.40 we rose above, which was easily done, as it was scarcely 1,500 ft. high.

After 1.15 p.m. the fog began to thin out, so that at 2.45 we were able to sight the coast of Greenland. But only at three o'clock, when it ceased altogether, could the land be seen clearly. We deviated slightly from our course, steering towards the coast to reconnoitre. Two hours later, while we were flying over a pack frequently broken by little channels, the wan, ice-covered mountains of north Greenland came in sight. At 5.29 p.m. we were close by Cape Bridgmann: since leaving the extreme northern point of Amsterdam Island we had covered about 430 miles in 11 hours and 40 minutes, at an average speed of 36 m.p.h.

Having recognized Cape Bridgmann, we turned back and

steered for the Pole, along the 27th meridian W. of Greenwich.

At six o'clock, a few miles from Cape Bridgmann, the sky—until then covered with clouds—cleared up.

With the blue sky above, the radiant sun lighting the inside of the cabin, and the wind astern increasing our speed, the journey to the Pole proceeded in joyous excitement. All on board were happy, and contentment shone from every face.

One of the Naval officers stood at the steering-wheel, whilst the other two divided their time untiringly between solar observations and measurements of drift and speed. Trojani and Cecioni, as usual, manned the elevator-wheel.

Malmgren was standing up, with his spectacles on, to mark on a chart fixed to the wall of the wireless cabin the meteorological data which Biagi, as he intercepted them, came to communicate to us. Pontremoli and Behounek attended imperturbably to their instruments, without troubling in the least about what was going on around them. One would have thought they were working in the quiet of their laboratories.

The three mechanics were at their posts, vigilant and attentive as ever: Pomella in the stern engine-boat, Caratti on the left, and Ciocca on the right. But only the stern engine and one of the side ones were in motion.

Arduino was walking backwards and forwards along the gangway, to supervise the mechanics and check and regulate the consumption of petrol.

Alessandrini, after visiting all the accessible parts of the ship during the first hours of flight to make sure that nothing was wrong, and pulling up the handling-ropes that dangled outside—to prevent their offering an unnecessary resistance to the air and getting coated with ice—had come down into the cabin, some time before, to help Trojani and Cecioni and take a spell at the steering-wheel.

With such a strong wind astern we advanced rapidly towards our desired goal. At 6 p.m. we had reached the 84th parallel; by 10.30 p.m., 88° 10'.

The region over which we were flying was unknown to man. It lay between the route of the *Norge*, to the right of us, and that of Peary, to the left. Not a trace of land in sight, although the visibility was exceptional, as we could see clearly up to 60 miles all round.

The height at which we were sailing gradually increased: at 6 p.m. it was 750 ft.; at 8 p.m., 1,500; at 10 p.m., 1,650; at 10.30 p.m., 1,800.

I was delighted at such splendid visibility occurring unexpectedly after the 8 hours' fog which had made the first part of our voyage so trying. But the strong wind, although it helped us on our way to the Pole, made me regretfully consider that I should have to give up the descent we had planned.

Meanwhile I watched Malmgren at work. He was now tracing the curves of two cyclonic areas which apparently existed, one above the Arctic Ocean towards the Siberian coast, the other above the Barents Sea.

Which was the best route to follow, after leaving the Pole? This was the problem which had been preoccupying me for some time.

The notion of sailing against a wind as strong as the one at present behind us did not at all appeal to me, especially as I feared it might be accompanied by fog. So I thought that, having reached the Pole, it would be better to fly before the wind to the Siberian coast, or steer for the coast of Canada, where the meteorological bulletins forecast fog, it is true, but with atmospheric calm.

I discussed it with Malmgren, who dissuaded me.

"It would be better to return to King's Bay," he said. "Then we shall be able to complete our programme of scientific research."

I remained undecided. I knew from long experience what a hard—and often intolerable—strain it was to fight for hours against a strong wind, and so instinctively I shrank from it. But Malmgren reassured me.

"No!" he said. "This wind will not last long. When we are on our way back it will drop, after a few hours, and be succeeded by north-west winds."

Eventually I was won over and followed his advice.

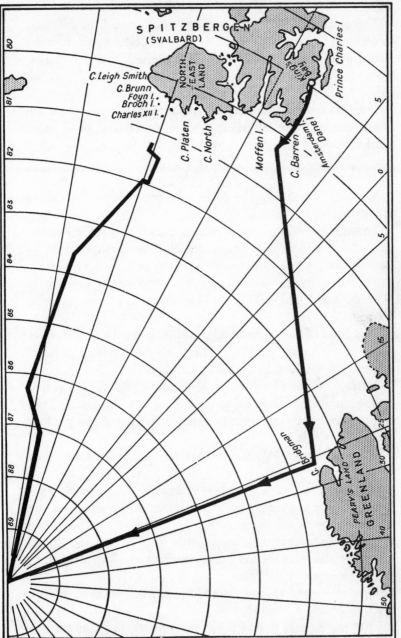

The *Italia's* Flight to the North Pole

The conversation on this subject was resumed, in dramatic circumstances, four days later. On May 27th, on the pack after the catastrophe, Malmgren asked me if I thought that all would have been well had we followed out my idea of reaching the mouth of the Mackenzie. Probably it would, because the airship would have been spared the torment of a prolonged struggle against the wind—but who can tell whether, on this route too, some other peril would not have been lying in wait for us?

At the Pole

Whilst I was talking to Malmgren we continued to draw rapidly nearer to the Pole.

Towards ten o'clock there was an unexpected change in the sky, which until then had been blue all over. In front of us, an hour or two away, a barrier of cloud over 3,000 ft. high rose from the horizon, standing out against the azure of the sky above. With its weird outlines it looked like the walls of some gigantic fortress.

That band of cloud, dark and compact, had a menacing aspect which struck my imagination. "There's no getting through that!" I thought. "We shall be bound to turn back."

At 10.30 we encountered a bank of thick cloud. And as at that moment it did not suit us to lose sight of the sun—height measurements being more than ever necessary—we rose above the fog, to about 2,400 ft.

We were then at 88° 10′. Another 54 miles and we should be at the Pole.

Meanwhile the Naval officers were making their solar observations. We were getting nearer and nearer to the goal, and the excitement on board was growing.

Twenty minutes after midnight, early on May 24th, the officers who were observing the sun with a sextant cried: "We are there!"

The *Italia* was at the Pole.

We had covered 425 miles from Cape Bridgmann at an average speed of 62 m.p.h.

I had the engines slowed down and ordered the helmsman to steer in a circle.

It was impossible, alas! to descend on the pack, but we had a promise to keep: to deposit on the ice of the Pole the Cross entrusted to us by Pius XI, and by its side the Italian flag. We prepared ourselves in religious silence to carry out this gesture—so simple and yet so solemn. I ordered Alessandrini to get ready.

Then I had the engines accelerated once more, to pass under the fog. It was 12.40. Twenty minutes later we were in sight of the pack. We went on circling round at a reduced speed until the preparations were completed. I had had a large tricolour cloth fastened to the Cross, to catch the wind and guide it down.

At 1.20 a.m. I leaned out of the cabin and let fall the Italian flag. Then followed the *gonfalone* of the City of Milan, and a little medal of the Virgin of the Fire, given me by the inhabitants of Forli. For the second time our tricolour spread itself over the ice of the Pole. Beside the flag we dropped the Cross. It was 1.30, and we were about 450 ft. up.

At the moment when these rites were completed, I felt a thrill of pride. Two years after the *Norge* flight we had come back to the Pole, and this time the bad weather, from Italy onwards, had made it much more difficult.

Inside the cabin, now that the engines were almost still, a little gramophone was playing an old folk-song: "The Bells of San Giusto", bringing back memories, taking us all of a sudden to Italy, to our homes. We were all moved: more than one had tears in his eyes. Zappi cried: "Long live Nobile!" I was grateful to him, as I was to Malmgren, when he came and said, clasping my hand: "Few men can say, as we can, that we have been twice to the Pole."

Few men indeed: six Italians and one Swede.

Meanwhile Pontremoli had come to tell me, in his beautiful, musical voice, the value of the horizontal component of the terrestrial magnetic field measured at the Pole.

THE CATASTROPHE

The Return from the Pole

WE left the Pole at 2.20 a.m. on May 24th, navigating along the 25th meridian E. of Greenwich at a height of 3,000 ft.

A solar observation made soon after leaving the Pole had permitted us to check our position, but afterwards the sky had become overcast and the sun had disappeared. Below us a bank of dense fog stretched out of sight.

We sailed between clouds and fog solely by aid of the magnetic compass; but, with a strong wind blowing and no possibility of checking our drift and speed, it was like moving in the dark. So at 10.20 I decided to dive under the fog. Between 600 and 900 ft. the pack reappeared, and we were then able to take our first measurements: speed, 26 m.p.h.; drift, 18 degrees to port. That meant there was a strong south-west wind, making us deviate eastwards.

For some hours we slightly modified our course, to penetrate farther into the unexplored zone east of the 25th meridian. Then we turned once more to the right.

For nearly 24 hours we kept on flying under the fog. Visibility was at first rather bad, but at 10.50 we noticed an improvement. At 1.30 p.m. I noted in the log: "*Visibility 12-15 miles on each side.*"

There was nothing striking in the aspect of the pack—pallid and uniform, with its snowfields, hummocks, and numerous crevasses. Only at 4 p.m. the monotony was interrupted by a large channel running east and west.

Now and then flurries of snow enveloped us and cut off our view of the pack for some minutes. The wind, as it filtered through the joints of the pilot-cabin, sounded like a prolonged whistling. We felt the stuff that covered the framework quiver under the pressure of the air.

Each man went about his work in silence: the vivacity and cheerfulness that had accompanied our outward voyage had now disappeared. From time to time a loud crack, like a rifle-shot, unexpectedly shattered the stillness. Pieces of ice, flung violently from the propellers, were striking the sides of the ship and tearing little rifts, which were hunted for and promptly repaired.

Ice was forming all over the outside of the dirigible—and much more abundantly than usual. It got worse on the afternoon of the 24th, and then, after a short respite, came on again still harder in the evening. Between 9.45 and midnight we noted in the log: "*Fog, snow, and ice.*"

We were making little headway. From 10.20 a.m. to 6.20 p.m. the measurements taken gave an average of only 28 m.p.h., which meant that we were fighting a wind that was generally about 20 m.p.h. but often rose to 30. Malmgren was vexed at this. Ever since the day before, he had been convinced that the south wind would soon be succeeded by northerly winds which would help us back to King's Bay. But this forecast was not fulfilled; in fact, the contrary wind seemed to grow even stronger.

Yet Malmgren would not own himself beaten. He urged me to put on speed: "Let us get out of this zone quickly," he said. "Afterwards, things will go better."

I agreed. As a rule I kept only two engines working, at 1,200 r.p.m.: one of the side engines and the stern engine run by Pomella. I gave orders to speed them up to 1,300 revolutions, and at the same time had the third engine started between 1,100 and 1,200 r.p.m.

So our airspeed reached about 60 m.p.h. or even more, though our average ground-speed remained only about 37 m.p.h. Evidently the wind, instead of abating during the latter hours, had grown even stronger.

And so about 3 a.m. on May 25th, worried by the high petrol consumption and the strain which the increased speed was putting on the structure of the ship, I decided to reduce speed. But Malmgren, whose anxiety was steadily growing, came to me and said: "We aren't going ahead. It is dangerous to stop here. The weather might grow still worse. We must get out of this zone as quickly as possible."

Between the two evils, I chose the one which seemed the lesser. Once more I had the engines accelerated, and by 4.30 on May 25th we had returned to our former speed. Thus we continued on our way, with all three engines working, against the raging hurricane.

On the morning of May 25th the bitter struggle against the wind went on without respite.

For nearly 30 hours a stiff head-wind of 24 or 30 m.p.h. had been blowing. We advanced with difficulty, swerving now to one side, now to the other. It had become extremely difficult to keep on our course. Often the squalls got the upper hand of our helmsman, producing deviations of 20 or even 30 degrees.

Wind and fog. Fog and wind. Incessantly. And from time to time flurries of snow.

Everyone on board went about his business in silence. Some looked tired. The damp, grey, chilly atmosphere surrounding us weighed on our spirits. For a whole day and more we travelled thus. Not a glimmer of light through the fog above us; fog and cloud all the time. And below us, the colourless, monotonous pack.

Zappi and Mariano had charge of the route, dividing their attention between the steering-wheel, the speed-measuring apparatus, and the table on which the charts were spread. Trojani and Cecioni took turns at the elevator. Malmgren helped the Naval officers, taking long spells at the steering-wheel. Behounek, calm and impassive as ever, was beside his instruments. Pontremoli and Lago had gone to sleep some hours before in the fur bags laid down towards the stern. I was supervising everything, more or less, but for some time my attention had been given to checking the speed and to the radio-goniometrical reports, which served to determine our position.

There was great uncertainty as to this. We were making far less headway than our speed measurements indicated. Obviously, the zigzag course into which we were driven diminished our actual progress along the route. Only so could it be explained that we had not yet seen the land that ought to have been sighted some hours previously.

It was a really difficult situation. But—as always in similar circumstances—the difficulties had excited my energy: I did not feel tired, but even more alert than usual.

I divided my time between the navigation table, the wireless cabin, and speed measurements. When I got Biagi's reports I myself marked them on the map. Now and again I went into the front of the pilot-cabin to see that everything was all right. Then passing by my child's photograph—an old photograph which had already accompanied me on the *Norge* and had been fixed up again on the wall this time—I gave it a rapid glance. Maria's lovely eyes looked back at me. I was struck by the sadness of their expression—they seemed to be misted with tears.

Given the uncertainty as to our position, the radio-goniometrical data had assumed a vital importance. The trouble was that the radio did not tell us the exact spot where we were, but only the direction in which the *Città di Milano* heard our signals most strongly. So one could trace a bearing on the chart, somewhere along which the airship was at that moment; but where on this line, we did not know.

Towards seven in the morning my anxiety at not yet seeing land grew still keener. By this time, if we could rely on our calculations—according to which at 1.30 a.m. we had been 100 miles NE. of Moffen Island—we should have already sighted the coast. But there was nothing to be seen. In front of us, to the extreme limit of the horizon, nothing but frozen sea.

I felt more than ever the need of checking our position: we must reckon with the drain on our petrol caused by the forced speed at which we were travelling; that was still my chief worry.

I was anxious to put an end to this uncertainty, somehow or other. So it occurred to me to order that for half an hour at least, we should travel westwards, at right angles to the line given by these reports, instead of straight along it, as we had done until then. The angle between the two observations made at the beginning and end of this course, would give us an approximate idea of our position on the line, and so of our distance from King's Bay.

At 7.40 a.m. we were on a radius from King's Bay passing about 10 miles NE. of Moffen Island. I gave orders to steer westwards. At 8.10 the new observation showed that the radius had approached the island by 3 or 4 miles. This experiment had not lasted long enough to give a reliable result, but I dared not go on with it because the wind, blowing hard on the bow, reduced our speed too much.

So we resumed our course towards North-East Land, steering southwards. The wind seemed even stronger.

At 9.25 I was standing by the door of the wireless cabin waiting for news when suddenly I heard someone cry: "The elevator wheel has jammed!" I ran up at once and saw Trojani—who had been for some time at this helm—trying to turn the wheel, to raise the nose. But he could not manage it. The controls of the helm were blocked.

I realized the gravity of the danger. We were at a height of 750 ft. The ship, being down by the nose, was dropping. In a few minutes we should strike the pack.

There was nothing to be done but to stop the engines—which I did at once. When I looked out and saw the three propellers at a standstill I breathed once more. There was nothing now to fear, for the ship was so light that soon it would stop sinking and go up again.

As I had foreseen, the moment the engines were stopped the descent slowed down abruptly, and about 250 ft. from the pack it ceased altogether. We began to rise gently.

In the meantime Cecioni—who had been asleep in the keel— came down into the cabin, and by my orders paid out the ballast chain, which was lying on the floor. As the chain was heavy this little operation took some time, and I thought it would be much better to let the chain hang out, ready in case of need. At that moment I had not the faintest idea how soon the event would justify this small precaution.

While we were slowly rising, Viglieri had released the elevator by a sharp blow. I ordered Cecioni to take it to pieces and examine the mechanism. As he worked, the airship went on rising. Some time before I had opened all the air-valves, so that the gas-pressure had been reduced below zero. Now it showed signs of going up again. I kept an eye on the pressure-gauges.

Soon we were swallowed up in fog. At this moment Mariano came to me and said: "Don't you think, sir, we might take the opportunity of getting above the fog and taking the height of the sun?"

I agreed, all the more readily because the fog around us was becoming steadily more luminous, showing that it was thinning out. Besides, Cecioni had not yet finished his work.

During the ascent I saw the pressure-gauges register a slight rise. At a certain point I noticed that the pressure in the last compartment of the stern was much higher than in the others. I then let out a little gas, to equalize the pressure in this compartment with that of the others. We were still going up.

At 2,700 ft. we at last emerged from the fog and found blue sky. A glorious sun flooded the cabin with its rays. Mariano and Zappi made their observations.

Cecioni had finished. On dismounting the casing of the elevator he had found nothing wrong with it, so probably the obstruction had been caused by ice forming on the inside. In any case, the helm was now working perfectly well.

We were at 3,300 ft. by this time. The gas began to dilate, making the liquid rise rapidly in the pressure-gauges; but before they reached the height at which they were normally kept when flying, I ordered two engines to be started—the centre and the left.

It was 9.55 a.m.

We set off again, and flew for a few minutes longer above the fog, scanning the horizon in front to see if by any chance the highest peaks of the Svalbard were rising up in the far distance out of the mist. But there was nothing to be seen. Nothing, as far as our field-glasses would reach, except the sea and the fog.

I then decided to come down to the height at which we had

until lately been sailing. It was essential to find the pack again, so that we could go on checking our drift and speed.

We plunged back into the fog and slowly descended until the frozen sea appeared clearly in sight. We were about 900 ft. up.

The Crash

My first thought was to measure our speed. We had only two engines working, but it seemed to me all the same that we were making a bit more headway than before.

Our first measurement, in fact, showed a velocity in relation to the pack of about 30 m.p.h. The wind had gone down, then, and there was no need to start the third engine. I was relieved at this, for it deferred our anxiety about the petrol. I was also glad not to have to go on straining the ship by an excessive speed.

Once more I turned my attention to the course, with Mariano and Viglieri. Combining the position given by the recent height measurement with the radio-goniometrical report at 10 o'clock, we had located our position with approximate certainty. We were apparently 45 miles NE. of the Ross Islands and 180 miles NE. of King's Bay.

On the basis of this distance I calculated that we should reach the Bay between three and four in the afternoon, and intended to announce this by wireless a little later on.

Everything on board was now in order and each man had resumed his post. Malmgren was at the helm, with Zappi giving him instructions from time to time. Cecioni had not left the elevator since he had tested its casing. Beside him, between the pressure-gauges and the engine controls, stood Trojani.

In the rear of the cabin with me, sitting round the navigation table, were Mariano and Viglieri. One of them was taking speed measurements with the Goertz apparatus clamped to the side of the table. Behounek stood behind us, making observations with his instruments. Pontremoli and Lago, as I said before, had been asleep for some hours up in the stern.

The mechanics were all awake, in their respective engine-boats. Arduino, helped by Alessandrini, was in the gangway, superintending the inside of the ship.

We were flying between 600 and 900 ft. up. The dirigible was still light, so to keep it at the proper height we had to hold the nose down.

At 10.30 I again ordered a speed measurement. When this had been taken I walked to the front of the cabin and looked out of the right-hand porthole, between the steering-wheel and the elevator. To test the height, I dropped a glass ball full of red liquid, and stood there, timing its fall with a stop-watch.

While I was attending to this, I heard Cecioni say excitedly: "We are heavy!"

I turned with a start to look at the instruments.

The ship was right down by the stern, at an angle of 8 degrees to the horizon; nevertheless, we were rapidly falling.

The peril was grave and imminent. A short distance below us stretched the pack. I at once gave the orders which had to be given, the only ones that could save the ship in this emergency—if that was possible: to accelerate the two engines, start the third, and at the same time lift the nose of the dirigible still higher. I hoped by these means to overcome the unexpected heaviness.

Simultaneously, I shouted to Alessandrini to run out on the top of the ship and inspect the stern valves, as I thought gas might be escaping—the only explanation that occurred to me at the moment of this serious and rapid increase in weight.

Meanwhile, the mechanics had carried out my orders. Pomella and Caratti had speeded their engines up to 1,400 revolutions and Ciocca, with surprising promptness, had started his own. The ship began to move faster, and tilted at an angle of 15 or 20 degrees.

The dynamic lift obtained in this way must certainly have represented several hundredweight.

But unfortunately we went on falling. The variometer—on which my eyes were fixed—confirmed it; in fact, we seemed to be dropping even faster.

I realized that there was nothing more to be done. The attempt to combat the increased weight by propulsion had failed. . . . A crash was now inevitable; the most we could do was to mitigate its consequences.

I gave the necessary orders: to stop the engines at once, so as to avoid fire breaking out as we crashed; and to drop the ballast-chain. Sending Cecioni to do this, I put Zappi in his place.

It was all that could have been ordered; it was ordered promptly and with absolute calm. The perfect discipline on board was unbroken, so that each man carried out my orders as best he could, in the vertiginous rapidity of the event.

In the meantime the pack was approaching at a fearful speed. I saw that Cecioni was finding it difficult to untie the rope which held the chain. "Hurry up! Hurry up!" I shouted to him. Then noticing that the engine on the left, run by Caratti, was still working, I leaned out of a porthole on that side, and at the top of my voice—echoed, I think, by one of the officers—repeated the order: "Stop the engine!" At that moment I saw the stern-boat was only a few tens of yards from the pack. I drew back into the cabin.

The recollection of those last terrible instants is very vivid in my memory. I had scarcely had time to reach the spot near the two rudders, between Malmgren and Zappi, when I saw Malmgren fling up the wheel, turning his startled eyes on me. Instinctively I grasped the helm, wondering if it were possible to guide the ship on to a snow-field and so lessen the shock. . . . Too late! . . . There was the pack, a few yards below, terribly uneven. The masses of ice grew larger, came nearer and nearer. . . . A moment later we crashed.

There was a fearful impact. Something hit me on the head, then I was caught and crushed. Clearly, without any pain, I felt some of my limbs snap. Some object falling from a height knocked me down head foremost. Instinctively I shut my eyes, and with perfect lucidity and coolness formulated the thought: "It's all over!" I almost pronounced the words in my mind.

It was 10.33 on May 25th.

The fearful event had lasted only 2 or 3 minutes!

ADRIFT ON THE PACK

After the Crash

WHEN I opened my eyes I found myself lying on the ice, in the midst of an appalling pack. I realized at once that others had fallen with me.

I looked up to the sky. Towards my left the dirigible, nose in air, was drifting away before the wind. It was terribly lacerated around the pilot-cabin. Out of it trailed torn strips of fabric, ropes, fragments of metal-work. The left wall of the cabin had remained attached. I noticed a few creases in the envelope.

Upon the side of the crippled, mutilated ship stood out the black letters ITALIA. My eyes remained fixed on them, as if fascinated, until the dirigible merged in the fog and was lost to sight.

It was only then that I felt my injuries. My right leg and arm were broken and throbbing; I had hurt my face and the top of my head, and my chest seemed all upside down with the violence of the shock. I thought my end was near.

Suddenly I heard a voice—Mariano's—asking: "Where is the General?" And I looked around me.

I had never seen such a terrible pack: a formless, contorted jumble of pointed ice-crags, stretching to the horizon.

Two yards away on my right, Malmgren was sitting, and a little farther off lay Cecioni, moaning aloud. Next him was Zappi. The others—Mariano, Behounek, Trojani, Viglieri, and Biagi— were standing up. They appeared unhurt, except for Trojani, whose face was stained by a few patches of blood.

Here and there one could see wreckage—a dreary note of grey against the whiteness of the snow. In front of me a strip of bright red, like blood which had flowed from some enormous wound, showed the spot where we had fallen. It was the liquid from the glass balls.

I was calm. My mind was perfectly clear. But now I was feeling the seriousness of my injuries—worst of all, a terrible convulsion in my chest. Breathing was a great effort. I thought I had probably sustained some grave internal injury. It seemed that death was very near—that maybe I had only 2 or 3 hours to live.

I was glad of this. It meant that I should not have to watch the despair and slow death-agony of my comrades. What hope was there for them? With no provisions, no tent, no wireless, no sledges—nothing but useless wreckage—they were lost, irremediably lost, in this terrible wilderness of ice.

I turned towards them, looking at them with an infinite sadness at heart. Then I spoke: "Steady, my lads! Keep your spirits up! Don't be cast down by this misfortune." And I added: "Lift your thoughts to God!"

No other words, no other ideas, came to me in those first unforgettable moments when death seemed imminent. But suddenly I was seized by strong emotion. Something rose up from my soul —from the depths of my being: something stronger than the pain of my tortured limbs, stronger than the thought of approaching death. And from my straining breast broke out, loud and impetuous, the cry: "*Viva l'Italia!*"

My comrades cheered.

Beside me on the right Malmgren was still sitting silent in the same place, stroking his right arm. On his face, frowning and ashen pale, a little swollen from his fall, was a look of blank despair. His blue eyes stared fixedly in front of him, as if into the void. Lost in thought, he seemed not even to notice the other men around him.

I had been very fond of this young scientist, ever since we had shared in the *Norge* expedition. And lately my affection for him had grown. He had become my most valued collaborator—the only one to whom I confided my plans, my ideas, my thoughts. I attached a good deal of weight to his judgment and advice. Some days previously we had decided the general lines of our future flight—the bold scheme which, if carried out, would have utilized to the utmost the possibilities afforded by our ship and crew. . . . But now all our plans had come to naught.

Wishing to speak to him, I said softly: "Nothing to be done, my dear Malmgren!"

Nothing to be done! . . . A painful confession for men of action!

He looked at me and answered: "Nothing, but die. My arm is broken."

Suddenly he got up. He could not stand erect, for his injured shoulder made him stoop. Once more he turned to me and said in English: "*General, I thank you for the trip. . . . I go under the water!*"

So saying, he turned away.

I stopped him: "No, Malmgren! You have no right to do this. We will die when God has decided. We must wait. Please stop here."

I shall never forget the look he turned on me at that moment. He seemed surprised. Perhaps he was struck by the gentle and affectionate seriousness of my tone. For a moment he stood still, as if undecided. Then he sat down again.

But suddenly a ray of light pierced the darkness. I heard Biagi cry: "The field-station is intact!"

By this he meant the little emergency wireless set which had been placed on board precisely in a case of a descent on the ice.

I began to hope again. If we could send wireless messages—if we could ask the *Città di Milano* for help, perhaps all was not lost. My comrades might yet be rescued.

Then I called Mariano.

"I feel myself dying," I told him. "I think I have only a few hours to live. I cannot do anything for you. Do all you can, yourself, to save our men. . . . God help you! God grant you may return to Italy. . . . What a pity if our country were to lose men like you!"

He answered gently: "Yes, General! Set your mind at rest. . . . There is still hope. We have found the wireless, and very soon we shall be in communication with the *Città di Milano*. And we have picked up a case of provisions too. We can hope."

Then all at once the memory of home came back to me: "When you are in Italy, do what you can for my child and my sisters' children!"

"Yes, General—don't worry. . . . I'll see to it," he replied, and then added: "I've always been fond of you. . . . In my own fashion—but always."

I was delighted with the optimism and energy that this young man was showing in such terrible circumstances.

Suddenly my glance fell upon a large dark heap in front of me, between two hummocks of ice, and about 10 or 15 yds. away. I recognized one of the two waterproof bags in which Pontremoli and I had put everything that might be useful in case two or three of us made a descent at the Pole, as I had thought of doing. One of the bags was inside the ship; the other, strapped to the ceiling of the wireless cabin, had fallen amidst the wreckage.

I pointed it out to Mariano: "Get that sack opened! You will find valuable things inside—a tent and provisions. There's a sleeping-bag too. Please bring it here to me and get me into it, if you can. Then I shall be able to die there in peace."

Shivers of cold were running through my body. Unlike the others, I had not a heavy coat lined with lamb's-wool.

They brought the sleeping-bag to the spot where I was lying, and little by little slid me into it. This was not easy, because my right arm, leg, and foot gave me excruciating pain at the least movement. Besides, I was on top of a hummock, where there was not even enough flat surface for me to lie comfortably.

Once inside the sack I thought of Titina and called to her. The dear little thing was scampering gaily to and fro on the ice, happy to be free at last and no longer in the air . . . so happy that she was not even surprised at this novel method of landing, and still less disconcerted at the terrible aspect of the pack. I called her to me, but she refused to understand and continued to frisk about, wagging her tail and sniffing the air.

I recommended her to the care of one of the men.

Having done this I put my head inside the bag and lay motionless, waiting for death to steal over me.

Half an hour passed thus—perhaps even longer. But death did not come. In its stead I felt life gradually creeping back. It did me good to lie still. The effects of the violent shock on my lungs were beginning to wear off.

All of a sudden I began to wonder what my comrades were doing. I put my head out of the bag to have a look.

Mariano, Viglieri, Trojani, and Behounek were wandering about on the ice picking up materials. Biagi, having improvised a wireless mast, had begun to transmit. Cecioni, sitting up, was still cursing his luck. As soon as he caught sight of me he called: "I've broken my leg, sir!" I noticed he had bandaged it as best he could.

Malmgren, gloomy and ashen pale, was still motionless in the same position. He sat there, nursing his right arm, and staring fixedly in front of him. On the other side, on my left, Zappi was lying stretched out. He had been slightly hurt about the face, and was complaining of a pain in his chest, just by one of his ribs: "Do you think it's broken, General?"

"If it doesn't hurt you much when you breathe, that means it isn't broken," I hazarded in reply. But to tell the truth I was not at all sure of the accuracy of this remark.

Meanwhile I heard Viglieri, Trojani, and Mariano discussing the best spot to pitch the tent. It must be put up as quickly as possible because the cold was intense, and the wind (although only blowing 12 or 15 ft. to the second) made us feel it still more.

At last the spot was chosen—a sheet of ice about 50 yds. square— some yards away from me and on a lower level. Trojani, helped by some of the others, set to work.

Once the tent was ready they carried me there. The going was painful. More than once I had to set my teeth, not to cry out with the agony of my fractures. But at last they dragged me inside and laid me at the back of the tent, along the wall facing the entrance.

Then they carried in Cecioni and put him beside me. They

slit up my fur bag, and thus opened it made a bed for us both.

Meanwhile Mariano, Viglieri, Behounek, and Trojani went on looking for provisions. Some of the tins had fallen through the holes in the framework where the cabin and the stern engine-boat had been. Later on it was suggested that Arduino and the others, on their own initiative, had thrown down stuff to lighten the ship, but this does not seem probable.

By the evening about 150 lb. of provisions—pemmican and chocolate—had been collected. This would suffice for 25 days, allowing a ration of 11 oz. per head.

Biagi had already sent out the first S.O.S., trying in vain to call the *Città di Milano*; then a flaw had developed in the apparatus which he had been unable to set right.

A little later everyone gathered in the tent and Mariano distributed $\frac{1}{2}$ lb. of pemmican to each. Some of them began to masticate it, not without signs of distaste. Cecioni and I put ours aside: we had no appetite.

Then they gave me the news of Pomella's death. They had found him seated on the ice near the wreckage of his engine-boat. He had taken off one of his leather shoes. There was no sign of suffering on his face—no apparent injury.

Pomella was very dear to me; yet that tragic night his loss left me indifferent. It was not hardness of heart—but involuntarily I reflected that it was better for him to have died then and there and escaped the lingering death reserved for us. For my part, I envied him his lot.

Then having speculated a little about the fate of the other six we settled down to sleep. Nine men, huddled up together in that cramped space. A tangle of human limbs. Outside, the wind was howling, and one could hear the canvas of the tent flapping with a lugubrious rhythm. Cecioni rambled on until weariness overcame him. It overcame me too, and I fell asleep.

Waking on the Pack

I slept heavily for several hours, though from time to time I was awakened by a stab of pain in my leg or arm. When I opened my eyes my comrades were still curled up asleep, one on top of another.

The tent was square: 9 ft. each side. A wooden pole supported the point of the pyramidal roof. At each corner of the base were two ropes pegged into the snow.

I was glad of the care I had given to the minutest details of this tent. But being meant for four people, it was too small for the nine of us. Cecioni and I alone took up more than a third, seeing we had to keep our legs stretched out and motionless. Seven people had to fit into the remaining space, besides the wireless batteries, which I had advised them to bring inside to preserve them from the action of the extreme cold, as according to Pontremoli's experiments this would considerably diminish their efficiency. On the other hand, there were advantages in being crowded up like this, since at any rate it made the night cold much more bearable.

Mariano, Viglieri, Behounek, and Trojani got up and went out at once to finish collecting the scattered stores from the pack and to hunt in the wreckage for anything that might be useful. This had to be done as quickly as possible in order to stow these things away safely before they were lost in crevasses or hidden under the snow.

Malmgren, Biagi, and Zappi remained in the tent with us two invalids. The two latter, aided by Cecioni, began to take the transmitting apparatus of the radio to pieces and hunt for the flaw. At last the trouble was located and repaired, and an hour or two later Biagi was able once more to send out the S.O.S. that Mariano had prepared.

He transmitted it at the 55th minute of each odd hour, as we had arranged with the *Città di Milano* for short-wave communications during flight. Immediately after sending it, Biagi would listen-in for the reply—but in vain. Nobody heard us.

The condition of the injured had improved. Zappi was still rather out of sorts, but convinced by this time that his rib was merely bruised. So after helping Biagi mend the wireless he turned to the medical duties, for which I had made him follow a special course in Rome. He examined Cecioni's leg, contrived splints with two wooden boards, and carefully bound it with bandages cut from the varnished cloth covering the pilot-cabin.

Having attended to Cecioni, Zappi went on to bandage my own leg. To tell the truth it seemed rather strange to me at that moment to bother about curing our injuries when I saw no possibility whatever of being rescued.

Malmgren appeared much better than the day before. He was carrying his arm in a sling. Zappi had ascertained that it was only badly bruised. The shoulder also was bruised, and the blood had spread in large reddish patches under the skin.

From time to time someone coming to rest under shelter from the wind would tell us the results of the search. Some more provisions had been found: boxes of pemmican, chocolate, and malted milk. There were also a few tins of petrol and one of emaillite.

An important discovery was that of the instruments for astronomical observations—two or three sextants, a mercury artificial horizon, calculating tables and chronometers. Nothing was missing. We took the opportunity to make observations on the rare occasions during the day when the sun broke through the clouds. These measurements showed our position to be: 81° 14′ of latitude N., 28° 14′ of longitude E.

But apart from the brief intervals when the sun shone out upon the desolate pack, the fog and wind continued without respite.

And so we passed the long, dreary day. At one moment a few pieces of chocolate were distributed, but nothing else. Nearly everybody still had some pemmican left from the day before. But for my part, I again ate nothing.

The lack of response to our S.O.S. had profoundly disheartened my comrades. Their optimism during the first few hours, when having found the emergency wireless set miraculously intact they had succeeded in putting it in working order, had now vanished. It had been a bitter blow, and they were beginning to despair.

Our receiver, however, was working perfectly, so that at nine that evening we intercepted the news bulletin from the station of San Paolo at Rome, from which we learnt that people in Italy were getting seriously alarmed at our silence.

By nightfall we were in a state of utter depression. The weather —still abominable—harmonized with our frame of mind and made it worse. For the second time after the crash my companions huddled up together, trying to sleep.

As for me, from that time onwards I had a long spell of insomnia. It was a great effort to bear the nervous distress of Cecioni, who at times seemed almost mad. He could not reconcile himself to the idea that he might die out there. Wide-eyed with terror, he would throw his arms round my neck and ask me if there were any hope. I tried to calm and encourage him.

That night our disturbed rest was suddenly broken by a noise like a long-drawn-out crash. It seemed as if something were shaking the tent. Someone shouted: "All out!" They took Cecioni and me by the shoulders and dragged us out over the snow. By the time we got outside the noise had ceased. Pieces of ice, driven by wind and current, had clashed together, making all this din; but now everything was quiet again. It was snowing a little. Once more I was struck by the strange and terrible aspect of the pack: unexpectedly—I don't know why—it occurred to me that a landscape on the moon must be very similar.

The peril being over, we went back into the tent.

Malmgren turned to speak to me: "This is a bad position," he remarked, "we ought to change as soon as possible. It would be dangerous to stop here. We had better look for another flat place, safer than this. The very fact that the ice here is so broken and jagged means that it is more exposed to the action of the winds and currents."

My comrades settled down to sleep again, still more depressed by this incident. Biagi and I remained awake.

At the appointed time he went out of the tent to transmit our desperate call for help. Immediately afterwards he came in again and fitted on the head-piece of the receiver, which had now also been put in a corner of the tent near the door.... A few minutes of deep silence... I was fixedly watching the wireless operator....

"Nothing, Biagi?"

"Nothing!"

Then he wearily curled up beside his little box, trying to sleep until the next attempt.

The tent relapsed into a mournful silence, rendered still more oppressive by the rhythm of the canvas flapping in the wind.

We Prepare to Hold Out

The rest had cheered my companions up. Next morning (May 27th) they got up more than ever decided to hold out to the last.

It is true that our signals, repeated every 2 hours, remained unanswered. But I told the others to be patient: sooner or later we should be heard. Meanwhile everything possible should be done to improve the conditions of our transmitting-station. First of all we must make certain that the wave-length was really 32 metres. This test was made by Biagi, tuning our station to San Paolo, which used the same wave-length.

In the meantime we decided to regulate our daily life. A certain quantity of provisions had been collected, but the search must be continued. Some cases of pemmican and chocolate had been found in the snow 100 or 150 yds. away from our camp. There might yet be others, and we must make haste to find them.

We discussed how we should share out the work.

"The General will decide about meals," said Mariano.

I accepted. It was the only thing I was fit to do. I settled meal-times and rations: ½ lb. of pemmican and a few pieces of chocolate.

Someone would have to provide drinking-water. Malmgren, who had completely pulled himself together, offered spontaneously, saying: "I'll see to the water!"

This was one of the most important tasks, and by no means as easy as it appeared at first sight. We had to hunt for fresh-water ice and then melt it.

Malmgren used an empty petrol-tin, filling it with pieces of ice and lighting a fire underneath. At first this was done with petrol, of which we had found two tins full, but as we had no stove, most of the heat was wasted, so later on I ordered that the petrol should be spared and pieces of wood and rags used instead.

The fact remains that we never had enough drinking-water. It was one of the things we wanted most. The precious liquid was distributed at meal-times in the lid of a thermos-flask, which circulated from one to another.

On the 27th, for the first time, we had a hot pemmican soup—an important event in our life on the pack. For 4 days we had not tasted hot food or drink, so when the steaming tin was brought into the tent we hailed it with exclamations of joy. An odour that appeared delicious pervaded the air.

Mariano in the centre, kneeling by the tent-pole, began to ladle out the soup, whilst the others crowded round him. A really picturesque scene.

I don't know why, but the image which kept on recurring to my mind was that of an encampment of brigands. Perhaps this was suggested by the appearance of my comrades—dirty, with beards already sprouting and fur caps on their heads. Nothing in them recalled the elegant youths whom I had known in Rome.

By the evening of that day my companions had finished gathering up the provisions, and we made an inventory. We had just over 280 lb. of concentrated food—enough to keep us alive for 45 days.

Forty-five days was a long time, and many things might happen in the interval. Sooner or later, I thought, our wireless calls would be answered. My companions now seemed less depressed than on the previous day.

During the whole of the 27th, at the prearranged hours, we sent out our S.O.S. in vain. The *Città di Milano* did not hear us. They merely repeated: "We imagine you are near the north coast of the Svalbard, between the 15th and 20th meridians E. of Greenwich. Trust in us. We are organizing help."

Trust in them! . . . But they were looking for us a long way from our actual position.

We discussed at length the reason why our calls had not been received. By this time we had fixed up our transmitting-station as well as possible. Perhaps it was too weak to be heard by the *Città di Milano*? This was Zappi's opinion. Biagi in his turn suggested that there was a "skip distance". But we were all agreed that the people on board the base-ship were not listening very persistently for us.

At nine that evening we intercepted very clearly the news bulletin of San Paolo, and found that the *Cittá di Milano* was going to leave King's Bay for the north coast of the Svalbard. We began to hope that, when the ship had come closer, it might at last hear us.

From that evening onwards we regularly received the San Paolo bulletin. This ended by being—next to meal-times—the most important event of the day. We anxiously waited for nine in the evening, to have news of what was happening in Italy, of the ideas about our disappearance, and of what was being done to rescue us. But as a rule we were disappointed. The news that could interest us was usually very scanty, whilst there were abundant accounts of ceremonies, speeches, and fêtes which naturally left us quite indifferent in our present situation; or at the most, by contrast, made us feel our misery more acutely.

And so came our third night on the pack.

THE COURAGE OF DESPAIR

The First Mention of a March

MALMGREN had not been wrong, after all, in predicting that on the route we followed back from the Pole the south wind would die down and be superseded by northerly winds, but unfortunately this forecast was only fulfilled a day later. From the evening of the 25th onwards, in fact, the wind had been blowing steadily from the NW.

In consequence the sheet of ice where we were encamped had drifted SE. with the whole surrounding pack. We noticed this on the morning of May 28th—the third day after our crash— when the sun once more broke through the clouds and we were able to take our bearings. We found we were at 80° 49' of latitude N. and 26° 20' of longitude E. In 2 days we had drifted no less than 28 miles! . . . I almost refused to believe in the accuracy of the astronomical measurements, so improbable did such a strong drift appear. But it was confirmed by the fact that Charles XII Island, which had formerly been right out of sight, was now on the horizon.

This discovery made a great impression on us. Even Malmgren was surprised at it, and thought the speed we had measured was really exceptional. When I asked him where he thought this drift would eventually carry us, he answered unhesitatingly: "Towards Franz Josef Land."

This unwelcome prophecy was confirmed by a navigation book picked up in the snow—the *Arctic Pilot*—the only book we had found, and incidentally the only one that, in our situation, could interest us. On page 264 we read: "*The principal direction of the ice-stream in North-East Land is towards the east*".

The eastward drift and the fact that our wireless seemed

incapable of making itself heard, aroused in Mariano and Zappi the idea of marching towards the coast.

After our meal that day, I heard this suggestion discussed for the first time. Mariano was talking about it to Malmgren. He proposed that we should set out on a march. Malmgren, indicating Cecioni and me, asked: "With them?" And when Mariano nodded, he replied: "No! That's impossible!"

Later on Zappi and Mariano came to speak to me. . . . They judged the situation desperate. The drift would carry us farther and farther from the zone where the *Città di Milano* was organizing rescue work. We could not depend on the wireless any longer.

I objected that the technicians who had chosen this set had surely tested it before handing it over to us.

"Yes!" replied Zappi. "They did test it, but under very much more favourable conditions. They even got in touch with Rhodes once, but that was at night."

I did not share Zappi's pessimism, nor was I convinced that the drift must inevitably carry us eastwards. At bottom, the matter depended on the winds. These might change, and one fine day we should find ourselves drifting before an easterly wind towards the region they were searching, instead of away from it.

In any case, Zappi and Mariano's proposal was clear enough: a group composed of the Naval officers and Malmgren should make for the coast and send help.

I replied that we would all gather in the tent, to discuss the proposal thoroughly and come to a decision.

Meanwhile, when the two had gone out, I had to start calming down Cecioni, who at the bare idea of our staying there alone became overwrought and began to cry like a child.

At this moment Cecioni had not the least idea that what he considered the worst luck of all would eventually prove a valuable factor in the salvation of himself and the rest of us. Had it not been for that broken leg there is no doubt that I should have energetically insisted on everyone leaving me, when I discovered later that nearly all my men thought that, in the circumstances, striking out for the coast was the sole way of escape. . . . And then we should all have been lost.

The whole of the 28th passed without our receiving any direct news from the *Città di Milano*. From San Paolo we heard that the ship had reached the north coast of the Svalbard, but this did not improve the wireless communication. Even, as if on purpose, now the *Città di Milano* was nearer, we could no longer intercept it, so that things were worse rather than better. Biagi again began harping on this theory of a "skip distance".

Later, having listened to the San Paolo bulletin, which Biagi, with the headpiece over his ears, read out to us, translating the signs word by word, Mariano and Zappi pressed me to hold a discussion on their proposal of sending out a patrol to reach the coast.

I invited them to define their idea.

They in their turn asked Malmgren to speak. Evidently the three had already gone into the question together, during their excursions to get some idea of the state of the ice and the difficulties of the march.

Malmgren spoke concisely: "All hope of the radio working must now be considered as lost; on the other hand, the drift is carrying us farther and farther from North-East Land. In these circumstances the only possibility of salvation lies in sending a patrol towards Cape North to meet the rescue expeditions."

Cape North, in fact, is near the 20th meridian east of Greenwich—the eastern limit of the zone where the *Città di Milano* announced that its search would extend.

"Who would go?" I asked.

Mariano promptly replied: "I'm perfectly ready to undertake it."

"And how many would you be?"

This time it was Zappi who answered: "At least four; the three Naval officers and Malmgren, who knows all about the ice and would be an invaluable guide."

Malmgren backed him up, proposing explicitly that Behounek, Trojani and Biagi should remain with us two invalids.

It seemed more than ever obvious that Mariano, Zappi, and Malmgren had agreed beforehand what to do. It came to this: they had arranged for everyone to leave whom they considered fit for the march. They excluded Behounek and Trojani, who in their opinion were not physically adapted for it, and would have ended by being a serious hindrance to the others. As for Biagi, I subsequently learned that Zappi wished to take him with them, but Malmgren had objected.

As soon as Malmgren had finished speaking Behounek interposed. The energy of his language surprised me. He spoke crisply, decisively: "For my part, I willingly remain with the General. But I do insist that one of the Naval officers stays with us. We must have someone who can take our bearings. Otherwise what's the use of the wireless operator?"

I agreed. Behounek was quite right. Trojani, Biagi, and Viglieri remained silent.

Then Cecioni spoke. . . . No! There was no need to separate. We ought all to march together. By easy stages of a mile or so a day we could reach the coast. With the wreckage of the cabin he would make two sledges: one for himself, the other for the General.

He spoke feelingly, and his words had a beseeching tone.

Then I spoke.

I told Cecioni that I approved of his idea of building sledges. This seemed to me no easy matter, but I did not doubt that, with his ingenuity, he could pull it off, even in present conditions. It was a good idea to construct these sledges: they might be useful in many ways. But he must not deceive himself. To carry the injured across this pack, as he imagined, was a wild-cat scheme which had little or no chance of success.

To Malmgren, Mariano, and Zappi I replied that I did not see any need to rush such a serious decision as that of dividing up our party. We had better see whether the drift would really go on carrying us first SE. and then E., as they maintained. That this must inevitably happen was open to doubt. Things might change. There was no use in being precipitate: it was much wiser to wait. And there was another reason: I was convinced that sooner or later our wireless appeals would be heard.

My conclusion was that we had better wait a few days more before deciding that any of us should march towards the coast.

Meanwhile I proposed that next day Cecioni, helped by the others, should set to work at once to build a sledge out of the cabin wreckage. Immediately it was finished we could try to shift our camp some 4 or 5 hundred yards nearer the coast, on a safer and more level site, as Malmgren had suggested. So I asked Mariano and Malmgren to go next day to look for a fresh camping-ground.

Making Sledges

Next morning (May 29th) Charles XII Island had disappeared from the horizon. In its stead we could see two islands to SW., very close together.

They were Broch Island and Foyn Island.

So we were still drifting. Later we took the height of sun and found we had turned a trifle farther E. We were at 80° 41' of latitude and 27° 12' of longitude. Since the 26th we had drifted 29 miles SE.—nearly 10 miles a day.

The sight of the island only 10 miles away could not help exercising a potent attraction upon the men who intended to march, and they renewed their insistence.

Then Cecioni elected to have himself dragged out of doors, and set to work on the sledges—the most difficult undertaking imaginable, with nothing to use except some steel tubing from the cabin framework.

That morning I remained alone in the tent. All round me I heard my companions moving and talking on the sheet of ice.

Mariano and Malmgren had gone off together.

Cecioni was hammering away at tubes and plates, and, as usual when he was at work, continually grumbling at the others, who, according to him, were not helping enough. Behounek and Trojani, patiently accepting his abuse, wandered up and down to hunt in the wreckage for the things he needed: pieces of aluminium plating, wire, sticks.

Zappi and Viglieri were busy rearranging the provisions and the other objects which made up our whole resources. Every two hours Biagi sent out his S.O.S., running back at once into the tent to listen to the receiver. In between whiles he helped Cecioni.

I heard them talking about the scanty news of the pack—especially a channel which had opened some 100 yds. away.

From time to time someone came into the tent to rest, or to bring in something he had picked up in the snow: maps, gloves, a woollen cap. Amongst other things they found a canvas bag containing hundreds of rifle cartridges. But the arms, alas! had all remained on board.

And since, now we were near the islands, numbers of seagulls and wild geese were flying round the tent, I often heard Biagi regretting he had no rifle.

This question of arms was the main subject of conversation when, towards two or three in the afternoon, we gathered to take our ration of pemmican and chocolate.

Again we began to discuss the fate of the dirigible. Had the smoke seen by some of the men half an hour after the crash really been a signal, as they had thought at first? Or must we rather think the ship had caught fire on striking ground? And if it had, what could have become of our comrades?

These were questions to which no one could reply. At any rate, we all agreed that the dirigible must have descended or fallen quite near us. Someone hazarded the suggestion that two men should be sent out towards the place where the smoke had been seen, which we reckoned to be not more than 6 miles away. In this manner we should have definite news of our comrades, and could also fetch the rifles.

Naturally the idea was given up at once: a march across the pack was too difficult and dangerous, and the result too uncertain, to make it worth the risk.

We were still discussing when evening came. The wireless remained silent.

During the last 24 hours, having noticed that we heard San Paolo better than the *Città di Milano*, we had modified our S.O.S. by adding: "Answer via IDO 32"—i.e. "Answer via San Paolo on the 32-metre wave-length". . . . But nobody replied—neither the *Città di Milano* (which we were again hearing well) nor San Paolo. Evidently they thought us dead, since they devoted nearly all their time to transmitting newspaper reports and private tele-grams.

The Anxiety to Start

After hearing the San Paolo bulletin at 9 p.m. on May 29th (the fifth day after the crash) we reverted inevitably to talking of Mariano and Zappi's proposed departure.

Cecioni resolutely opposed the idea, whilst the two Naval officers declared that no time should be lost.

For my part I insisted that they had better put it off a few days longer. Perhaps the *Hobby* would hear our radio when it got up to Cape North. Besides, the question of the drift, which was worrying them so much, was not so serious as they thought.

Mariano and Zappi interrupted: "Yes! But whilst we put it off, the provisions are growing less."

The remark was pertinent. I remained silent awhile, and then went on: "No! Better put it off a few days. I want to demonstrate to Cecioni that his idea of the whole party moving together is unfeasible. He has made a sledge: let us test it. Tomorrow we can experiment by shifting the camp 500 yards. We shall see the difficulties in practice."

They shook their heads. "No! Marching all together over this pack is an impossibility. You ought to have seen it and walked on it, as we have done. It is terrific. The whole time one has to scramble, slide, crawl, and at every step one risks falling into a crevasse, as has already happened. To carry a heavy man like Cecioni over it is an absurd idea. We had better stop wasting time and decide straight away to start."

"All right!" I said. "But with what aim?" To reach the coast and then send help? Could this be done? Would they arrive in time? And where and how would they search, without knowing where we had drifted meanwhile? In any case, if a patrol were to go for help, I thought it should be reduced to a minimum; two were enough. With the scanty provisions and clothes at our disposal two men could be adequately equipped. Two would be better than three. If one of them fell ill the other must leave him his share of provisions and go on.

Mariano remarked: "No! There should be three at least. Then if one fell ill the second would stay with him and the third go on."

Zappi insisted on four: the three officers and Malmgren. Anyhow, at least three: Mariano, Malmgren, and himself.

I put another important question: How many miles a day did Malmgren expect to cover on this pack? How many days would it take to reach Cape North?

"On a pack like this," said Malmgren, "I think we could manage about six miles a day; but nearer land, where the ice will probably be smoother, we might cover nine. Anyway, as an average we can take the speed of the first few days, when we are fresh but marching under difficulties. Later on we shall be tired, but to make up for it the way will be easier."

We looked at the map. They proposed the following route: Foyn Island, Cape Brunn, Cape Platen, Scoresby Island, Cape North: about 100 miles. So they ought to reach Cape North in 15 or 16 days.

One by one I questioned my men, to find out who wished to go. Mariano, Zappi, and Malmgren, of course, said they were ready, and Viglieri and Biagi were also willing. Only Behounek and Trojani declared that they would "stay with the General".

This done, I adjourned the decision. "Tomorrow we will try to shift the camp 500 yards," I said. "Afterwards, we will see."

It was getting late, and my comrades settled down to sleep. Malmgren, who until then had lain at the side of the tent, to the right of the entrance, changed his place that evening to find a more comfortable position for his injured arm, and lay down at the feet of Cecioni and myself.

Very soon the others drowsed off. Cecioni, between sleep and waking, murmured a little from time to time. Mariano remained awake for a while. I watched him: he had changed. He no longer seemed the same as on the first day. Something in him escaped me. These discussions stood between us, for his eagerness to be off, leaving some of his friends on the pack, had displeased and surprised me.

I alone stayed awake. From time to time Cecioni woke from

his light, troubled sleep and convulsively clutched my arm, clinging to me as if to an anchor of hope. . . . A hushed interchange of words—a prayer—an exhortation. Then all was silent again.

A light wind puffed out the silk of the tent, and the rhythm, as it beat like waves lapping on the shore, seemed a lullaby for the sleeping men.

The Polar Bear

Lying awake, with so many thoughts whirling in my brain, I watched for the sun to shine out. The double silk of the tent was so thin that the shape of the disc gleamed through it. The moment it appeared I would ask Zappi to make an observation and check the position resulting from previous measurements.

At bottom our main obsession was the drift.

Suddenly the sun came out.

I signed to Cecioni to wake Zappi, who was sleeping next him. Zappi in his turn called Mariano, and they went out together to make the observation.

A few minutes passed. Then all at once Zappi looked in at the entrance, saying excitedly in an undertone: "*There's a bear!*"

Everybody woke. Malmgren sat up and turned to me, saying: "Give me the pistol; I'm going to hunt it."

I gave him the Colt with some cartridges. He loaded it and went out, advising us to keep quiet. The others followed. Someone helped Cecioni and me to crawl out. In our excitement we felt no pain from our injuries.

Outside, the cold was bitter but not troublesome, as the northwest breeze was so light that it hardly stirred the air. The sun had gone in again, and the sky was covered by clouds. The clear, transparent air produced that delicate radiance I had so often noticed during the Arctic nights, which made the bluish icecrags stand out so well against the whiteness of the snow.

The bear was 20 or 30 yards away on the opposite side of the tent, towards the islands. Once more Malmgren whispered: "Hush! Don't move!" Then he went forward cautiously, grasping the pistol.

We stayed silent near the tent-door. In the meantime we had armed ourselves. The most formidable weapons—a knife and an axe—had, I think, been taken by Mariano and Zappi, who were now warily following Malmgren. The rest of us, armed with a file, a large nail, a bit of metal tubing, stopped where we were, motionless, holding our breath and eyeing the bear. I hugged Titina close so that she should not bark.

Whilst Malmgren was stealing up to it I leant forward to watch. The beautiful beast was behind a hummock, looking curiously at us and slowly wagging his head.

Suddenly a shot rang out. I saw Malmgren dash forward, followed by Mariano and Zappi. Somebody shouted: "He's hit!" Two more shots followed hard on each other.

The poor brute had tried to escape when the first bullet hit him, but he was mortally wounded: after a few steps he fell and lay still.

The spot where he was lying was about 40 yards from the tent, a fine sheet of ice, two or three times the size of our own. We christened it forthwith "the bear floe".

My companions went to cut up the animal and skin it, as Malmgren said this should be done at once, whilst it was still warm.

Cecioni and I crawled back, as best we could, to our places in the tent. There was joy in our hearts, but we remained silent till the others came back. Their hands were blood-stained and they were all excited.

The adventure was discussed in detail. Everyone had been surprised at the pacific behaviour of the bear and at Malmgren's skill in shooting it through the heart at 15 yards. I complimented him, adding: "You see, the Queen was right!"

I was referring to a conversation the day before, when Malmgren had declared that we should never manage to kill a bear with the Colt revolver. On this I had remarked that our Queen—who was a fine shot and had hunted bears and seals in the Svalbard—when discussing the subject one day with me had recommended this type of pistol as excellent, even for big game.

This great event of the night, May 29th-30th, raised our spirits and put an end to our taciturnity.

The curious fact that nothing had been found in its stomach except for some rags of paper printed in English had given rise to all kinds of conjectures. At the moment it did not occur to anyone that the famished bear had (as we afterwards found out) swallowed several pages of one of our navigation books.

Then we began to reckon up the increase in our supplies. Our situation had greatly improved: we had (apart from the liver, which is poisonous) between 350 and 400 lb. of fresh meat. So there was no longer any need to hasten the departure of the three.

With these happy thoughts in our minds we settled down to sleep, while one of the men went to mount guard outside, as we now thought advisable.

It was the first night that we had lain down with relief in our hearts, and hopes that were roseate, even if rather vague.

"BOTH PARTIES WILL DIE!"

The Decision

THE argument of the dearth of provisions, which in the discussion the day before had prevailed over my wish to postpone the proposed departure of Mariano, Zappi, and Malmgren, was now worthless; so I was very much surprised when Zappi said next morning that the group ought to start at once. His impatience struck me as peculiar.

Afterwards I learned the explanation: the drift had carried us still farther SE. In fact, the latest observations gave a latitude of 80° 26′ and a longitude of 27° 23′. Upon marking this position on the map we found that compared with the day before we had travelled about 5 miles SE. towards Foyn Island.

That morning the island was very close: the distance was calculated on the map as about 7 miles.

During my talk with Zappi I was struck by his state of nerves. I realized that nothing would shake him in his idea. He wished to go, and was surprised at my putting difficulties in his way. I noticed that he could not even follow out an argument, but rejected every demur at sight. He was irritated at the time he was being made to lose—the delay in carrying out the plan he and his friends had conceived.

The argument about provisions having collapsed, he had another one ready that morning: it was essential to reach Cape North quickly; otherwise the men searching for us, having got there without finding anyone, would straightway return. This fear was exaggerated. I pointed out that they certainly would not leave Cape North without at least putting down a *cache* of provisions.

When Zappi had gone out, Mariano in his turn came to insist on starting.

In face of Mariano and Zappi's firm conviction that the last hope of rescue for them and for us lay in carrying out their plan, I felt I had no right to oppose it any longer. So I decided to consent, and told Zappi to go and get ready.

As for the other two, I really wanted one of them to stay with us. Trojani and Biagi, too, had remarked that as Malmgren was the only one conversant with life in the Arctic his presence would be invaluable to those staying behind. Our experience the night before was clear proof of this.

I called Malmgren and told him what my comrades desired, adding that I myself thought either he or Mariano should stop.

Malmgren replied: "I think it essential that the group should have a guide who knows all about the ice. Marching on a pack like this is arduous and risky in the extreme. They must have somebody practical." He seemed to be reflecting for a moment. "In any case," he added, "I will do as you wish—stay here or go with them, whichever you prefer."

I asked him about his injury. Was he fit to march, with an arm in that condition?

Yes, he said, his arm was much better. It had only been badly bruised, not broken, as he had thought at first. Of course, he would have to carry less on his back than the others; but he could certainly manage 30 or 40 lb. without difficulty.

After this chat I told Malmgren that I had no further objections to make. He could get ready to start with Zappi. As for Mariano, I would talk with him later and induce him to stay.

That day (May 30th) we started a series of meals founded on bear. For 3 weeks or more we ate hardly anything else: it was our staple food.

After the broth had been drunk and the meat gnawed, Mariano turned to go out.

"I want to speak to you alone!" I said. He did not answer.

From that moment he took care not to come back into the tent, but all at once I heard him talking to Zappi outside. "No!" he said loudly, "we two should go, as we are such great friends." Evidently this was meant for me. Malmgren must have already mentioned my wish that Mariano should stay. That was his answer.

I understood. Any attempt to modify an idea which had been maturing for days in the minds of Mariano and Zappi was quite hopeless. They meant to go together. Whatever I had said, I could not have held back either of them. So I decided to object no longer.

I gathered everybody in the tent and told them that the three would leave. The next thing to do was to divide up the stores and clothing.

Zappi had already drawn up in his pocket-book a list of what he thought the men who were leaving should take. The first item was "half a tent". But, as it was somewhat difficult to split our tent in two, this was not even mentioned. On the other hand, we gave the three the woollen blanket with which till then we had all protected ourselves as best we could against the night cold.

Then we discussed provisions. Malmgren was the first to speak. He proposed that the pemmican, chocolate, and malted milk should be divided proportionally to the number of persons. They would leave us the fresh meat as well. This was agreed upon.

Next we talked about arms. They would have liked the pistol, but Cecioni, Trojani, and Viglieri protested.

We would let them have the knife and axe.

As spare clothing, we settled to give them the wind-tight suits, some pairs of *finsko*, and all the woollen things we could possibly do without.

We also shared our charts and instruments. It was decided that each of them should have a pocket compass and a watch. I gave them one of the chronometers, but advised them not to take the sextant, as they wished. It would only have proved a useless encumbrance.

Having settled all this I asked when they intended to start.

"This evening," said Malmgren. "We must go as soon as possible."

"I am afraid of this wind," he added. I don't know what he meant, but probably he was referring to the drift.

After this Mariano and Zappi went out to begin their preparations. Malmgren remained.

For some time we were silent.

All at once I asked him to tell me frankly what he thought would happen to those who were leaving and those who were staying behind.

"They do not understand," he said (referring to the two men who had just gone out), "how difficult and dangerous a march on this pack is." Then he added as an afterthought: "Some years ago a perfectly equipped German expedition was lost on it to a man."

"And we?" I asked.

"You will have the drift. That will carry you towards the east."

He paused a moment; then, lowering his voice as if to be heard by me alone: "Both parties will die!" he concluded.

He said these words as tranquilly as I listened to them. It was as if we were discussing matters in which we had no personal interest.

Biagi Wants to Go Too

Malmgren went to help his friends get ready, and I remained alone with Cecioni. Soon afterwards Viglieri and Behounek came back. Viglieri sat down on my left beside Cecioni. Behounek stayed near the door.

Not quite half an hour had passed when Biagi came in. He was in a bad temper. He sat down silently in the corner facing me, frowning and sombre. I noticed it, and asked him affectionately: "What's wrong, Biagi?"

He answered: "I'm fit to march too."

I gathered from this that Biagi thought the men who were leaving had a better chance of survival than those who were staying behind. If this was so—and it was so—my duty was clear, and I must do it unhesitatingly: invite the wireless operator to leave as well, and anyone else who wished to go.

Turning to Biagi, without a shadow of resentment or surprise I said gently: "If you think it better to go, then you shall go. I myself wish it, and ask you to do it, if you feel like that. Don't think I shall mind. You mustn't worry about me. You have done your utmost to make your radio work: if it hasn't succeeded that's not your fault. I am grateful for your devotion. You've been working for a week now without stopping. You needn't have any scruples about leaving. Go and get ready."

My tone was such that Biagi was persuaded. His face cleared and he immediately went to make his preparations.

As he stepped out, Viglieri, who had been sitting silent, said quietly: "But then I should like to go too."

This was logical. There was no reason why Viglieri should stay, when the wireless operator was leaving. But in that case it was better that the other two should go as well.

I had been thinking for some time about this possibility—that everyone except the two invalids should go—and had planned how to organize the march. As for Cecioni, I was by this time sure that I could induce him to resign himself to staying alone with me.

Then I called Malmgren, Mariano, and Zappi into the tent. I spoke firmly.

"Biagi is coming with you," I said. "But, from the moment that your departure is reckoned the only means of saving yourselves, I consider that all the other able-bodied men should accompany you. I will stay here with Cecioni. During the march you will split up into two groups, if necessary."

Mariano and Zappi objected that "the two invalids could not be left alone."

"Don't worry about us!" I retorted. "Cecioni will keep calm. I shall look after him. But I intend that whoever wishes to go, shall go. Now I am going to question them, one by one."

I started with Viglieri. He hesitated a moment, then suddenly made up his mind and said placidly: "It has been arranged that the three shall leave. I don't think it necessary to go back on that decision."

Behounek and Trojani supported him: "We are staying here with the General."

So it was only Biagi who was going with the three.

"All right," I said. "Go and get ready then."

Mariano, Zappi and Biagi went out.

Malmgren stayed behind. After a momentary silence he sat down resolutely at my feet.

"Well!" he said, "if they leave, I stay."

I looked at him in surprise. "Why, Malmgren?"

"I could never go back to Sweden and say that I left the leader of the expedition and another sick man here without any help. It would be unworthy of a gentleman. No! If Biagi leaves, I remain. He represents the only hope you have."

Only a few minutes had passed when I saw Biagi come in again. He stayed by the door, sitting cross-legged like a Japanese and looking at me.

"Forgive me, sir!" he said smiling. "It was a moment of weakness. But I'm not going. You might need me for the wireless."

Later on, Trojani (and Biagi himself) told me of the discussion outside the tent which had led to Biagi changing his mind. Zappi had frankly expressed the opinion that "a strapping, resourceful young fellow like Biagi would be very useful, so they had better have him with them".

But in consequence of Malmgren's ultimatum and some remarks made by Mariano, Biagi had of his own accord decided to stay.

The Departure of the Three

Part of the stores and other things which the three were taking were put in Pomella's knapsack, and the rest made into bundles, to be fastened on their backs. In spite of his injured arm Malmgren had his share of the load—30 or 40 lb. The others had about 60 each.

The net weight of the provisions was 120 lb., consisting of 72 lb. pemmican, 40 lb. of chocolate, 6 lb. of malted milk, and 2 lb. of butter.

As spare clothing they had a complete wind-tight suit; 7 pairs wind-tight shoes; 4 or 5 pairs of *finsko*; a woollen combination found in Pomella's knapsack, and several pairs of thick wool socks and gloves. Besides this they had a woollen blanket, 2 bottles of petrol, half the spirit from the compasses, a cord to rope themselves with, and some pieces of varnished cloth from the inner and outer lining of the pilot-cabin.

Each of them was wearing a thick combination, a very thick wool suit, an Iceland wool jersey, and a complete lambskin suit, covered with solid cotton stuff. Their equipment was completed by a woollen mountaineering-cap, a fur cap, woollen and fur gloves. The latter were made on the Russian plan, with an additional flap to protect the fingers without hampering their movement.

We had only one pair of snow-spectacles, kept in Cecioni's knapsack. I made him give them to the men who were leaving. As footgear each had 3 pairs of thick socks (one being the type used by skiers in Norway), surmounted by catskin slippers and *finsko*.

When Malmgren was ready he came back into the tent and sat down to speak to me. He was affectionate—full of little attentions. The decision reached after so much discussion had stimulated him and done him good. For a man of action like himself, this staying still to wait for death, counting up the days of rations left and cursing at the wireless, was undoubtedly what had so utterly depressed him. Now that he had braced himself up for a march he was a different man.

He began by saying: "We shall march as fast as possible. In about a fortnight I hope to reach Cape North. Thence we will push on to King's Bay. The moment we arrive I will get into touch with the Tromsö Geophysical Institute and the Oslo Institute for studies on Spitsbergen. First of all I will get information about the winds which have been blowing each day in this region, whilst the Oslo Institute will tell me all they know about the drifts and currents north of North-East Land. So I shall discover, more or less, where to find you again."

"And then?" I asked.

"Then I will come back to look for you myself, with Swedish aeroplanes. Do you think one could land here on the pack? I do. I have seen a flat ground some hundreds of yards farther on; but possibly by that time there will be a lead, like the one which opened close by, where a seaplane could moor."

Then he went on eagerly. "Mind you keep the balls of aniline dye. They will be useful for colouring some rags red. Put 4 of these improvised red flags at the corners of a square 200 yards each side, with the tent as its centre. Then we shall be able to see you better from a height."

He had realized that the simplest and quickest way of fetching off the injured was by air. All at once, hoping that we would soon get well, he advised us: "Keep quite still. Then your fractures will heal sooner. In 3 weeks you, too, may be able to march and get to Foyn Island. And there you can wait. Anyhow, if you do march follow in our tracks. Then we shall know where to find you."

He was deceiving himself. At that moment he seemed oblivious of the difficulties which he himself had pointed out.

"Save the pemmican and chocolate," he went on. "They will be useful when you set out. Meanwhile eat up the bear-meat and the sugar. This is too heavy and no good on a march."

There was a pause.

"Put aside the wireless for 20 or 25 days," he added. "Spare the batteries until we have had time to get there and send a boat. Then it will be possible to hear you."

Then it was my turn to ask his advice, since in him I was losing the only ice-expert. "Ought we to change our camping-ground?"

"Yes, it would be better. You should find a safer spot. I am amazed we have been able to stay here until now without having trouble. And keep your eye on the lead. If it comes within fifty yards, get out of here as quickly as you can."

Then seeing Cecioni silent and miserable, he added: "We are making straight for Foyn Island. If I see that the lead stretches right up to it, we will turn back and fetch you. Cecioni can make a raft with the empty petrol-cans for us to carry you on."

Then Malmgren asked what message I wanted to send to Italy.

"Tell them," I said, "that my comrades and I are staying here calmly, waiting for God's will to be done. If we can be saved, so much the better; if not, we will wait serenely for death, satisfied to have done our duty. Only see that they look after our families."

Malmgren held my hand: "All right, General! In any case," he added, "remember that the greater number of lost expeditions have been saved at the last moment."

This was my dear comrade's parting advice. It remained

impressed on my mind, and several times I had occasion to recall it.

But the men who were leaving were themselves fated to experience the profound wisdom of Malmgren's remark. For Mariano and Zappi were rescued only when they had come to the very end of their tether . . . and Malmgren, too, might have been saved if he himself had put more faith in the precious counsel he gave us.

The party had said: "If you have any letters for your families give them to us." Everyone had hunted for paper and settled down to write, except Trojani, who, thinking it perfectly useless, had handed me his fountain-pen.

An unforgettable scene. . . . The stuffy tent was suddenly filled with memories of our dear ones far away: in the silence that had settled on us one heard the scratching of pencils on paper. Viglieri was writing to his mother; Behounek to his fiancée and his sister: Biagi and Cecioni to their wives. I turned to look at them. Behounek was the one who struck me most. I had always seen him so self-contained that I had ended by considering him incapable of emotion. Yet now tears were running down his cheeks as he wrote. The others also were weeping. Only Trojani remained impassive, as he carefully wrapped up a sum of money for his wife.

Then I looked at Cecioni. The poor man had put down a few lines and then been too upset to go on. I glanced at what he had written: it revealed all his despair, his anguish at never seeing his loved ones again. "No, not like that! It isn't certain we shall die here," I said to comfort him. "You must write differently. Hand it over! I will write, and you shall copy it out." And this is what was done.

Then I started writing on my own account. A great calm possessed me. I wrote to my wife seven pages of advice, suggestions for the child's education and counsels for her health. Then I comforted her, to help her bear it if I did not come back.

"Perhaps God wills that we shall embrace each other again one day; that will be like a miracle. If not, do not mourn my death, but be proud of it. Be certain that I shall have done my duty quietly to the last."

Then I wrote a few lines to Maria: "You must keep Mummy from crying, if I don't come back again. Titina is perfectly happy here, but perhaps she would still rather be at home." . . .

We handed our letters to the men who were leaving.

And now the separation was at hand.

When all was ready my comrades gathered in the tent. Everyone was very sad. I distributed the last meal in common: three tablets of malted milk and some lumps of sugar.

Then Mariano and Zappi slipped in between Cecioni and myself to embrace me. There were tears in their eyes.

I made a point of embracing Malmgren too.

Then I heard Mariano say, as he took leave of Cecioni: "If the lead stretches up to the island we will come back to fetch you. In any case, don't worry. We will march swiftly and bring help." These assurances comforted Cecioni and alleviated his distress at the separation.

Having said good-bye the three went out and fastened the bundles on their backs. The others followed to help them.

I heard more leave-takings. And now, at last, they had started on their march and were moving away.

"Good luck!" I called. "God go with you!"

Viglieri, Trojani, Behounek, and Biagi followed them for some time with their eyes. Then they came in again.

We were silent.

SIX IN THE RED TENT

The Day After

THE departure of the three seemed to have taken a weight off our minds. For the last three days we had been kept in a state of worry, wondering whether we ought to agree to their enterprise. The consequent discussions; the insistence of those who wished to leave and the objections of the rest; the impatience of the former and discontent of the latter, had all heightened the tension—bad enough in itself—produced in our little camp by the drift and the silence of the wireless. The uncertainty was increased and the discussions made acrimonious by Cecioni's pleading that we should all march together, and his stubborn opposition to any plan that would divide up our forces.

For a few hours after the parting we felt still lonelier in that great icy wilderness, still weaker in face of those vast forces of Nature which had us at their mercy. Two of the strongest had gone, and with them Malmgren—the only Arctic expert. We were reduced to six, two of us crippled by serious injuries. Of the other four, not one had any previous experience of life on a frozen sea.

Yet the day after the departure our spirits were high.

One thing which helped to set our minds at rest was perhaps a momentary respite in the eastward drift. That morning, in fact, having travelled slowly NW. during the last 24 hours, we were still nearer to Foyn and Broch Islands.

I set myself eagerly to reorganize the camp, allotting each man his task. Viglieri was to overhaul the provisions, make an exact inventory of them, and guard against the danger of their falling into a crevasse by roping the various packages together. He was also to determine our position by means of solar observations.

The cooking was entrusted to Trojani and Behounek, who

from the first had shown striking aptitude for this work and were steadily perfecting their talent. Nor did I overlook Cecioni. It is true his broken leg prevented him from moving about, but to make up for this his arms were first-rate. As sewing-materials and some pieces of felt had been found, I suggested that he should make slippers for our companions who had to move about on the ice. He enthusiastically took up this new occupation, revealing unsuspected ability. I did my best to help, but I must admit that there was a great difference between my slippers and those that he made.

The *chef d'œuvre* of our shoemaker was a fine pair of shoes for Viglieri's by no means small feet, made from the solid waterproof tool bags.

All the fit men, too, were to take it in turns to stand guard over the tent, the necessity for which had become apparent after the cracking of the ice and the bear's visit. I arranged a watch of 2 hours, later increased to 3.

I did not think it advisable to follow Malmgren's parting advice to put the radio aside for 3 weeks or so. Like Mariano and Zappi he thought our transmitting station too weak to be heard by any possibility at King's Bay, and that we had better save our batteries until the three had reached their goal and could send a boat fitted with wireless up to Cape North, near enough to communicate. Until then, according to Malmgren, we ought not to exhaust our batteries by further useless attempts.

Nevertheless, though I hoped they would reach the coast, I did not think they would arrive in time to send us help. More by instinct than reason I felt that our only hope lay in the wireless; consequently we must make every effort to go on calling, until someone answered us.

Even if the *Città di Milano* did not hear us, some other station might. The whole civilized world was in suspense. Hundreds of wireless stations were certainly listening for us, and sooner or later, if only by chance, one of them would pick up our call.

To make it more likely, I thought we had better transmit our S.O.S. for half an hour or an hour at a time, instead of 10 minutes, as we had done until then.

The evening the men left I ordered Biagi to check that our wave-length was exactly 32 metres, by carrying the receiving apparatus about 100 yards away from the transmitter and connecting the two. Biagi found that everything was in order.

I then wrote a short message in Italian and in French and gave it to him. "From tomorrow onwards," I said, "you will send it out every day for an hour on end."

Biagi, as usual, carried out the order without discussion, and to this we owed our salvation.

One thing that helped to cheer us up, after the misery and depression of the first weeks on the pack, was certainly (as I have said before) the better weather. The wind, which for 5 days had made us drift south-eastwards, had at last dropped and been succeeded by a light easterly breeze that drove us steadily to the west, nearer Foyn and Broch Islands. In fact, on June 3rd we reckoned we were only 4 miles NNE. of Foyn and 5½ miles NE. of Broch. This was our closest to the two little islands.

Of the two, Foyn Island, which was always the nearer, soon became our favourite. In the end we called it simply "The Island".

"The Island" regulated our moods, which changed with its distance from us. When its silhouette stood out clearly on the white horizon-line we were happy; it saddened us to see it fading into the distance. And when it disappeared altogether pessimism overcame us, and dreary days began; we felt lonelier, more abandoned than ever in the white desert around us.

Away from "The Island" everything was grey, uniform, silent, desolate; near it seagulls came to keep us company, attracted by the smell of the camp. They settled on the hummocks near us, and for hours and hours together filled the air with their raucous cries.

These signs of life, however slight, cheered us up immensely. We felt less alone. Perhaps also, involuntarily, we thought that if there was life around us there was also a chance of prolonging our own, when one day our provisions were exhausted.

Here on the pack the hard, implacable law of the struggle for existence had us all under its sway.

One day, whilst the lead near us was still open, some seals came out of the water to enjoy a ray of sun. Biagi came to speak to me: he had a plan of his own. But the charming beasts, fortunately for themselves, disappeared and were not seen again. Then our wireless operator had the idea of fishing in the lead. Cecioni made some hooks. But the attempt failed, and was not repeated.

Our main hope lay in the bears, which we dreaded and yet desired. After the one killed by Malmgren, four others visited us in the course of a month, almost always when we were near Foyn Island.

The second visit also took place at night. Biagi was on guard, and was filling up his time by sending the customary S.O.S. I was the only one awake inside the tent, when suddenly he dashed in, crying, "There's a bear! Where is the pistol?"

The pistol, to be always handy, was kept hanging on the tent-pole. Biagi took it and went out. We heard a few shots, and immediately afterwards his exclamation: "He's got away!"

In a minute or two he returned to tell us that he had only noticed the bear when it knocked against one of the wires of his radio. It was near the corner of the tent where I was lying, and was busy snuffling at a fire-extinguisher. Barely half a yard had separated my head from its powerful claws!

Biagi returned the pistol to its place. The tent-pole had many uses. Right on top was a little picture of the Madonna of Loreto, presented to the *Norge* expedition, which had again accompanied us on this one. It had been found on the ice, a day after the crash. Below the pistol was a small calendar, on which we marked off the passing days. Lower still were hanging the *finsko* which Viglieri, Behounek and Trojani (Biagi was the only one who had leather shoes) took off and put there to dry when they lay down to sleep after finishing their spell of guard-duty.

This episode convinced me still more of the absolutely harmless nature of the white bears. They had no intention of hurting us. It was only out of curiosity that they approached our camp, and I believe they were quite astonished to find themselves attacked by us—and once even by Titina.

This happened one evening, when we were all at supper inside the tent. Suddenly we heard our little dog barking furiously. When the men ran out to see what on earth was happening, they watched the curious spectacle of Titina chasing a poor bear who had come to investigate our camp. She only gave up when the bear saved himself by diving into a lead and swimming away.

Drifting South-East Again

From June 3rd to 6th our nerves were put to a very severe test. The north-west wind sprang up again and blew us steadily south-eastwards. Soon we had lost sight of Broch Island, and Foyn was fading rapidly into the distance.

Although this north-west wind had helped us at first by carrying us nearer land, it was now our worst enemy, because it drifted us away from the meridian of Cape North—the extreme limit of the zone where they were searching for us. To make matters worse, it was always a strong wind, and lasted a considerable time.

Biagi was still sending out our S.O.S., which I insisted on his transmitting for a long time together, but in vain. He was nervy and thoroughly out of temper: it seemed at times that he even doubted his own competence.

Silence from the wireless, and a south-eastward drift . . . the nightmare had begun again! Once more Malmgren's prophecy obsessed my mind: once more I saw the gesture with which he had traced out on the map the route we should probably follow towards Franz Josef Land.

Seeing my comrades gloomy and worried I tried to cheer them up. . . . We must trust in Providence. Up till then we had been preserved by a series of coincidences verging on the miraculous. It seemed to me impossible that we should have been saved and granted two months' provisions merely to prolong our agony. And, then, there were millions of people in the world praying for us: I believed in prayer, and above all in the prayers of children. Surely some beneficent action must be exercised by the millions and millions of thoughts and hearts that were turning towards us all over the world.

This line of reasoning, which helped to make these long,

terrible days bearable, had more effect on Cecioni than on any of the others; but I would see the faces of Viglieri and Biagi also lighten. Trojani alone remained plunged in pessimism; in spite of all my efforts, I never managed to coax a smile from him. It is true he did his job with a zeal and efficiency which might have surprised some people, but not me, who had selected him. Yet it was rather through discipline than because he saw any use in helping us, by his efforts, to hold out to the very last.

To tell the truth it was not surprising if my comrades did not all bear our terrible adventure as calmly as I did. In nerving themselves to the enterprise perhaps they had not sufficiently reckoned with the possibility of disaster, as I had done. It was from this in the main that my tranquillity was derived. The catastrophe had not taken me spiritually unawares, because when I first embarked on the venture I had counted all the risks.

"After all," I kept saying to the others, "we can die quite tranquilly up here. We have done our duty, and very nearly achieved everything on our programme. We have flown for 134 hours over the Arctic circle, almost all across unexplored territory. We can boast of having organized the first really scientific aerial expedition, and most of the results are in safety, even if we ourselves are lost. We have fulfilled the mission confided to us by the Pope, and Italy knows this. The Cross and our national flag have descended upon the Pole. These are only symbols, it is true, but very lofty ones—symbols of the beauty and poetry of our enterprise."

These talks, I noticed, did my companions good. Perhaps my words corresponded to their own unexpressed feelings. I would see their faces light up—even Trojani's.

The other three Italians were more serene: though anxious and sometimes sad, they showed no sign of that invincible pessimism that dominated Trojani. More than anything else, they were miserable at the lack of proper footgear. By this time the *finsko* were saturated, and in these circumstances doing sentry-duty in the snow had become extremely trying.

This watch outside the tent in the wind and cold was bad enough in itself; and it was still worse to have to interrupt one's

sleep to replace the man who was coming in to rest. To remain
2 or 3 hours alone, keeping an eye on the cracks as they opened
and taking care not to be caught unawares by a bear, soon became
a very exacting duty. Viglieri and Biagi tried to make it more
bearable by digging in the snow in the hope of turning up some
provisions or any other useful object. As for Behounek, he stood
still and immovable on the same spot, particularly after an
occasion when, wishing to inspect beyond our own piece of ice,
he had fallen into a crevasse and taken an impromptu bath. Not
hearing him walk about and fearing he might have met with a
fresh accident I used to ask him now and then: "Nothing new,
Behounek?" "Nothing!" he would reply placidly.

But the gayest of all was Biagi. One morning when we were
in sight of the islands I heard him singing *Gina, My Lovely Gina!*
It was a delight to listen. Very soon Biagi's cheerful mood spread
all round, infecting the others, until even Trojani began to sing.

Happy at this unexpected cheerfulness I gave the two singers
a special ration of sugar; but I must admit that not even this could
induce them, in the days that followed, to send their song ringing
out over that fearful expanse of ice; and the reason was that (as
I have said) from June 3rd to 6th we were thoroughly discouraged
by the cursed wind which drove us farther and farther SE.

We waited impatiently for the sun to break through the clouds
and enable Viglieri to make an observation, hoping to find that the
drift had stopped or changed its direction. But these hopes were
disappointed: for days and days on end the sun never appeared:
besides, whenever the air cleared a little we could see Foyn Island
steadily receding. Already, scanning the southern horizon with
field-glasses, we sighted the coast at Cape Leigh Smith.

Very often I caught myself immersed in gloomy meditations.
Where should we end up? Perhaps in a few days we should reach
Cape Leigh Smith, pass it, and drift on inexorably eastwards
away from land. All possibility of help reaching us in time—even
by chance—would vanish. And then at last I too should have to
give up hope in the wireless, since (if our theory was right) the
farther away we were the less probable it became that our S.O.S.
could be picked up and understood. What were we to do?

This was the agonized question I asked myself, and the answer was, that we two invalids had no right to sacrifice the rest of the party. If all hope in the wireless must sooner or later be abandoned my duty was to let the others try to save themselves by a march. Obviously, in the circumstances this would be full of difficulties and unknown risks. But however desperate it might be, it was the last hope for the four other men.

And so the extreme decision matured in my mind: if we went on drifting south-eastwards, as soon as we were near Cape Leigh Smith I would order the four able-bodied men to leave us and strike out for land. As for Cecioni, I would try to make him accept the decision with as little suffering as possible.

Having spoken to Cecioni, I questioned Behounek and Trojani. It was unnecessary to ask the other two, as I knew they would obey a peremptory order.

Trojani answered: "I will do what you command," and the reply pleased me. But when I asked Behounek if he felt fit to undertake a long march, he said trenchantly, "I don't know why you ask me this. I have come here with you, and I'm not going away without you."

It is not without emotion that I record Behounek's answer. This man's noble spirit did not belie itself. I already admired him for the imperturable calm he had shown throughout. Never a word or a gesture of disheartenment.

Half starved as he was, with the shoes dropping off his feet, the Czechoslovak scientist had not forgotten his instruments. He had hunted for them in the snow, put some of them to rights, and resumed on the pack the observations that the catastrophe had interrupted.

So that when I asked him some days later if he could take up some of his measurements again it was a pleasant surprise to hear him reply: "*Mais oui, mon Général! J'ai repris les observations il y a quelques jours.*"

And to think that in those days our fate appeared so hopeless that we had not scrupled to use as firelighters some rolls of film, although they contained valuable records of our last flight!

THE MIRACLE OF THE RADIO

Schmidt

IN spite of everything I would not lose faith in the wireless, and took care to insist on Biagi transmitting our S.O.S. unceasingly, especially at 8 p.m. (Greenwich time), when innumerable stations were listening for the time-signal broadcast on the 32-metre wave-length from the Eiffel Tower.

My wireless message, sent out in Italian, French, and sometimes English, read as follows:

S.O.S. *Italia*, Nobile. On the ice near Foyn Island, north-east Spitsbergen, latitude 80° 37', longitude 26° 50'. Impossible to move, lacking sledges and having two men injured. Dirigible lost in another locality. Reply via IDO 32.

But unexpectedly, when not one of my comrades believed any longer than anyone could reply to our appeal—just when our discouragement at the inexorable eastward drift was at its worst—there came the news we had awaited so eagerly for nearly a fortnight, day by day, hour by hour: the news which revived our vanished hopes and set our little lost camp on the floe in a ferment.

It was the evening of June 6th.

Biagi, with the head-piece over his ears, was transcribing the San Paolo bulletin, as usual, in a note-book, when suddenly he exclaimed: "They've heard us!" and went on writing. And word by word as he wrote, I read:

"The Soviet Embassy has informed the Italian Government that . . ."

They were speaking of the young Russian Schmidt, who had picked up some fragments of our S.O.S. at Archangel the evening of June 3rd.

I could hardly contain my joy. At last my prophecy had come true! Someone had heard us, if only by chance!

Archangel was too far away for the signals of our little station to be heard clearly; but that did not matter. The essential was that the alarm had been given, that at last someone was convinced we were still alive and able to make ourselves heard.

At eleven next morning I ordered Biagi (who was repeating his usual efforts with far more zest than before) to transmit our S.O.S. for an hour on end.

While Biagi was broadcasting outside the tent Viglieri and Behounek were asleep inside. Trojani was wandering about to prepare the next meal.

As usual, he had brought in several large slices of meat for Cecioni to cut up into tiny pieces. Then he had gone out again to light the fire.

Meanwhile, straining my ears for Biagi's signals, I glanced now and again at my watch to see if the hour was up. I was surprised to find that he was going on beyond the stipulated time. It was the first time Biagi had not carried out my orders to the letter, and—I don't know why—I was glad of it.

All at once I heard him repeating some words he had intercepted, "We have received your call and the word 'Francesco'." But he attached no importance to it, and took off the head-piece, saying: "The *Città di Milano* is talking to San Paolo."

On the contrary, we learned later that it was to us the message was addressed. They had intercepted a few words of our call.

This call was substantially the same as the one Schmidt had picked up fragmentarily 4 days before. The only change was that we had added after "Foyn" the word "*circa*", to indicate that the co-ordinates which followed were approximate and not exact. This little alteration gave rise to a misunderstanding, because "Foyn" and "*circa*" were run together and interpreted as "Francesco".

That evening we awaited the San Paolo bulletin more eagerly than usual. We knew that the Soviet Government had ordered an inquiry, to find out if our S.O.S. had really been picked up, and we hoped to hear it confirmed. It was vital for us to know whether they had really heard us at Archangel.

We were all in the tent, except Trojani, who was doing sentry-go outside, as he often was at that hour. Biagi began to copy out the bulletin in his register, writing and speaking at the same time, as was his habit. Suddenly we heard: "A wireless amateur in the United States . . ."

The news referred to a certain American dilettante, who declared that he had intercepted a radiogram of ours, in which we said we were near the 84th parallel, right out in the Arctic Ocean.

This news—probably invented straight out by some wretch in search of notoriety—thoroughly upset us, as we were afraid that it might make people sceptical of the Russian report, which was true.

A little later on, intercepting the telegrams which the Italian journalists at King's Bay were sending to Italy, we heard news which at once made us forget to be angry with the American wireless amateur: that morning (June 7th) the *Città di Milano* had heard some fragments of our call for help: "S.O.S. . . . Francesco. . . ."

So we had reason to hope, although it was by no means reassuring that they thought we were in Franz Josef Land, instead of north of Spitsbergen.

Next day we went on transmitting; but to prevent any further mistake we altered the call as follows:

S.O.S. *Italia*, Nobile. Longitude 28° E., about 20 miles from the NE. coast of Spitsbergen.

The solar observations which we had at last been able to make gave us our position 80° 30′ latitude N. and 28° longitude E. In 5 days we had drifted 18½ miles SE.—an average of nearly 4 miles a day.

When evening came we listened for the San Paolo bulletin. Nothing of importance. Biagi took off the ear-phones to chat with us, but a few minutes later he began to listen-in again, wishing to intercept the Press news. Suddenly he gave a start, crying: "They are calling us!"

And he began to translate the signals. It was San Paolo, saying that the *Città di Milano* had picked up our message that morning. I remember that moment as if I were living through it now. . . . We hung on the wireless operator's lips, holding our breath lest the sound of it should disturb the reception. We wanted to hear everything, word by word. All four of us stared fixedly at Biagi.

He went on: "The *Città di Milano* heard you well this morning and has received your co-ordinates." Then he added: "Give Biagi's registration number."

The communication came to an end. Then it began again from the beginning: "*Italia! Italia!*" . . . Now we could contain ourselves no longer. Our joy overflowed. At last we were in touch with the world! The miracle of the wireless had been achieved. My own tenacity in willing, and Biagi's in executing, had been at last rewarded. The agonized suspense of our families would cease, and they would know where we were. . . . I called Trojani inside.

We all looked radiant: the lines graven by the previous days had been blotted out. How splendid it was to see my men laughing again—dirty, grimy, and ragged as they were! The laughter lit up their bearded faces, clouded with all the dirt of a fortnight. Mutually, we lifted a grateful thought to Providence for this hour of indescribable joy.

We celebrated the event by distributing to everyone 5 pieces of sugar, 10 malted milk tablets and 2 oz. of chocolate. We had never treated ourselves so generously. Laughter, chatter, comments filled the tent. . . . The General had been right: at last the wireless had worked! I was congratulated, and Trojani repeated his embarrassing question: "But you, who can read the future— can you tell us whether we shall see our families again?"

This was difficult to say. I did not want my comrades to give way to a facile optimism and be taken unawares by events.

"You must get ready now to put up with another lot of anxieties and uncertainties. We have still to go through some hard trials. It's not over yet!" I warned them.

In fact, one period of misery and suffering had come to an end and another was beginning. Nevertheless, our hearts were now

so high that we did not even feel the menace of that relentless
SE. drift.

A Happy Sunday on the Pack

The precise wording of the message from San Paolo was as
follows:

Italia, IDO. It is exactly 9.55 p.m. At 7.23 p.m., G.M.T., the *Città
di Milano* heard you clearly, receiving your S.O.S. and co-ordinates.
The *Città di Milano* will call you at the 15th minute of every hour
on the 900-metre wave-length, to ask confirmation of your co-
ordinates, and Biagi's registration number as a check.

But we could only receive on the short-wave length! So I
hastened to reply on the same evening (June 8th):

We confirm longitude 28° E., latitude 80° 30′ N. Giuseppe Biagi
86891. We only receive on short wave-length. We are on the pack
without sledges and with 2 men injured. Dirigible lost in another
locality towards E.

This message was duly received. It was surprising that the *Città
di Milano*, which had never once picked us up during 13 days,
could now hear us so clearly!

I wished to profit by this easy communication to tell the *Città
di Milano* everything I thought it essential for them to know. On
the morning of the 9th I telegraphed:

We confirm that we have checked by solar observations 28° longitude
and 80° 30′ latitude. We are on the pack, drifting slowly SE.

It was necessary to make it clear that our bearings had been
checked by observations. Our position was so far from where the
Città di Milano had till then imagined us to be that it would be
only natural if they wondered whether the co-ordinates we gave
were wrong.

At 9.45 a.m. we received the following fragment:

Be ready to make a smoke-signal. Aeroplanes will be . . .

I replied:

We are on the pack, drifting slightly with the wind. Dirigible lost
in another locality towards E. We have 2 men injured, with broken

legs. We will make smoke-signals and fire Véry lights as the aeroplanes approach. Remember that our batteries may run out in a few days, but we shall still be able to receive.

This last warning seemed to me necessary to avoid our silence being once more interpreted as showing that we were dead. I was also anxious to give some idea, at once, of our circumstances. So I continued:

We have provisions for 50 days on very short rations. We lack foot-gear, arms, ammunition, medicines, sledges, boats, and a stove.

For this was the first and gravest problem to solve: to improve our conditions so that we could hold out on the pack to the utmost possible limit.

It might have been quicker to say that we were in need of everything; but I thought it urgent to let them know what they ought to send us at once by the aeroplanes, which they said would soon fly overhead.

Meanwhile, to give the airmen something to go on, I sent information about the weather we had been having:

The sky is generally cloudy here, but under the clouds, at 1,500 ft., there is good visibility.

Then I gave news of the men who had left:

Three of óur companions are marching along the coast towards Cape North.

Ten days had already passed, and if they were making the progress they had reckoned they ought by now to have reached the coast.

Here I had to stop because the *Città di Milano* warned us at 10.27 a.m.:

Call us again this evening at 6.55 p.m. G.M.T. We will call you at the 55th minute of every hour to give you news. Now there is a disturbance. Impossible to receive from you.

This disturbance was probably due to the working of the local station at King's Bay: if so, Romagna could have had it stopped for the necessary time.

At 8 p.m. I managed to get my message through, adding the phrase:

We have dyed our only tent red.

According to the first messages from our base-ship, in fact, the aeroplanes, now they knew our bearings, might arrive at any moment. So we painted wide red stripes over the pyramid of the tent, using the coloured liquid in the glass balls that had served during our flights to check the altitude, some of which had fallen intact.

After 2 or 3 days, under the strong sunlight, these stripes faded out and soon disappeared. All the same, they sufficed to create the legend of the "Red Tent"—which was really a drabbish white.

At 8.30 p.m. I added further news:

There are six of us here. Three are on the march, as I have said. We know nothing of the others, as they have been carried away on the dirigible, which may be about 20 miles away towards E.

These first days of communication with the world (June 8th-12th) were undoubtedly the happiest we passed on the pack. Everything helped to cheer us up, even the wind, which had veered to the south-east and was gradually driving us back to the position we had occupied a week before.

Once more Foyn Island was near—even nearer than on May 30th, when the three had left us. So the event seemed to prove that I was right, and that their pessimism with regard to the drift had been unjustified.

Our good spirits went so far that, for the first time in all those days I decided to wash my hands with a little piece of soap and a towel that Cecioni had found in his bag. Of course, with our scarcity of fuel, water was out of the question, so I got Biagi to bring me some snow in a wooden box, and by rubbing hard with the soap and snow I contrived to wash myself. This first wash on the pack is one of the events that stand out in my memory. To see the dense, blackish liquid dripping off my hands into the receptacle below was an indescribably voluptuous sensation; even the men around were watching my hands in surprise and admiration as they gradually regained their natural colour.

Our dinner that Sunday was no more abundant than usual, but the seasoning of our good spirits made it seem exceptionally delicious, and high praise was given to Trojani, whose clever cooking had obtained such tasty gravy from the bear.

Yet I did not delude myself into being too optimistic. Amid all this merriment I privately reflected that our ability to communicate with the world, which had caused this exhilaration, was very precarious. Some accident might cut us off again: the only valve of our transmitter might break, or our batteries run out.

So I thought it necessary to send the following message that day:

Our situation on the pack is still precarious, but our spirits are high. So far, powerful drifts have carried us principally south-eastwards. Therefore it is extremely important to reach the nearest point of land at once, where we shall be able to wait patiently a long time for further help.

It is necessary, then, for dog-teams to reach us very soon. If they are delayed you had better at once send ahead a rapid patrol, with expert Norwegian guides, to reach us and accompany us to land, conveying the 2 injured men. Having each a broken leg they cannot walk.

Would dog-teams be able to get across this rugged pack? Certainly if they were light enough and had taken caïques and collapsible boats for crossing leads. But, above all, they must be guided and provisioned by aeroplanes on the way. So I added:

Several sledge expeditions should be sent, to be prepared for every emergency and make it easier to find the tent. Aeroplanes should guide the sledges to our camp. The seaplanes ought to establish a fuelling base as far up as possible.

Then I again thought about the sledges and added:

If possible, provide one of the sledge expeditions with wireless receiving apparatus, so that it can hear our co-ordinates and other news.

Having given this advice, I continued:

It is important to help us hold out and make our position safer, by sending aeroplanes at once to revictual us. Our provisions are now reduced to 200 lb. It would be most useful to send about 200 lb. of pemmican, or their equivalent; a rifle with ammunition; a packet of medical requisites for 2 fractured legs, with instructions and advice from a doctor; and a collapsible boat.

But the thought that we might eventually drift a long way eastwards kept on worrying me; in this case these requisites—without which we could not hold out—could only be brought by an aircraft that could fly a long way. So I added: "You should at once procure a flying-boat with a considerable flying range."

Then I harked back to the limited capacity of our batteries with the warning: "We will communicate the changes in our bearings so long as the batteries allow us." To give some idea of the devilish pack on which we had fallen I added: "The pack here is extremely broken." But this very condition made it possible that leads (like that of some days before) might open in it: "Leads often open, large enough for a seaplane to moor." Finally, to make them see why we needed rifles and ammunition, I told them: "We have been visited three times by bears." Farther on in the note-book, where these messages were written, I added: "Of course, the patrol and the sledges should signal their approach by repeated rifle-shots, or other more effective means. We will light smoke-signals and fire shots in answer, if you send us the rifles."

I quote these radiograms just as they were written, not only for their intrinsic value as documents written in such unique circumstances, but to give a concrete idea of the way my brain worked during those first few days of contact. These messages, however, could not always be transmitted at once; often, if only to spare the batteries, we had to abridge and sometimes even to suppress them, as happened to a report describing the catastrophe.

To prevent its getting lost I tied the pencil with which I wrote these messages round my neck with a bit of string; and I still keep it, as a souvenir of my efforts to give good advice. This, however, seemed so superfluous to the Commander of the *Città di Milano* that on receiving the message he replied:

You had better economize your batteries. It is our business to speed up the rescue work.

But then, as a happy ending to this splendid day, it gave us good news:

Three Swedish planes are on the way. Captain Riiser-Larsen is in the *Hobby* near Moffen Island, but blocked in the ice. The Russians are preparing a large ice-breaker, whilst we are trying to reach you with dog-teams, and to meet your 3 comrades who are making for Cape North.

The Problem of Rescue

On the evening of June 11th the news was even better:

The Swedish expedition, with 3 aeroplanes and a base-ship, is *en route* for King's Bay. The *Hobby* has got clear of the ice near Mossel Bay and is going ahead, with Riiser-Larsen and two small planes on board. They hope to push far enough eastwards to reach you by air. The *Hobby* has 2 dog-teams. Maddalena has started from Italy with a flying-boat "S.55". Major Penzo is starting shortly with another machine. Today a Russian ice-breaker will put out from Archangel with two planes—one a bimotor that has a long flying range. Another large ice-breaker is ready to leave.

Later came news that Finland also was sending a trimotor with skis, and that Germany too had offered men and machines.

So we began to have a complete idea of the various expeditions that Italy, Sweden, Norway, Russia, and Finland, with the same enthusiasm and generous eagerness, had prepared to save the *Italia* castaways. This international solidarity moved us deeply, especially from the four European countries which, being nearer the edge of the Arctic Circle than other lands, know its perils and feel its fascination.

During those bright days from June 8th to 12th, I went on thinking over the rescue problem, studying its difficulties and considering how to overcome them. Above all, I tried to answer the questions: "How are we to leave the pack and come back to civilization? How are they to find the wreckage of the airship and save our six comrades, if they are still alive?"

The Russians had gone to work enthusiastically, sending the *Malyghin* along the E. coast of Spitsbergen, and getting ready to send the *Krassin* along the west. But for my part I was very doubtful whether the *Malyghin* could push far north, because during our flight to Severnaya Zemlya I had been struck by the compactness of the ice along the E. coast of North-East Land, and I thought it would be a tough proposition even for a powerful ice-breaker.

But, whatever chances their ships might have of success, we were full of admiration for the dash with which the Russians had acted, and we fervently hoped they would get to us. The idea of returning home comfortably, on a ship which had come all the way to pick us up, was particularly attractive.

As for the seaplanes and aeroplanes with skis, it would not be difficult, I thought, to find a suitable landing-ground, or a lead for mooring, within 2 or 3 miles of our camp. The main difficulty would be to find us. It is true that, so long as the wireless held out, we could give our co-ordinates, but this was not enough. Our tent was a tiny speck lost amid the jumble of ice-crags piled one on another and intersected by countless crevasses.

So we must prepare smoke-signals to help the pilots find us. Many things would be used for burning, but we searched for something that would produce the blackest and thickest smoke.

"It's an interesting problem, our rescue," I remarked one evening.

Trojani, pessimistic as usual, rejoined: "It's a beastly problem! If they don't hurry up, they won't solve it."

We Shift Camp

Malmgren's advice to find a safer camping-place had always been present in my mind. But there was no large, solid sheet of ice close by; or so my men reported. Besides, after the alarm on the night May 27th-28th, more than a fortnight had passed, without any real danger threatening us. Even the large lead which had opened, during the first few days, about a hundred yards away, had been closed for some time, and no others had formed which could seriously worry us. So I had decided to stop where we were until something forced us to move.

On June 12th and 13th a strong west wind drove us nearly 10 miles eastwards. Once more I felt that we were sailing at the mercy of the wind—a strange sensation, intensified by the flapping tent-cover and the rapidity with which the islands faded into the distance.

During these stormy days, of course, my men were all out ot temper. The wireless, too, worked so badly these 2 days that we never managed to get a reply from the *Città di Milano*. We talked even less than usual: only the voice of the wind was heard. And on the 13th, when the storm was over and the sky cleared up a little, we found that we had lost sight of the islands; then the silence and solitude of the pack added to our depression. Even the seagulls, whose crying had hardly ever ceased, had left us.

On taking solar observations that day we found we had once more reached the meridian of Cape Leigh Smith, where we had been on June 8th, but this time we were 7 miles farther north. This was our farthest from the islands and the coast of North-East Land, after the departure of the three.

On the 13th, too, we had a false alarm. In the deep silence of the pack, we imagined all of a sudden that we heard the humming of an aeroplane . . . a delightful sensation, which quickly changed when we realized that the noise was due to the vibrations of the Alpini pennant hoisted on the wireless-mast.

The wind veered that day to the NE., so that we drifted south-westwards towards Foyn Island.

The day before the strong wind had stirred up the ice round our tent: amongst other things, a lead 7 or 8 yards wide had opened not far away. This was carefully watched by our sentries, in case it widened to the extent of putting our encampment in danger.

The peril materialized on the afternoon of the 14th. Already a few sheets of ice had broken away from the mass and were floating about in the lead, and now the same fate had overtaken a block next our own.

The alarm was given by Trojani. We all came into the open,

ready for any emergency, including Cecioni and I, who crawled
out as best we could. Once outside, we discussed what to do.
Some of the men maintained that we ought to shift camp, whilst
others thought that it was not urgent. After listening to the
various opinions I made up my mind it was wiser to move at
once. So I decided to camp on the "bear floe", which was (as
I have said) about 40 yards away.

Whilst the four others were beginning to shift the stores
Cecioni and I waited, sitting on the ice outside the tent. The sky
was grey: a few snowflakes were slowly falling.

I looked around. Until then I had never had a chance to con-
template at my leisure the fearful spot where we were encamped.
I had only been outside the tent for a few minutes—once on the
night when the ice had moved, and again when the bear was
killed.

The dreary sight made a great impression on me. The ice on
which we had been living for 18 days was churned up and dirty.
Here and there were puddles of water, and everywhere was
wreckage: pieces of twisted tubing, rags, broken instruments.
A short distance away some reddish streaks on the snow revived
the memory of the catastrophe. All around us an indefinable
dreariness in the atmosphere weighed on the soul.

I thought I would try to crawl, wishing to spare my men the
fatigue of carrying me, especially as I saw they were sad and disheartened. But in a very few yards I found myself on the brink of
a crevasse. No! it was impossible to move alone! Humiliated,
I went back to my place.

Then they came to me. They laid me on Cecioni's shapeless
sledge and carried me as if in a litter. There were four of them, yet
they had to stop now and again for a rest. In the end they covered
those 40 yards. Sweating and out of breath they got to the "bear
floe", put me down on the ice and left me there with my thoughts,
whilst they went back to bring Cecioni, then the tent, provisions,
wireless, and all other necessities.

All things considered, the pack was less terrible here than in
the spot we had left, chiefly because there were no traces of the
catastrophe. Everything was immaculately white, except for a

few footprints here and there, and the bear's skeleton jutting up from the snow.

In three hours all was ready, and we settled into the tent. At first we felt rather uncomfortable, as one is for a day or two in a new house, before getting one's things back into place. But very soon we got used to it, and in the end we were glad of the change, like a man who has given up an old home where everything reminds him of some terrible misfortune.

So on the evening of Friday, June 14th, we installed ourselves on the "bear floe".

Fresh Troubles with the Wireless

When the *Città di Milano* told us that they would only listen-in for us at 8.55 p.m. every day, we were considerably put out by the choice of this hour, as it prevented our intercepting the Press bulletin sent out daily at this time by San Paolo. But of course we made no objection.

All day we lived for this hour. I used to think over what news to give and what to ask for, and write it down, waiting impatiently for the moment of communication. What a disappointment it was when the hour came and we found it was no good transmitting, because the *Città di Milano*'s reception was defective!

Obviously one daily appointment, which might so easily miscarry, was too little. So on June 13th I had telegraphed:

I consider at least 2 communications a day necessary, so that we can warn you in time of changes in our co-ordinates.

And later on I insisted:

One single daily appointment is quite inadequate, for often the reception, as during the last few days, is very weak. Besides, some accident might possibly prevent us from transmitting at the time arranged.

Then, not being sure if they had yet grasped that we were drifting all the time, I said:

Let us know when an aeroplane is coming, so that we can tell you our position in time and give you visibility news.

At this point a fresh doubt struck me: if we failed to communicate the changes in our position how would the pilots set about finding us? So I added:

To get some idea of possible changes in our position the pilot should take into account the wind which has been blowing since the last communication.

But on the evenings of June 13th and 14th my insistences on having these warnings transmitted were useless. The *Città di Milano* only picked up a few fragments; in fact, at 10 p.m. on the 14th it telegraphed:

We cannot hear you any longer. We are trying to guess what you want. So we will call you at the 55th minute of every hour (Greenwich time) to give you news, and receive it from you if necessary.

Yet things were no better on the 15th. It is true the base-ship called us punctually every 2 or 3 hours, as it had promised, but only to say: "We have nothing new to tell you. Good-bye till the next hour!" Then instead of listening to the news we wanted to send them, they switched off at once, to get in touch with San Paolo.

This day, too, we failed to transmit a message of mine, saying that the NNE. wind had driven us within 7 miles ENE. of Foyn Island (latitude 80° 35′ and longitude 27° 30′); nor could we tell them that we must have some floats as soon as possible, because the ice was beginning to break up, and at every minute we risked losing something in the crevasses.

This was exasperating. To have to wait a whole day for nine o'clock, and then find we could not communicate at this hour, whilst at others the reception was so good that one could easily have heard and made oneself heard, became unbearable. I wrote:

The single daily appointment compels us to waste energy when we hear you badly or you hear us badly, as happened yesterday. So I once more beg you to fix at least 3 daily communications: not only calling us but above all listening to our answer.

I insisted:

When you call us you must listen-in too, because we might have urgent news to communicate.

But it was like preaching in a wilderness. Nobody listened to us.
The words that came so clearly to our ears every 2 hours, seemed
almost like mockery. One would have thought some malicious
spirit had wished to invent a new form of torture, by making us
wait impatiently for the 55th minute of every even hour, just to
repeat, "Nothing to tell you. Good-bye till the next hour," and
immediately break off.

On June 17th I gave our position. For some days we had been
almost stationary, E. of Foyn Island, at a distance which worked
out on the map as 5 miles. I added:

For 3 days the weather here has been magnificent—calm, with
excellent visibility. Such conditions are not likely to occur again.
You should take advantage of them, to send us at once the minimum
of things we have asked for: above all, floats, stores, footgear, and
firearms. Our situation is still dangerous.

MANNA FROM HEAVEN

Fine Weather on the Pack

THE fine weather had really come at last. From June 12th onwards we had ten magnificent days on end, with a pure blue sky and a calm, clear, quite transparent atmosphere. These were ideal flying conditions.

During these days we remained almost stationary, drifting a mile or two at the most: in the main we stayed where we were, E. of Foyn Island.

On the afternoon of the third fine day (June 17th) a great event took place: we saw the first aeroplanes.

There were two of them, and they came flying towards us from the south.

Our miniature world was at once roused to wild excitement.

I gave orders to kindle a fire for making a smoke-signal and to shoot off the Véry lights; but all this was no good, because when the two planes were within a mile or two of us they turned back again.

Later we learned that they were the Norwegians: Riiser-Larsen and Lützow Holm.

Through the Press notices we intercepted we had eagerly followed the first adventurous flight of Lützow Holm and the advance of the two pilots in the *Hobby* to Cape North. Their promptness in coming to our help had moved me deeply, and although my old comrade of the *Norge* had declared to a journalist that his plane was too small to carry the things we needed, I was sure that he would not come empty-handed, and that he might even descend on the pack if he descried a suitable landing-field.

I telegraphed at once to the *Città di Milano*:

Today we saw 2 aeroplanes coming in our direction, a mile or two south of us, without reaching us. Weather conditions, especially visibility, are exceptional. Take advantage of it to send the minimum of things we have asked for. Ask Riiser-Larsen to come back this evening before the weather breaks up. If he leaves, let us know, so that we can prepare our scanty signals. At the first opportunity send us some more effective means of signalling our presence.

But the Norwegians could not return that night as a flaw had developed in one of their engines. We heard this early next morning:

The aeroplanes will set out again some time today, as soon as they have changed an engine. We shall certainly reach you. Don't worry. Riiser-Larsen reports that the ice is compact right up to Cape North.

This last news was reassuring: it meant that the men who had left us on May 30th would not find their way barred by open water. So we were daily expecting to hear that they had arrived at Cape North.

The glowing optimism of the phrase, "We shall certainly reach you", also made an agreeable impression. I too felt sure that sooner or later one out of the many aeroplanes mobilized to help us would get to our camp. The essential was that they should come in time.

By means of the wireless, and the journalists' reports in particular, we had followed this mobilization of aircraft. As soon as the news of our disappearance in the Arctic sky was received in Norway, Amundsen had decided to come to our help. On June 16th he had left Caudebec-en-Caux, in France, on board the flying-boat *Latham*, piloted by Guilbaud. With him were Dietrichsen, his old comrade of the 1924 expedition, and the Frenchmen de Cuverville, Brazy and Valette. On the 17th the *Latham* had arrived at Tromsö, and next day it flew on northwards. But on the same day two more flying-boats coming to our help were at Tromsö, and I had hoped that they would all cross the Barents Sea together. But unfortunately the rescue expeditions were acting independently and there was no co-ordination between them; so that each aircraft crossed that stormy sea alone. Had it been otherwise we should not now be mourning the disappearance of the celebrated Norwegian explorer and his valiant comrades.

Without losing a moment Maddalena set out from King's Bay at 4.25 a.m. (Greenwich time) on the 19th in search of us. At 6.20 he passed Cape North, and at 7.5 appeared on our horizon. We saw him circle twice to the NW., coming within a couple of miles of us; then, at 7.30 he turned away and disappeared.

I sent the following message to the *Città di Milano*:

If you wish to succeed you should carefully follow my advice. Start from Foyn Island and take a true course of 59 degrees. Advance 12 miles in this direction, then turn back to within 5 miles of the island. Repeat this several times systematically, each time altering the course laterally as much as necessary. At least 2 aeroplanes should be used, flying parallel to each other. In any case, Maddalena should have enough petrol to fly overhead for at least 4 hours. Repeat the attempt during the day. Meanwhile fix up a wireless on Maddalena's flying-boat, worked by an efficient operator. Observe with the sun at your back. Today we also saw Riiser-Larsen, but he was too far east. Tell him all I have said.

But the people at King's Bay had already thought of putting back the wireless which had previously been taken off Maddalena's machine, and they gave us a code by which to guide the seaplane to the tent when it was near enough.

During these preparations one of the Norwegians came back a third time alone.

Once more, in suspense made up of hope and fear, we watched the aeroplane turn towards us from Foyn Island and come gradually closer. It travelled in zigzags, so that we were sure it would find us in the end. But, alas! we were disappointed again, for within a few miles of us the pilot turned round, and our smoke-signals and Véry lights failed to catch his eye.

I then wrote the following message for the Norwegians, which, however, we could not get through:

Riiser-Larsen. Three times you have come very close to us. I am deeply grateful for all you are doing. I suggest that you start from Foyn Island and take a true course of 55 degrees. You will find us a few miles from the island. Be careful to have the sun at your back.

I was convinced that our humble smoke-signals and Véry lights were quite useless if the pilots had the sun in their eyes. Riiser-Larsen, for his part, made the helpful suggestion that we should flash mirrors towards the aeroplane as it approached. The trouble was that we had none, but I managed to make one from the tin-foil round some of our scientific instruments. Besides this, a petrol-tin answered the purpose fairly well.

The First Revictualling

Four times already an aeroplane had approached our tent without sighting it. Of course, I had known for some time how hard it was to find us amid the pack; but in practice it seemed even more difficult than I had expected. Even Behounek, who up till then had shown the greatest faith that they would reach us, began to doubt it. We were eagerly awaiting the return of the Italian flying-boat, in the hope of guiding it to our camp by giving the necessary directions in the wireless code sent us by the *Città di Milano*.

On June 20th at 6 a.m. (Greenwich time) Maddalena left King's Bay. As soon as we heard this I ordered Viglieri and Trojani to prepare the smoke-signals and Véry lights, ready to send them off the moment the aircraft was near enough, and told Biagi to stand by with his wireless. Everyone left the tent. Cecioni and I crawled out alone, pulling ourselves along with our arms.

Each man took up the post assigned to him. Trojani stood ready to light the fire prepared with petrol, oil, rags, and paraffin. Behounek planted himself solidly on the ice, grasping a shining tin, to flash the sun's rays towards the flying-boat. Viglieri, whom I had asked to follow the movements of the machine and tell Biagi what signals to transmit, jumped on a hummock and stood on the look-out. Cecioni, sitting near the tent-door, held himself in readiness to use the mirror that I had made out of tinfoil.

I was seated on the sledge beside Cecioni. I remember that to protect my eyes—still painful from snow-blindness that I had contracted one night when I stayed on guard outside the tent—I had made myself a kind of visor from a piece of coloured paper.

At 7.35 we got into touch with the plane by wireless. At 8.15 we heard the first throb of its engines. We waited anxiously.

At last the aircraft appeared and the signals began. It seemed at first not to hear us, then all at once it began to obey our orders: "Turn so many degrees to the right", "Reverse your direction", "Turn so many degrees to the left". . . .

In a few minutes we managed to bring the flying-boat towards us: "The tent is on your course, less than 2 miles in front. Go ahead!" And the plane obediently went straight on. A moment later it caught sight of us. We saw it swoop down to about a hundred yards. . . . "VVV. . . . You are on top of us!" We were feverish with excitement. Here it was! The throb of its engines grew louder, and now we could clearly see the colours painted on its wings. It was very close . . . was passing overhead. . . . One or two men leaned out of the cabin and wildly waved their arms in greeting. My throat was constricted with excitement. I wanted to shout, but I only waved an answering greeting with my hand. The others were shouting and laughing. Even Titina rushed madly about the ice, barking.

The flying-boat overshot us and went on, the sonorous hum of its engines growing fainter. We expected it would turn back at once to throw down provisions and other things. Following it anxiously, we saw it wheel round, but in the wrong direction. It passed some distance from us and then changed its course again, as if searching round; but it was a long way off. It had lost sight of us!

We persevered with our signals. Biagi kept running to and fro, between the transmitter outside the tent and the receiver inside, sending his message and then rushing to put on the ear-phones; to find out if it had been heard. At last, after half an hour, the aircraft picked us up. We drew a breath of relief as it began to obey our orders with docility. We guided it back in our direction till it sighted the tent. It came straight for us and in a few seconds was overhead.

"KKK", I ordered Biagi the moment the plane was above us. This was the code-signal for "Drop the provisions!" and I hastened to give the order for fear they should lose us again. We saw someone leaning out of the back of the cockpit to drop parcels. The first packets fell and we greeted them joyously. Then the flying-boat turned and started to throw out afresh. It was not losing us now.

We followed the parcels with our eyes to see exactly where they fell. Then the cascade ceased and the aircraft swiftly turned homewards.

Viglieri, Biagi, and Trojani started on their search.

This was not easy. A few of the packets, scattered amidst the masses of ice, were not found, whilst others had fallen into crevasses.

When everything possible had been collected and the inventory made we found we had 6 pairs of shoes, a few provisions, 2 collapsible boats, some smoke-signals, 2 sleeping-bags, 2 rifles— which broke as they crashed on the ice—and a few batteries, also half shattered.

That evening (June 20th) I sent the following message to the *Città di Milano*:

Today we see Foyn Island at 250°.

Thank you for the thrill you gave us this morning, when we saw our country's colours overhead.

Tomorrow you should send us more batteries, better packed than those of today, which all arrived broken.

You should also send some more boats, or floats of any shape; pemmican, cakes, a Primus stove, some solid fuel, medicines, a pair of *very large* shoes for Viglieri, cigarettes, chocolate, snow-spectacles, handkerchiefs, and the wooden parts of 2 rifles to replace the others, which smashed as they fell.

This will make us much more comfortable.

I must state that the rising temperature these last few days is steadily disintegrating the ice. So I fear its present condition may prevent the sledges reaching us in time unless they are equipped at all points and guided by experts. Over this I think you should put yourself entirely in Amundsen's hands, as he is the only expert collaborating with you. My own opinion is that, together with the sledge expeditions, you should consider the possibility of taking us away by air, one by one, before the heat increases and the fogs set in, or we drift too far from your bases and from land. Maddalena might accompany the ski-plane.

I suggest that you have Sora's patrol watched by aeroplanes, as his march on the pack may be brought up short by large leads.

Take advantage of the continued fine weather and our almost stationary position, either to send more provisions at once or to try to fetch us away by air. Act with every means at your disposal simultaneously. Tell Riiser-Larsen that this morning we saw him flying along the coast.

This evening, too, at 8.15, we saw 3 machines at 230°, towards the island, which began to circle round within a mile or so of us, and then turned back.

Give me news of Mariano.

As soon as we receive the batteries I will send you detailed advice for looking for the dirigible.

Note that this morning's experience has shown the difficulty of finding us, even when our co-ordinates are known. If our position were only known approximately it would take at least 4 aeroplanes to find us.

The man of action had fully reasserted himself in me. Once more I was the leader: I wanted to see all my men saved, now that there was a chance.

And I was so taken up by this anxiety to have my comrades rescued that often I forgot myself—as if I had not been there, badly hurt and as helpless as Cecioni. In fact I added further on:

Urge the Swedes to take at least Cecioni off by air, as his broken leg cannot be cured here.

Maddalena and Penzo

My advice to send the flying-boats back again quickly with the other supplies that were so indispensable was received by the *Città di Milano*, but not put into practice so promptly as I had hoped. I was expecting that the two Italian airmen would take advantage of the splendid weather and come out together on the afternoon of the 20th (as we had been told they would), but we awaited them in vain.

At last, next night (June 21st-22nd) the *Città di Milano* asked: "Tell us what weather you are having and what visibility." I replied: "The weather here is perfect and the visibility exceptional. Come at once."

We prepared to receive them. A festoon of white and red flags was hoisted on the wireless mast, whilst I had some maps painted red and spread out on the sides of the tent-roof.

Soon after the planes had passed Cape North we got into touch with them by wireless. A quarter of an hour later they were in sight.

This time the planes found us without difficulty. They obeyed our wireless orders with docility, and as soon as they caught sight of us circled round the tent once or twice to bring themselves to the right height and direction; then at once they began to drop their parcels.

Now there was plenty: down from the sky rained every good thing imaginable. Passing alternately overhead, the two planes dropped packets of every size and shape in all directions. Some, falling free, plummeted straight down like rocks; others swung gracefully down upon large silken parachutes.

As they dived down over our heads to make each throw, we could clearly see the men leaning out to look at us; and among them I noticed a cinematograph operator turning a handle. This detail struck me.

When all the parcels were thrown, at 11.10 Maddalena's flying-boat turned homewards. Penzo stayed a few minutes longer. Suddenly we saw him swoop down within a few yards of the ice, as if he meant to land, so that we held our breath for a moment, fearing that something had gone wrong with his engine. But as he passed over the tent he called out an *"Arrivederci!"* rose again, and flew away.

Viglieri and Biagi, helped by Behounek, began to pick up the parcels. It was a hard job, which was only finished after 2 or 3 hours' tramping about on the ice.

Our meals that day were more abundant and less regular than usual.

For once in a while the bear-meat was replaced by cakes—to the great delight of Behounek, who was so nauseated with it that he often refused it and went hungry. Then my companions began to smoke, whilst Cecioni pulled one of the sheaths from the packet of medicines, adapted it, and fitted it on his right leg.

Meanwhile I dressed and bandaged Behounek's right arm, which had been troubling him ever since the crash, though he had never even mentioned it. We had only found it out now by pure chance, because Biagi had accidentally knocked against it, wrenching from him a cry of pain.

And so the day passed rapidly, amidst the delights of smoking and of reading the letters and newspapers which had showered down with the other things, without my companions noticing that once more the wireless had fallen silent.

AN AEROPLANE LANDS ON THE PACK

The Red Parachutes of the Swedes

O N June 22nd at 7.30 p.m. (G.M.T.), a great event unexpectedly broke the monotony of our life on the pack.
Two seaplanes, flying the Swedish colours, approached
the tent, located us by means of our smoke-signal, and came flying overhead. Very skilfully they dropped 5 parcels of extremely
well-chosen provisions, each fastened to a small red parachute.

On the brown-paper wrapping of one parcel was written in
English:

If you can find a landing-ground for aeroplanes fitted with skis (min.
250 m.), arrange the red parachutes in T-shape on the leeward side.

Now, some days before we had discovered a suitable floe, of the
required dimensions, and providentially it was quite close—not
more than 150 yards away. According to Trojani and Viglieri's
report after their inspection, the ground was ideal—absolutely
flat, without cracks or unevenness. But they must make haste,
because if the temperature rose the snow would begin to melt and
landing conditions would no longer be so favourable.

I prepared a message in English for the Swedes, thanking them
and telling them about the landing-ground, but it was impossible
to send it, because for several days wireless communications with
the *Città di Milano* had been abominable.

By this time the radio had become the worst of our torments.
Every time a call went unanswered our spirits sank, and if the
silence went on too long we grew thoroughly discouraged. The
optimism I was trying so hard to instil into my comrades vanished
and a dreary silence settled on the tent. Then there were criticisms,
grouses, recriminations against the *Città di Milano*, for not yet

having realized the necessity of making every effort to listen to our calls and requests. They had ice-breakers, seaplanes, aeroplanes with skis, sledges at their disposal; but they did not know the conditions in the part of the pack where we had fallen. We could have made useful suggestions, if only they had taken the trouble to listen to us.

Several times I had tried to summarize my advice in concise messages, without ever succeeding in getting them transmitted. The last of these was received fragmentarily by the *Città di Milano* on the morning of June 23rd, and said among other things:

I think the dangers of our position have not been clearly realized. Of the 6 men here, only 4 are able-bodied. If the ice were suddenly to break up, it would be impossible to move. It is urgent to fly Cecioni off, followed by Behounek and the others. But there is no time to lose. Perhaps you have not sufficiently realized that when the fogs come, neither sledges nor aeroplanes will be able to reach us; nor, perhaps, shall we be able to give our position. If the pack breaks up, with Cecioni crippled and Behounek unfit for a march, there is no hope of saving my companions. Take away Cecioni and Behounek: the others, perhaps, could fend for themselves amid all the dangers of this pack. Keep me posted about your plans, because I could give you useful advice. And listen-in for us at least twice a day, at whatever times you like but under the most favourable conditions, so that we do not exhaust our batteries in unanswered calls.

After transmitting part of this message the wireless fell silent; in spite of Biagi's persevering efforts we could not hear anything more. The hours passed in an exhausting suspense. I saw the discontentment on my companions' faces. A painful silence hung over them all.

My thoughts reverted to the Swedes. They had promised to come back. Would they come that evening? I had repeatedly assured my comrades that the simplest and quickest method of escape was to leave by air. The more convinced I became of this possibility, the more bitterly I commented on the mistake that was being made in wasting valuable time. Meanwhile I had often considered the order in which we should leave the floe, if the Swedes managed to land.

There was no doubt that the injured ought to go first—I mean, Cecioni; as for me, I left myself out of count. All my thoughts were for my comrades. Once Cecioni had gone, I would not in any case have stood in the way of their salvation. From the day of the crash, and many times afterwards, I had kept on saying to the others: "Don't worry about me. I won't hinder you in any circumstances whatever."

This determination is reflected in a scrap of the message quoted above.

That was why I had decided to leave last of all. But then I reconsidered it: staying to the end would mean a very serious risk to the man who came to fetch me. So the last to go must be the wireless operator, and the last but one Viglieri—the only man capable of locating the tent by astronomical means. The next after Cecioni should be Behounek, who was heavy and rather weak-sighted, and seemed to me the least fitted for a march. And then Trojani.

When I told Behounek my decision, he thanked me with great simplicity.

The Swedes Land on the Pack

It was now evening. The sky was still blue and a light NW. breeze was blowing. The hour fixed for communicating with the *Città di Milano* (five minutes to nine) had passed without our receiving any news. From time to time the silence was broken by someone asking me the state of the barometer, which had been slowly falling for some days.

We sat down to supper. My companions were all rather depressed, and everyone was silent. More than ever annoyed at the silence of the radio and the lack of news, I began to turn over in my mind an old idea: to have our boats ready loaded with provisions and materials, and a few weeks later, when the pack had broken up, to embark all together in the biggest boat and steer through the ice to the nearest shore. Once we had touched land, wherever it might be, I considered we were safe. I was not even alarmed at the idea of wintering there.

I was thinking over these things and waiting till the end of supper to speak to my comrades, when a slight humming came to our ears. We all started.

It was a moment of great excitement. We guessed that it was the Swedes, who had come to fetch us.

Viglieri and Biagi dashed out of the tent and stood listening. The throbbing grew louder, and now it came more distinctly— a slight rhythm familiar to our ears: "The aeroplanes are coming!"

Dragging myself along the ice, I also left the tent, followed by Cecioni. Now the rhythm of the engines came clearly, rejoicing us like the sweetest music. I looked round for the planes, but the masses of ice round our encampment hid them. Viglieri, Biagi, and Behounek, standing up, were scanning the horizon.

"There they are!"

Two aeroplanes were coming towards us. The rhythm grew steadily more sonorous. I gave the order: "Make a smoke-signal!"

The smoke rose, dense and black, and the aeroplanes wheeled. They had seen us.

"Viglieri and Biagi! Go straight to the field, both of you, and lay down the landing-signal. Hurry up! Run!"

Run! It was all very well to say this! As the crow flies, the field was about 150 yards from our camp, but to cover this short distance one needed rare acrobatic skill. Here and there were crevasses, sometimes hidden by snow, hummocks to climb, channels or little pools to cross, using a piece of ice as a raft, which often threatened to overturn under a man's weight. Although they had already made the journey several times, Viglieri and Biagi would do well to reach the field in a quarter of an hour.

I watched them go. Meanwhile the aircraft began to circle overhead. Then I turned to Cecioni, who was beside me at one corner of the tent, and ordered: "Get the sledge ready at once!"

The sledge was all in a muddle. A number of loose parts had to be tied together.

"Trojani! Look in the box for the wire! Quickly!"

Trojani, who had a temperature, was lying in his sleeping-bag inside the tent. He found the wire and brought it out.

Whilst Cecioni was busy tying up the disconnected parts, I

watched the flight of the planes. One of them—the seaplane—stayed high in air and circled widely round our encampment. The other gradually came lower, continuing to manœuvre round the landing-field.

I followed it anxiously with my eyes, giving news to my companions. . . . Now it was flying over the field—coming lower —skimming the ground—disappearing behind the masses of ice. All at once it rose again. Perhaps it had difficulty in landing? Then I guessed that the pilot was trying to get some idea of the state of the field. There he was, flying round once more, and yet again. The aeroplane swooped down afresh and seemed to touch the ice.

I followed the manœuvre, holding my breath. Yes! Now it had touched and not risen again. It skimmed along the ground. . . . It had landed—and landed safely!

I drew a long breath of relief, and irrepressible joy filled my heart. The long, unutterable torment was at an end—the alternatives of hope and despair, the wearing suspense, the anxiety about the radio. . . . At last we were in contact with humanity. Very soon we should greet the lucky man who, alone of all those who had been trying during a whole month to reach us, had succeeded in his purpose.

I looked once more at the aeroplane. One could see the propeller slowly turning and hear the quiet throbbing of the engine. Then Behounek, who was on the watch, told me that Viglieri, Biagi, and a stranger were coming towards us.

Lundborg

Eagerly awaiting his arrival, I spurred Cecioni up to finish his preparations. At last the men appeared. The stranger, dressed in flying-kit, had a pleasant expression—a frank, rather rugged face and blue eyes. Viglieri introduced him to me: "Here is the General!" The stranger saluted respectfully. I answered by thanking him in the name of us all; then, feeling that words were inadequate to express our gratitude, I asked Viglieri and Behounek to lift me, so that I might embrace him. Then they laid me down again.

Lundborg began to speak: "General, I have come to fetch you all. The field is excellent. I shall be able to take away the lot of you during the night. You must come first."

"But that's impossible!" I replied, and pointed out Cecioni: "Take him first. That is what I have decided."

Lundborg answered firmly: "No! I have orders to bring you first, because we need your instructions to start looking for the others."

Then I remembered that, only two or three days before, the *Città di Milano* had asked me to give "data and instructions to search for the airship", which I had not been able to send, owing to the bad wireless communication. Instinctively I considered Lundborg's words in relation to this request. So the seaplanes were ready to start their search? We had to take advantage of the weather, which was still fine: a clear sky, perfect visibility, calm. Perhaps it was a case of snatching a few hours, for such favourable conditions could not last long: the barometer had been going down for some days.

Still, though the vision leaped to my mind of those seaplanes ready to start and impatiently awaiting my arrival, I was reluctant. I did not like the idea of coming back to *terra firma* before my companions, even when I thought it simply meant anticipating them by an hour or two. For sentimental reasons I would rather have followed and not preceded them. So I insisted firmly: "Please take him first. That is my decision."

"No, General, don't insist!" replied Lundborg. "We will take you to our base not far from here; then I can come back quickly for the others."

As I showed signs of protesting again he interrupted me curtly, as if to cut short any further discussion: "No! I can't take him now" (indicating Cecioni); "he is too heavy. It is impossible, without leaving my companion behind, and I cannot do that. Later on I will come back alone to fetch him. Besides, it would take too long to carry him to the plane, and we have no time to lose. In a few hours I will bring you all away. Please come quickly." And he pointed to the machine, of which we could see the propeller still revolving: "Do please hurry up!"

Viglieri and Behounek pressed me to go. Biagi said: "You had better go first. It will set our minds at rest." Cecioni interposed: "You go! Then, whatever happens, there will be somebody to look after our families."

I hesitated a moment longer. I did not like the idea of going, but, on the other hand, I felt I could not waste the pilot's time in a futile discussion. I crawled into the tent to question Trojani: "Yes! It's better so. You go!"

Then I made up my mind. I would go.

This was not easy. It needed far more courage to go than to stay, but in the circumstances I felt it my imperative duty to give way to Lundborg. It was no good protracting the argument. He was getting impatient; in any case, he had declared he could not take Cecioni. As for Viglieri and Biagi, they were outside the discussion, for I had already decided they should be the last to leave. The choice lay then between Behounek, Trojani and myself. But Lundborg declared that I was wanted, before they could begin searching for the others, and there was no doubt my presence and advice would be useful. I could not take the responsibility of refusing. So I decided to go.

I said good-bye to the three men who were staying at the tent. Then Viglieri and Biagi took me, one by the arms and the other by the legs, and began to carry me. Sometimes I tried to help them by putting my sound leg to the ground and leaning on it to give myself an impetus. All the same, the others were so utterly exhausted that from time to time they were obliged to stop. Lundborg, who had gone on ahead, noticed, hurried on to the field, and sent back his friend Schyberg to help us. With his aid, we at last contrived to reach the landing-ground.

When Lundborg and Schyberg had tested the engine, I was carried to the aeroplane and lifted on board. I gave Viglieri and Biagi my final instructions:

"As soon as we have gone, move Cecioni at once to the field, so that he is ready to start. After Cecioni the others will leave in the following order: Behounek, Trojani, Viglieri, Biagi. Meanwhile you, Viglieri, take command for these few hours. . . ."

One last, touching farewell to my two comrades: "Good-bye,

until later. I shall be waiting for you. . . . and, whoever comes last, don't let him forget the little picture of the Madonna. . . . Good-bye!"

The machine wheeled on its skis, pushed by Viglieri and Biagi, until it was head to wind. The engine throbbed faster. We began to move, sliding along the snow. All at once I felt that we were in the air, and a moment later I leaned out to look down. Below us was the pack—that terrible pack on which we had fallen a month before.

My eyes travelled in search of the tent, but at first I could not find it. Schyberg pointed it out—a wretched little object, a scrap of soiled material, almost invisible against the whiteness of the ice. There was an ache at my heart as I thought of my comrades still there on that one tiny piece of ice lost among so many others. The only sign of life was the festoon of white and red flags hoisted on the wireless mast.

I remained a few moments absorbed in watching. The night was bitterly cold, and the keen air blew on my dirty, bearded face with an ineffable sensation of cleansing. The dreadful expanse of ice was all broken by crevasses and little channels. Here and there were brief flat stretches, which might serve as landing-grounds for aeroplanes. Now we were approaching Foyn Island. I turned round to gaze at it with curiosity. It had been our lighthouse in that ocean of ice. We had spoken of it dozens of times a day. All our hopes had been bound up with that little fragment of land: a hilly mass covered with snow, greyish in places, where the rocks cropped up.

It was cold. Schyberg insisted on my nestling down at the bottom of the cockpit and covering myself as well as possible with a rug. I made him show me on the map where we should land. Then I gave myself up to my thoughts, hugging Titina close, so that she should not get mixed up with the controls. And I waited for the brief fantastic flight to come to an end. . . . A little more than an hour passed. I felt the engine slow down. We were coming to earth. . . . A slight jerk and the swish of skis on the snow. We had landed.

On the Shore of Murchison Bay

I leaned out to have a look. The spot was deserted, the ground covered with snow. I saw two or three strangers coming to meet us—tall, lean men in flying-kit. They greeted me joyously and helped me down. Then, taking me in their arms, they carried me about a quarter of a mile to the sea-shore, where two sea-planes were moored.

As we approached the shore the layer of snow on the ground gradually lessened, then spread out, and finally disappeared altogether. In the midst of the shingle were scattered pieces of yellowish drift-wood.

Other young airmen were waiting for us, one of them busy warming up food on a little petrol stove. Several sleeping-bags and a few provisions were lying about. In the centre a wood-fire was crackling merrily.

They put me on the ground. Then, seeing that I was cold, they wrapped me in a shawl and very gently slipped me into one of the fur bags, taking care not to jar my injuries. They were all round me, full of kind solicitude. They gave me food and drink. Someone offered me a cigarette. I took it and smoked—for the first time in seven years.

Meanwhile I watched the strange scene, bewildered, as if in a dream. These tall, blue-eyed strangers who moved around me, smiling, brought back to my mind vague recollections of mythology.

Lundborg and Christell were talking to me: "You know, we flew with our planes to greet you over Stockholm, when the *Italia* came up to Spitsbergen."

Then I remembered the Swedish seaplanes, which had come to meet our ship and circled round to welcome us: "Yes! I remember. We took some pictures of your planes. Some day I will give you them."

And then Tornberg, the leader, began to speak: "I am very glad you have come. You were needed here. Up to now we have had all kinds of difficulties, but things will go better now, with you. We shall be able to get on with the search for Mariano's party and begin looking for the airship. Your presence will make everything easier. The *Città di Milano* is on her way to Virgo Bay, and in a few hours the *Quest* will arrive here. We will have a meeting with the Captain and decide what to do." (The *Quest* was the Swedish base-ship.)

I listened to him rather absent-mindedly. My thoughts reverted to the five men out there in the tent. They were waiting for Lundborg to come back. "When are you going?" I asked him. "Very soon," replied Lundborg, and a beautiful smile lit his sun-burnt face. Then at last he got up: "I'm off!" ... I saw him going away with some of the others, and mutely accompanied him with my good wishes.

Tornberg, Christell, and the other officers who stayed with me wriggled into their fur bags and settled down to sleep, after wishing me a good night. In between us the little wood-fire went on burning.

But sleep would not come. I was overexcited. A thousand thoughts whirled in my head. I saw Lundborg arrive at the field near the tent and start back again with Cecioni. Very soon they would be here. ... And then the rest, one after another. ... I already imagined I could see them sleeping in their fur bags on my right, in a row one behind the other. ...

As the hours passed my excitement grew more intense. I kept glancing at my watch and calculating the time. Then I turned to look at the Swedes, amazed that they could sleep so quietly. Their deep breathing echoed loud in the utter stillness, accompanied by a gurgle of water lapping against the seaplanes. A brief cry of alarm broke the silence—one of the fur sacks, too near the fire, had begun to burn. When the little blaze had been stifled, all was quiet again.

I waited—waited in ever-growing anxiety. Suddenly I gave a start—the throb of engines had come to my ears. I woke Christell, who put his head out of the bag and sat up. A seaplane appeared in the sky—the machine that had accompanied Lundborg. Christell looked out. Then he told me casually: "The Fokker has overturned," and tranquilly lay down to sleep again. A moment later I learned that the pilot was unhurt.

It was a terrible blow. I was separated, then, from my men! They would have to stay on there, no one knew how long. And Lundborg remained a prisoner with them! All my joy was suddenly turned to grief and I felt sick at heart.

Then I pulled myself together to meet the misfortune. I looked facts in the face. Something must be done. We must examine the situation coolly and decide what to do. My comrades, and Lundborg himself, were waiting, full of confidence in me. I felt that they were reassured because I was there. But there was no time to lose. I must stifle my misery—and act.

I turned to Tornberg, who was now lying next me. His tender, thoughtful expression attracted me immensely.

"What are we to do now? Has the Swedish expedition any other planes with skis which could go out there?" . . . No, there was none; but there was a Finnish plane.

"But the best thing," said Tornberg, "is to send for some light sporting planes. The 'Moth' is a suitable type. They can be got in England. You ought to ask the Italian Government for them at once. And you can count on the Swedish Government, too, doing everything in its power."

Then I turned over in my mind the things my companions wanted. The seaplanes had brought us a great many provisions, but other essentials were lacking. Above all they needed pemmican. I mentioned it to Tornberg, who replied that the Swedish expedition had some and would send it along that very evening.

Then he asked if I wanted to wait for the *Quest*, which was late, but due in a few hours. "No! Don't let's waste time! I want to go on board the *Città di Milano* at once."

And so Tornberg and Christell took me in one of their seaplanes to Virgo Bay.

ON THE *CITTÀ DI MILANO*

At Virgo Bay

OF my arrival at Virgo Bay I remember little, except the rather desolate view of grey mountains sprinkled here and there with snow, circling the little bay that is so inseparably linked with the memory of Andrée's expedition. Then the deck of the *Città di Milano*, crowded with sailors. A motor-launch came to meet us. I was lifted into it and brought on board ship, amid the cheers of the crew. But there was a sadness in my soul which even the warmth of this reception could not dissipate. I only remember the face of an officer with tears in his eyes, and the journalist Aponte, who wanted by main force to kiss my hand.

They carried me down to the cabin. I cast a rapid glance into the mirror: I looked frightful, unrecognisable.

Losing no time, I asked Tornberg, Christell, and the Captain of the ship to meet in my cabin and decide what was to be done: telegraph to Rome for the little sporting planes with skis, and in the interval arrange to fit skis to the Finnish trimotor. Once more I begged Tornberg to send an aeroplane that night to the camp and throw down the pemmican and other provisions that I knew were urgently needed. Immediately after this meeting I sent the following message to my companions:

Don't be anxious—I am here. The Finnish trimotor is being fitted with skis, but as a precaution we have ordered 2 or 3 small planes from England. You will receive 6 more batteries from the Swedes, some smoke-signals, a tent, various medicines, dried milk, 110 lb. of pemmican and some solid fuel.

My body was in the *Città di Milano*, but my spirit remained out there with my beloved comrades. It was as if I had been violently torn away from my family. Though I had already endured so much, I seemed unable to bear this separation.

Such was my state of mind, when the Captain of the *Città di Milano* came to me and said: "People might criticize you for coming first, General. It would be as well to give some explanations."

I was completely taken aback. Give explanations? I don't understand. So the Captain knew nothing of the order brought by Lundborg? I told him how things had happened, and a little later condensed the account in a wireless message sent to the Naval Secretary—a message beginning: "I have come to take up my post of command."

But I must confess that, although astonished at this demand—contrasting so oddly with the enthusiastic reception that the crew had given me on my arrival from the pack—I had not the least suspicion of the attack that was being launched against me, speculating upon Lundborg's accident. I did not know then that the altered behaviour of the Captain of the *Città di Milano* was due to instructions received from Rome, and to the fact that the powerful "quadrumvir" Balbo, catching the ball as it bounced, had made a move against me.

The Behaviour of the Fascist Government after the Crash

These instructions were a consequence of the attitude taken up by the Government in the very first days after the catastrophe. The disappearance of the *Italia*, the mystery which wrapped our fate, had moved the whole civilized world. Sweden, Norway, Russia, Finland—all the countries bordering on the frozen Arctic Ocean—in a generous impulse of solidarity had immediately decided to organize rescue expeditions. But in Italy the Fascist Government had made no move. On the day when the newspapers published the story of our disappearance, Balbo landed at Alcazar aerodrome near Madrid. He was met on the field by a professor of Aeronautical Law at the University of Rome, who gave him the sad news. Balbo, in a tone of absolute indifference, remarked: "Serve him right!" and gave orders that the Press should devote as little space as possible to the expedition, but publicize his own flight of sixty aeroplanes across the Mediterranean. A still more serious episode was reported to Viglieri after our return to Rome: at a banquet given during that mass cruise, Balbo had toasted the disappearance of the *Italia*!

This hostility explains why Italy was so tardy in organizing an aerial rescue expedition. The attitude of the Fascist Government had been severely criticized not only in Italy but also abroad. The King of Norway, when on a visit to Helsingfors he received the Italian Ambassador, could not help pointing out the inertia of our Government in face of the catastrophe. Still more explicit had been the Soviet Vice-Commissar for War, Kamenev, who in an interview published on June 12th in the newspaper *Izvestia* regretted that in Italy "the practical measures taken to help the castaways were so few that they virtually amounted to nothing."

But already public opinion in Italy had begun to make itself felt, urging that something should be done. Its mouthpiece was Arturo Mercanti, of Milan, who asked permission to go to our help with two flying-boats. Thanks to this initiative, it was finally decided to send to King's Bay Maddalena and Penzo, the brave officers who brought us supplies with their flying-boats. But in his letter to Mercanti, Balbo gave vent to a number of insulting remarks about me, explicitly affirming that ours was no Fascist enterprise, and that therefore there was no obligation to go to our help.

Lundborg's mishap had given Balbo the opportunity to launch a direct attack on me. In Rome, during a meeting of Ministers, he impugned me in the most violent manner. At the same time, the foreign Press was incited against me. In Paris, *Le Matin* published the cheapest slanders, excusing themselves on the ground that they were only repeating what had been said by "a high Fascist personage." Instructions were sent from Rome to the Italian Legations in various countries to prevent demonstrations of sympathy for me. The peak of insolence was reached by Balbo's paper, the *Corriere Padano*, which asserted that I had broken my leg when running to meet the Swedish aeroplane that had descended on the pack. This grave insinuation was made at a time when other Italian newspapers had already stated several weeks previously that my injuries had been caused when the airship crashed.

A Month of Hell on the "Città di Milano"

This behaviour of the powerful Fascist leader obviously had its effect on the atmosphere in the Città di Milano.

Absorbed in my distress at being separated from my comrades and my anxiety to save them and Lundborg, I did not at first notice the spite of these unimportant lookers-on at our drama; but gradually my eyes were opened to the reality.

The shock left me stunned. It was an unexpected and atrocious insult. With my record, after I had shown so often how little I cared for life and the dearest things in life, dared they insinuate that, in letting Lundborg bring me first, my idea had been to put myself in safety before the others, and not to hasten to the help of the men who had disappeared? Could they launch such a base accusation against a man who had urged his comrades on the pack to strike out for land, leaving him alone on the ice with another invalid?

It was an indescribable bitterness. My disgust with mankind was so complete that I decided to go out there again. Very soon the Finnish machine would be ready. I sent for Sarko and asked how many people he could carry. Four or five. I could go, then! He would tell me the moment he could start, so that I, too, could take my place in the machine and guide it to the tent, where I would get out to make room for my companions. I should stay behind . . .

In fact, the day after my return (June 25th), I sent the following message to my comrades: "I am coming to fetch you with the ski-plane as soon as it is ready to start and the weather is fine. Meanwhile, I have urged the Krassin to go ahead."

To go back to the tent on the ice, amid the floe which for a whole month had been my hell. . . . That was the obsession that gripped and held me.

Once and for all be it said: as chief of the expedition my post was there, on the Città di Milano, directing rescue work; not on the ice, where my injuries prevented me from helping my men in any way whatever, and actually made me a danger and burden to them.

The rescuer—the man who voluntarily exposes himself to the risk—is the best judge of the order in which he shall save them. And he did perfectly right in taking me first, if my life was the most important—if it was true that I, though seriously injured, could give valuable advice to help forward the search for the other castaways.

And be it also said, once and for all, that this decision was providential for my companions. It was great luck for them that I was in the *Città di Milano* after Lundborg's accident. One of the men rescued from the Red Tent declared: "If the General had not come before us, we should still be on the pack." If I had not been in the base-ship, and if—although feverish and racked by torments of body and mind—I had not found strength to act, to struggle, to stir up and advise the others, perhaps the *Krassin*—the splendid Russian ship—would have been led to turn back and refit, instead of gallantly pushing on to the Red Tent.

Why the "Città di Milano" did not pick up our S.O.S.

On quitting the pack, while I had left behind every article of clothing that was not strictly necessary, I had brought the two note-books containing the wireless messages received and sent. These books were a living testimony to our anxieties on the pack, a clear documentation of the terrible isolation in which we had remained. I wanted to take them with me, to make sure they were not lost.

It was only natural, therefore, that my first concern, as soon as I came on board the *Città di Milano*, was to improve the wireless communication with the tent. It was essential that the troubles which I myself had noticed and pointed out in vain should not continue. I knew only too well what torture it was for a handful of men cooped up on a piece of drift-ice to keep on calling and receive no answer, to tolerate this state of affairs any longer.

Calling Captain Romagna to my cabin, I told him quietly how necessary it was that the wireless operators in the ship should listen perseveringly for the calls from the tent, to hear my companions' news and attend to their requests. This should be done several times a day.

These hints were not received kindly. Romagna answered in the tone of a man who was convinced that the wireless service had always worked to perfection and amazed that anyone could find the least cause for complaint. So I had to speak out:

"Well then! Why did you never once hear us during twelve days following the catastrophe, when we called you incessantly for hours and hours on end, at the risk of exhausting our batteries? How was it that you never heard our S.O.S., while it was picked up by the Russians at Archangel, so much farther away?"

"But, my dear General," replied the Captain, "if logic is to count for anything, we were perfectly right in imagining—as we did—that it was impossible for you to transmit, and so it was a waste of time to listen for you."

Completely astounded, I begged him to explain how such a colossal blunder could ever have been made in the name of logic. Romagna explained—but I confess that his explanation bewildered me even more the the original statement.

"Well, look here, General—our last wireless communication with the *Italia* was at 10.30 on May 25th. Then, all of a sudden, there was silence. We put our wits to work. Could this silence be explained by some damage to the transmitting station? No! that was improbable, because there was an emergency set on board. So it was not a question of damage to the apparatus. Then how was it that you had not even managed to send out an S.O.S.? It was as plain as a pikestaff! The wireless operator had been unable to do it. So we came to the conclusion that Biagi was dead."

"And how could that have happened?"

My amazement was increasing, and my curiosity to know in what way Biagi could so unexpectedly have died was acute. I was all attention.

"You see, we thought Biagi had leaned out of the porthole, and at that moment the screw of the wireless had come loose and cut off his head."

This conversation, which I have reported quite literally, took place on the day of my return, but the question was of such vital importance that I returned to it later several times. And on each occasion he painstakingly repeated: "But if logic is to count for anything, how could we have come to a different conclusion?"

In fact the conviction of Biagi's death was so firmly rooted in Romagna's mind that nothing had been able to shake it—not even the episode of May 29th.

This is so characteristic that I must put it down exactly as it was repeated to me more than once by the wireless operator Pedretti and confirmed by other witnesses.

On the afternoon of May 29th, at 4.55 or 6.55 (I don't remember which) Pedretti was at his post in the wireless cabin of the *Città di Milano*. Beside him was the chief wireless operator, Baccarani.

Suddenly Pedretti leaped in his seat. He had intercepted the word *Italia*, and a little later: "Reply via Ido 32K" . . . the beginning and end of the message that Biagi sent out on the days following the crash. "Ido" was the code-word for the station of San Paolo at Rome, "32" indicated the wave-length, and the "K" in our wireless code meant "Hurry up! Answer us!"

Pedretti leaped in his seat and grabbed Baccarani by the arm, crying: "The *Italia* is calling us!"

"Nonsense!" retorted the other decidedly: "It can't be! It's probably Mogadiscio." (The station of Mogadiscio, in Benadir, used in fact to communicate with San Paolo every day.)

The conviction that we could not transmit was so profound and the suggestive force of Romagna's *logic* so strong, that no one in the *Città di Milano* seized on the hope held out by the words they had intercepted. They unhesitatingly rejected the idea that we were calling. This seemed so absurd that it never even occurred to anybody to telegraph to Mogadiscio, to find out if they really had been calling San Paolo at that moment. Most people would have grasped desperately at this thread of hope and not relinquished it until they had found out exactly what had happened. Aboard our base-ship, on the other hand, there was not a moment of doubt. . . . The message could not come from us, for Biagi was dead!

That is why, for days on end, nobody in the *Città di Milano* heard our S.O.S., until the Russian amateur Schmidt gave the alarm.

Anyhow, my protests were not useless. I eventually got them to listen-in several times a day to the calls from the tent. I myself undertook to keep in touch with my comrades; sent them news, gave them advice, and kept up their spirits as best I could. I made them tell me everything they needed. By means of the wireless they felt I was watching over them—at least, until my name was omitted from the telegrams.

For later on, under the pretext that these telegrams were picked up by strangers, Romagna's signature—without my knowledge or authorization—was substituted for mine. Only a little alteration, but it explains many things of greater importance.

The Pilots at Virgo Bay

In my long talk with Sarko, the Finn, the day I arrived on the *Città di Milano*, I had urged him to rush forward the fitting of the *Turku* with skis. The moment it was ready, we would leave together for the tent, to descend on the field where Lundborg had already landed twice.

How the news of my arrangement with Sarko came to Romagna's ears I do not know. The fact remains that he came to my cabin and said: "I have heard, General, that you intend to go with the Finns, but I must warn you that I have orders from Rome to prevent your taking part in any rescue expedition whatever. If you insist I shall be obliged to put guards at the doors of your cabin."

To put me under guard really seemed a trifle excessive—not to say ridiculous, when one remembers that the injury to my leg and foot prevented me from stirring without help. . . . But perhaps it was merely a figure of speech.

After Sarko, I sent for the Italian airmen, Maddalena and Penzo, to urge them to get ahead with their flights in search of the dirigible and the six men who had disappeared with it. And there was certainly no time to lose. Summer was drawing on, and with it the peril of long periods of fog.

Maddalena very much doubted the possibility of carrying out the necessary exploration. He spoke of the risks attached to it. These large flying-boats were not suitable—it was a job for small aeroplanes. Anyhow, his engines had already worked about 80 hours and ought to be changed. At the very most, he could only undertake one more flight.

I advised him to send at once to Italy for new engines. Meanwhile I suggested that, as soon as the weather was favourable, the Italian flying-boats and the Swedish trimotor should leave for the tent and throw down various indispensable provisions. From this point they could start a methodical search for the airship in the sectors I had indicated.

While the Finnish plane was being fitted with skis and the other flying-boats were preparing for the flight, someone came to tell me that people on board were very sceptical about landing on the field where Lundborg had capsized. They thought it highly dangerous, after Maddalena's unfavourable report on the size and condition of the ground. It was too small. A bare 200 yds. was absolutely inadequate for the Finnish plane. Worse still, its surface was extremely uneven and bumpy, strewn in places with blocks of ice. My informant added that, in consequence of this report, the Finnish airman was very much worried.

I expressed my astonishment. Why! Had not I telegraphed from the pack that the field was 325×250 yards, and absolutely smooth? Had not these dimensions been conscientiously measured by Viglieri and Biagi; and had not I myself seen as I left that the ground was dead flat? Did they, then, prefer to go by the mere visual impressions of an airman rather than by accurate observations made on the spot?

Once more I sent for Sarko, to reassure him about the field. I gave him exact details and again begged him to hurry up; for if the state of the ground had changed, the men below would warn us not to land. So there was no need for anxiety.

Sarko appeared convinced.

Then I sent for Penzo. This young pilot had attracted me

immensely from the very first. I had a confidential talk with him. The Italian Air Ministry, I gathered, had ordered our flyers to take as few risks as possible; but this was no reason for putting a stopper on the enthusiasm of the foreign airmen. Why discourage the Finns from attempting to land by pessimistic reports that contradicted my own information?

Then Penzo showed the stuff he was made of. He was miserable that circumstances had prevented him from doing more. He, too, would like to fetch off all my men, and might manage it with his seaplane, if he could find a canal of sufficient length near the tent. The width did not matter—10 yards would do—but it must be very long. Was there any hope, he asked, of a lead opening from one day to another?

Yes, it was possible. I told him about the large canal—some 60 yards wide, stretching out of sight—which had opened not far away, soon after the crash. There was nothing to prevent another one opening any day, especially now the snow was melting and the pack beginning to break up. If the planes with skis failed, an attempt might be made with seaplanes.

On June 26th I telegraphed to Viglieri:

As soon as it is fine—which will probably be in a day or two—both the Italian flying-boats and the Swedish trimotor will come to the tent, whence they will start searching for the airship in the direction 110°. They will drop on the field various things I have had prepared. Penzo has also decided that if during his flight he sees a lead near the tent, he will moor there and take you all off. The Finnish plane has been fitted with skis and is being tested. Send me brief news of the weather every day, especially visibility and wind.

In the meantime I thought it advisable that the Tromsö Geophysical Institute should supply us with special meteorological news; above all, warning of fogs.

Next day (June 27th) I telegraphed to the tent as follows:

The ice-breaker will be here tomorrow evening. Two more Swedish machines with skis ("Moth" type) will arrive on Sunday. The 3 large flying-boats and the Finnish machine with skis will leave here together, each with the programme already indicated. Tell me the position of the tent with relation to the field. The Finnish pilot and observer feel quite confident. The flying-boats are bringing you wireless parts, stoves, and waterproof stuff.

But I soon saw only too well that the doubts and scepticism of the others had infected the Finnish airman too; especially as the advance of the *Krassin* and the news that the little Swedish planes were due very soon had given rise to such extravagant optimism on board our base-ship that people saw no need to risk the Finnish machine in a landing on the pack.

Lundborg Wants to March to the Coast

On June 29th, at 6 a.m., Viglieri telegraphed:

Weather variable, but now seems to be clearing up. The sun sometimes pierces the clouds. Visibility from 5 to 10 miles. Light wind from the NW. Clouds about 1,500 ft. high. Landing-field still good, but you should come as quickly as possible, for it might get worse in parts.

I replied:

Everything ready. We are only waiting for better news of visibility. Keep on being patient. I quite realize the importance of not losing a single hour. I have given the pilot our signal-code.

Later Viglieri telegraphed again:

Our position 80° 17′ latitude N. and 28° 44′ longitude E. We sight Cape Leigh Smith at 215°. Wind calm. Visibility not very good. Trojani cured. The others well.

The position signalled had been reached after a fortnight of steady but slow drift SE. It was the most easterly position that had so far been noted, and also the nearest to North-East Land. In fact, the tent was hardly 9 miles from Cape Leigh Smith.

The protracted duration of this south-easterly drift must certainly have made the men on the pack think of Malmgren's prophecy that the tent would keep on drifting eastwards. This recollection, and their present circumstances, could not fail to depress them, especially as they had been waiting six days in vain for the aeroplanes to return.

In this state of mind, it was only natural that the sight of the coast so near should exercise an irresistible lure on those who were fittest to march.

In fact, at 6 p.m. that day the following telegram reached me from Lundborg:

Some parts of our field have yesterday and today become very bad. There is water under the snow and the water will make the ice very bad. There is a part where the ice now is better, but the weather is warm and I don't know how long it can be used. I will ask you, Sir, if we begin walking to Grosse Island and pilot put down food to us till the ice-breaker can save us. I ask you, Sir, on my question and if not today latest tomorrow answer. Perhaps you could help us with informations how to wait.[1]

This heartfelt appeal from a stranger, making me responsible for such a momentous decision, moved me deeply.

I at once answered:

Four planes are ready to start. Only they wait for visibility a little better. I have not well understood your question, but my opinion is that you shall wait there and not walk. Please tell if you think that conditions of the field are still good enough for landing tomorrow morning or tomorrow night.

At the same time I telegraphed to Viglieri:

I think some of you are getting unnecessarily alarmed. Let us know the moment there is sufficient visibility for the aeroplanes to start. You must hang on calmly where you are. It would be a mistake to set out on a march, and besides, I think it is impossible. The *Krassin* will be here tomorrow and take me on board. A Russian aircraft base has already been set up on King Charles Island. Go on being plucky. I am certain that soon I shall see you all again. When the aeroplanes come, if Maddalena's is with them, be ready to guide it by wireless if necessary.

In fact, the Italian flying-boats, the Swedish machine, and the Finnish plane were ready to start, but precious time was wasted in waiting for the ideal weather, which it was absurd to expect at

[1] *Translator's Note.*—This dispatch and the reply, written in English (the *lingua franca* of the Arctic), have been preserved in their original form.

that season. At 5.55 a.m. on June 30th came a message from the tent:

Visibility excellent. Wind calm. Clouds 4,500 ft. high. Weather perfect.

They should have decided to start on the spot. But they put it off till evening, and then again till next morning. By this time Lundborg no longer dared take the responsibility of advising the Finnish machine to land; so it stopped behind at Virgo Bay on July 1st, when the other three aircraft started. Unfortunately the weather had turned, and when a fog came down the pilots were forced back without reaching their goal.

This incident confirmed me in my old idea that we must shift the flying-boat base as near as possible to the zone where the tent was. By doing this not only would we have shortened the flight to be made before reaching the point to be explored, but one could also have flown more often—especially now that local fogs were forming so frequently. In fact, I had noticed several times on the pack that fog was reported from King's Bay when the weather around the tent was quite clear.

I explained my idea to Romagna. We must decide to shift the air base as near as possible to the north coast of North-East Land—for example to Murchison Bay, where the Swedes had established themselves with their ship *Quest* and their seaplanes.

Romagna wouldn't hear of it, thinking it too risky to take the *Città di Milano* over a sea of more or less unknown depth. These fears were perhaps exaggerated, because by advancing slowly and sounding with the modern equipment on board, it would have been possible, without undue danger, to reach the Swedes. Still, I did not insist, because, after all, it was not absolutely indispensable that the *Città di Milano* should accompany the flying-boats. These could join up with the Swedes, using the whaler *Braganza* as a refuelling base. In any case, there would be great advantages in reuniting the Swedish, Italian and Finnish pilots at a single base—if only that of working together in friendly co-operation.

The "Krassin" Goes Ahead

Immediately I arrived on the *Città di Milano* I had asked for news of the *Krassin*, telegraphing to the Italian Ministry at Oslo:

Please tell me if the Russian ice-breaker has arrived at Bergen. If so, urge it to start, as it is essential to reach the spot where the men are stranded as quickly as possible.

But the ice-breaker had left Bergen that very day (June 24th). Six days later it was off Virgo Bay.

The moment I heard this I put myself in touch by wireless with Professor Samoilovitch, the leader of the Russian expedition, whom I had known personally for some time, and asked him first of all to tell me his plans. How soon did he hope to reach the tent?

The same day (June 30th) Samoilovitch replied:

Impossible to make any exact forecast without knowing the state of the ice. Please telegraph me its thickness. We have now passed Prince Charles Island. Speed 12 knots.

I gave the required information. Round about the tent the ice in most places was a couple of yards thick.

Meanwhile I had decided to embark on the *Krassin*. When I told Samoilovitch this, he readily agreed, and telegraphed on the morning of June 30th, asking me to join him off the north coast of the Svalbard, where he would wait for me, as the *Krassin* could not enter Virgo Bay.

But this was prevented by Romagna, who, on the pretext of my state of health, refused to have me taken by a seaplane or a motor-launch to join the Russian ship.

The rapid advance of the *Krassin*, at first along the east coast of the Svalbard and then along the north coast, had raised the highest hopes amongst those on board our ship.

In fact, at 2 p.m. on June 30th, Romagna telegraphed without my knowledge to the tent:

This is to inform you that the *Krassin* is near Cape North. We hope to reach you in a day or two.

When I was told of this, I remarked that such a statement was hazardous in the extreme, since the ice north of North-East Land (I had seen it for myself on my flight of June 24th) was bound to oppose a great resistance to an ice-breaker—even such a powerful one as the *Krassin*. It was dangerous to raise the hopes of my men too much, for the consequent disappointment would leave them thoroughly discouraged. So on July 2nd I telegraphed in my turn:

I have not embarked on the *Krassin* because it passed us too quickly. I think you may catch sight of its funnels in about a week. In that case our faith and hope will have been justified.

I had given the flying-boats a letter I had written you, and am sorry you have not been able to receive it. Apparently the small aeroplanes have arrived. In any case, assure Lundborg that his compatriots are losing, and will lose, no time. They mean to establish a base on the coast, not far from Cape Leigh Smith.

On July 1st the *Krassin*, forging ahead at 4 or 5 knots an hour, sighted Cape North and the Seven Islands group. Here it met with its first serious difficulties. The Russians had meant to pass between the Seven Islands and the Cape, but on July 2nd a solid barrier of ice two yards thick forced the ship to return on its tracks and attempt to pass north of Ross Island, the most northerly of the group, where the ice was less impenetrable. The *Krassin* went on slowly, but it did contrive to get through. Our hopes revived. Everything encouraged us to believe that it would go on advancing—especially as our pilots, on their return from the flight of July 1st, had reported the existence of large and frequent pools of open water near the coast of North-East Land. Then I, too, became less pessimistic, and telegraphed to the tent:

The *Krassin* is getting on faster than I expected. So you can watch the thaw quite calmly. Tomorrow I will send you a list of the things I want you to ship on the ice-breaker. All the flags should be left, so that the place may easily be recognized, even after you have gone. *Au revoir*, then. Your families are well and confident.

But next day (July 3rd) the *Krassin* was blocked in a dense bank of ice, and stayed moored, after finding that its left screw was broken.

People on board the *Città di Milano* were all the more discouraged, as their enthusiasm during the first days of the *Krassin*'s advance had been so exaggerated. They began to run down the Russian leader, accusing him of rashness, because he had refused to take on board the Norwegian pilot whom Commander Romagna had persistently offered him. Gradually, the hopes set on the *Krassin* were abandoned by all, especially when it became known that its coal was running out. Trapped in a bank of ice, with a broken screw and little fuel on board, the ice-breaker, according to Romagna, had no alternative but to turn back as soon as it could get out of the fix.

But I well knew the spirit of the Russians, and, never having been carried away by the excessive optimism at the beginning of their advance, I now refused to be discouraged. The Russians would not turn back. They would not give up their part in the struggle, except through dire necessity.

THE END OF THE DRAMA

My Meeting with Riiser-Larsen

ON July 2nd Riiser-Larsen, my old friend of the *Norge* expedition, arrived at Virgo Bay. He and Lützow Holm, the other Norwegian airman, had come back from Cape North on board the *Braganza*. They had received orders from Norway to suspend their flights along the coast of North-East Land in search of Mariano's party, return to King's Bay, and embark on the *Hobby*, which was setting out to look for Amundsen, who had not been heard of since he had left Tromsö on June 18th, on board the *Latham* 47.

I had not really seen Larsen since July 1926, when we had separated at Seattle on our return from Teller. It is true we had met at Oslo some months before, but it had been a very frigid and formal meeting, because the dispute between Amundsen and myself had ended by estranging us from each other. I must confess that this estrangement had been very painful to me, for I was sincerely attached to all the Norwegians who had shared that memorable flight from Rome to Teller, especially Riiser-Larsen, whom I had known previously and with whom I had become more intimate.

My meeting with Riiser-Larsen is one of the most memorable episodes of my life in the *Città di Milano*. I was in bed with fever—partly physical but far more the fever of my sleepless brain perpetually reverting to the men in the tent and the others who were lost.

The cabin door opened, and I heard a well-known voice: "How do you do, my dear Nobile?" . . . Then I found myself in the giant's arms. I flung mine round his neck. I could find no words to express what I felt. My eyes filled with tears. . . . Someone who was present realized that this was a moment when we must be left alone.

"Dear, dear Riiser!"

Then I broke down completely—and so did my old comrade. For the first time I saw tears in his eyes. . . . There were so many things I wanted to tell him, but I was silent. I could not speak. I wanted to thank him—to say that I felt an indissoluble bond united all who had shared the *Norge* flight. I wanted to tell him my unhappiness at the misunderstandings that had arisen: all my sorrow for what Amundsen had said about me, and my regret at having had to defend myself. I wanted to express my gratitude for the chivalrous gesture with which Amundsen and he had wiped out those miserable little squabbles of the past. . . . This was what I longed to say—what I wanted him to read through my tears. But I was silent—I could not speak. . . .

Then we talked. He comforted me affectionately: I must wait in faith—everyone would come back. He asked me about Malmgren: "What provisions had they when they left?" "Just over 120 lb. of concentrated food, between pemmican and chocolate." "Oh, that's all right then!" exclaimed Riiser-Larsen, "you needn't worry about them. They have enough for 45 days."

I inquired after Amundsen. Riiser-Larsen was absolutely confident that he would be found.

Lundborg Saved

Commander Tornberg, chief of the Swedish expedition, had not been wasting time. With surprising rapidity, he had had the little "Moth" aeroplanes sent from Sweden and adapted for use.

On July 4th I was able to telegraph to the tent:

Tell Lundborg that Tornberg says the planes have arrived and he is ready to fly.

Between July 1st and 5th the tent, drifting to and fro, had described a large circle in counter-clockwise direction. On July 5th it was near Cape Leigh Smith, only $4\frac{1}{2}$ miles from the coast. Seeing land so near, my companions must inevitably have once more felt drawn towards it. In fact, at 7 a.m. on the day, Viglieri telegraphed:

Approximate position: latitude 80° 15′, longitude 28° 20′. Wind WNW., force 3 Beaufort scale, but going down. It is veering in the direction of the landing-ground. Visibility excellent. Clear sky. Landing possible.

Then he continued:

Don't let this chance slip. If there is a sledge expedition at Cape Leigh Smith it could reach us in a few hours. We are not trying to make for the coast, because we cannot abandon Cecioni.

I hastened to let Tornberg know this news, begging him to send the machines with skis as soon as possible. But this was unnecessary: the Swedes always acted with great promptness and decision. In fact, that very afternoon their seaplanes reached the tent and dropped abundant provisions and other things. The main object of this flight, however, had been to ascertain the state of the landing-ground. As this was good, a little "Moth" aeroplane piloted by Schyberg landed near the tent that night (2 a.m., July 6th) and fetched Lundborg away.

I received the news of this rescue with an outburst of joy. At last his imprisonment was over! And my own men would certainly be freed very soon; for I had no doubt the Swedes would return to the floe to take them off, one by one. So certain and imminent did this seem that Romagna came to ask my advice on the order in which they should leave. I replied that Biagi must, of course, be the last; otherwise the Swedish airman who came to the rescue would run an unnecessary and very serious risk.

But this discussion unfortunately led to nothing, because a few hours later the *Città di Milano* heard that the Swedes had given up any idea of returning to the pack. And so the hope of seeing my comrades rescued that day was disappointed.

Naturally this decision upset the Italians and provoked a good deal of criticism; but for my part I still had absolute confidence in Tornberg and his friends. So I prepared a telegram for Tornberg, urging him to take advantage of the good weather to fly the men off, one by one, and bring them to the nearest point on the coast.

But in the end this was not sent, because I heard that Tornberg was on the point of coming over to the *Città di Milano* for a talk with me. In fact, he and Lundborg arrived that afternoon at Virgo Bay in the Finnish plane *Turku*. They came down to my cabin together. I was still in bed with fever.

I was delighted to see Lundborg, and at once asked him for news of my men.

He said they were all fairly well now, but one after another had had a troublesome gastric fever. It would be as well to give them a change of diet. As for their morale, most of them were all right; only Cecioni had been rather depressed, especially the last few days. Lundborg remarked how important it was that they should often see aeroplanes flying overhead, as this cheered them up immensely. The truth of this I myself knew from personal experience.

At this point Tornberg said that their seaplanes could drop more provisions down to the tent that evening. I called the steward and ordered him to prepare the requisite things, and have them loaded on the *Turku*.

Then I again turned to Tornberg, bringing the conversation round to the point I had most at heart.

The situation was certainly rather delicate. I quite understood that the Swedes were reluctant to land again on the pack and risk having another of their men imprisoned there. It embarrassed me to have to press them, but I was determined to do it.

Tornberg spoke very frankly. Now that the high temperature had partially thawed the snow, the difficulty and danger of a landing had greatly increased. Was it worth while running such a risk? Or would it not be better to reach the tent in a ship? The Captain of the *Quest*—a man of great experience —had a plan which he considered certain to succeed. Why not try it?

I answered that not a single stone should be left unturned; so we must put the Captain's suggestion into practice. We could arrange about this later. But it would be a mistake to give up altogether any idea of reaching my comrades with small aeroplanes. I myself was still convinced that, in spite of the inevitable risks, this was the quickest and simplest means of getting the men off. After all, the Swedes had already shown that my conviction was well founded. Lundborg's accident was due, as he had explained, to engine failure; so that proved nothing against my opinion. Tornberg should also consider my comrades' state of mind. Until now they had borne up wonderfully, but from one moment to another their nerve might go. There was no doubt about it: another landing was worth the risk, if it would shorten their sufferings.

Tornberg listened. He seemed to be reflecting. Then, as if persuaded by my words, he said quietly: "All right! We'll land again. We will be ready to go any night. Just send us in time any useful information: the state of the field, visibility, etc."

Here Lundborg interposed: "When the temperature is fairly low, the field is always good for landing. It will be enough, then, if the men in the tent tell us the temperature."

At once I wrote the following message for them:

Every evening, not later than the call at 10.55 p.m. G.M.T., you should send news about the wind, visibility, state of the sky, and temperature. The last is needed for deducing the state of the landing-ground. If conditions are favourable, the aeroplanes will start at 11 p.m. G.M.T.

This having been decided, I thanked the Swedes, especially Tornberg—more by looks than words. Then I wrote a letter to my comrades and gave it to Tornberg as he left, asking him to drop it down to the tent with the provisions.

Discouragement

Though Romagna was not best pleased at the Russians and the Swedes taking sides with me when there were decisions to be agreed upon, he always ended by following my advice. So when I mentioned the Captain of the *Quest*'s idea, he straightway prepared the expedition of the whaler *Braganza*. As in the case of the *Krassin*, I asked permission to embark on it, but this was refused by the Assistant Secretary to the Navy, on the usual pretext of my health.

The *Braganza* expedition was prepared all the more eagerly, since for some days past the Naval officers had felt that this was the only practical means that remained of rescuing my men. As the *Krassin* was still blocked north of the Seven Islands group, and the Swedes, after bringing off Lundborg, had decided not to risk another landing to fetch the Italians, there was an atmosphere of pessimism on board, as unfounded as the previous optimism had been excessive.

Now the same day (July 6th) Romagna came into my cabin and announced that "Very probably the Admiralty would order Viglieri and his companions to set out for the coast, leaving Cecioni behind".

I protested. Such an order would be monstrous, and a colossal error. What would the world say to such a horrible decision? Who would dare to assume this awful moral responsibility?

"No! You won't do it! You'll have the whole civilized world against you!"

And fortunately there was no more talk of this.

In any case, this strange idea of ordering the other men to abandon Cecioni and march, shows the discouragement which the latest events had produced in our base-ship.

Certainly there was a moment when Fate seemed to set herself with the utmost ferocity against the shipwrecked of the *Italia* and those who were trying to rescue them. . . . Amundsen, Guilbaud and the other four in the *Latham* lost; the *Krassin* blocked at Cape North. The Russian pilot Babuskin had left the *Malyghin* for an exploration and not come back.[1] No news of Mariano, Zappi, and Malmgren. Sora had left for Foyn Island and nothing more had been heard of him. The tragedy had begun to spread in ever-widening circles.

But I had an unwavering faith that my men in the tent would at last be saved, and that in a few days we should have news of the other three. I refused to give way to pessimism. One or other of the rescue measures would, sooner or later, be successful.

[1] *Note.*—He returned safely a few days afterwards.

So I turned my attention to the *Krassin*, though everyone else on board had lost hope of its getting any farther. Romagna especially took care to keep on remarking: "Well! What do you expect them to do? Very soon their fuel will run out; then they will have to turn back to coal and repair."

But I refused to abandon hope. I knew the Russians would not give up the struggle so tamely.

On the evening of July 6th I telegraphed to Samoilovitch: "Please tell me whether you are advancing or not"; and next morning I repeated: "I should be very grateful if you would tell me your plans; above all, whether you think you can reach the tent."

At 5.15 p.m. on the 7th he replied:

Our Junkers trimotor is now out on the ice. Tonight Tchuknovsky will search out an aircraft base on the coast to fall back upon. Then a second flight will be made, to find an easier way through the ice for the *Krassin* and look for Viglieri's group. The *Krassin* will await the result of these flights, and go forward wherever it is possible. Please tell me the programme of the other expeditions.

This telegram was brought down to my cabin by Commander Romagna himself.

"We'll prepare the answer at once," he said, sat down at the little table and began to write:

We are getting ready the whaler *Braganza*, which is adapted for ice-breaking. A seaplane will be carried on board, and the ship will make for the coast of North-East Land to try to reach our men. The Swedish pilots——"

I interrupted him: "No! Not like that! The Russians might think that the Swedes and the *Braganza* have great chances of success, and that therefore they need not risk their ship in a dangerous advance. No! We must write quite differently." And I dictated:

All our hopes are centred on the *Krassin*. We beg you, therefore, to do your utmost to reach the tent as soon as possible.

In the meantime the situation was still further complicated by a magnetic storm.

Wireless communication between the *Città di Milano* and the tent had never been altogether interrupted, except during the first days after the catastrophe. In fact, since my return, the communications had noticeably improved. Every day—often more than once—I had got news through to my men and heard theirs in reply. Recently (July 2nd) good results had been obtained by substituting the 47-metre wave-length for the 32 used until then. The chief wireless operator and I had agreed on this change, after discussing the most suitable wave-length for the distance between the ship and the tent.

But unexpectedly, on the morning of July 7th, we failed, in spite of all our efforts, to send or receive messages. Soon we ascertained that communication had been cut off by a magnetic storm, which had affected wireless transmission (particularly on short waves) all over the Svalbard.

The effect of this complete silence on the spirits of my men can easily be imagined. They naturally supposed that their receiving apparatus had developed some irreparable flaw. So every day they wirelessed: "Our receiver is not working. Please send us another." But of course this appeal never reached us.

The "Krassin's" Venture

This irritating break in wireless communication was the one thing which brought home to us the value of the marvellous invention that enabled us to correspond daily with the tent, the Swedes, the Russians, and Rome. But at last the magnetic storm was over and the wireless began to work again, bringing us news of the extraordinary events by which the Polar tragedy, for the most part, was given such an unexpectedly fortunate ending.

On the morning of July 11th the tent telegraphed its position: latitude 80° 29', longitude 28° 27'. During these last days the drift had carried it 15 miles farther from the coast. Thus the event proved what a terrible mistake it would have been to order Viglieri and his companions to march towards *terra firma*, which, like the food of Tantalus, swiftly receded every time it seemed within grasp.

A little later that day came the surprising news:

Yesterday (Tuesday, July 10th) the *Krassin's* aeroplane flew for 4 hours over the NE. coast of North-East Land. On their return the pilots sighted a group of men on a hummock. Two were waving flags, and the third lying down. The position of this group was latitude 80° 42′ N., longitude 25° 45′ E. of Greenwich. A bank of fog came down unexpectedly and prevented the pilot finding his way back to the *Krassin*, so he headed for the coast and succeeded in making land near Cape Platen. The aeroplane was damaged during the landing. The 5 men on board have managed to reach the coast.

At 10.50 a.m. on July 11th the *Krassin* weighed anchor. She steamed ahead at full speed, making real headway through the ice, regardless of the damaged helm and broken screw. The pack, covered with old hummocks and banks of ice, was over 6 ft. thick, and the ship found it heavy going. Conditions improved towards midnight when, having passed Charles XII Island, they found the pack split by channels and were able to make much better speed.

There was keen suspense on board. All the crew, apart from the stokers and engineers, were on the bridge scanning the horizon. Samoilovitch had promised a money prize to the first who spotted the group of three men whom the pilot Tchuknovsky had seen; but such a promise was not needed to stimulate sailors who so ardently wished to see the dangerous voyage of their icebreaker crowned with success. From time to time someone raised his arm, shouting that he had seen something; but then, approaching the spot pointed out, they found nothing but a hummock or a slab of discoloured ice.

Blowing her siren at regular intervals, the *Krassin* pushed on through the blocks of ice that kept adhering to her sides; in her wake was a black strip of open water.

Suddenly the helmsman Breinkopf—normally silent and placid—flushed scarlet with excitement, shouted: "A man! A man! I can see him!" In a moment the whole crew had heard the news. Samoilovitch looked through his telescope. A long way ahead of the ship someone could be seen waving. This time there was no doubt: it really was a man. Amid general jubilation the *Krassin*, at 5.20 a.m., giving a long blast on her siren, steered towards the black dot. At 5.40 she was within 300 yards. Now the man could be seen clearly. He seemed to be signalling the *Krassin* to stop—perhaps because it would have been dangerous to come nearer. Another man was seen lying on the ice: his arms and shoulders moved, as though he were trying to hoist himself into a sitting position. Of the third there was no sign. Suddenly the standing man put a pair of binoculars to his eyes; a moment later they heard him shout: "*Krassin*, welcome!"

The ice-breaker stopped. When a ladder had been run out Breinkopf, the secretary of the expedition Ivanov, the doctor, Shrednievsky, and other members of the crew came out, bringing ropes, planks, a ladder and a stretcher. The rescuers made haste to arrive as quickly as possible, but for all their efforts it took them a long time to reach the floe where the two men were. It was a block of ice measuring about 8 × 10 yards. The first to get there was Ivanov, who, hastening towards the standing man, asked: "Malmgren?" The man replied: "No, I am Commander Zappi."

"And where is Malmgren?"

He said something in Italian, pointing down under the ice.

"Zappi," writes Samoilovitch, "looked a large, strong man. His fur suit was ragged and dirty. He had a thick beard. The other man was lying on a torn blanket in a hollow of the ice, and was too weak to talk. Only his eyes, shining with fever, were eloquent. His drawn, emaciated face was fringed by a reddish beard."

On the next floe—separated by a narrow channel from the one where the men were found—some pieces of stuff had been spread out to form the words: HELP FOOD ZAPPI MARIANO.

Mariano was lifted on to the stretcher, but Zappi refused help, saying he was strong enough to walk. Slowly, very cautiously, the caravan made its way towards the ship. It was a short journey but by no means an easy one, as a lead had opened and they had to improvise a bridge to cross it, and they often had to use the ladder to climb up blocks of ice.

When they got there, the stretcher with Mariano was carried on board, while Zappi, grasping tightly the hand-rope of the gangway, managed to mount it unaided.

"I was standing at the top of the gangway," relates Samoilo-vitch. "Someone pointed me out to Zappi as the chief of the expedition. He ran towards me, took my hand in both his own and pressed it in a long clasp, whilst he looked at me with deep gratitude in his eyes. At the same time Mariano, whose stretcher had been placed behind me, stroked my leg with his left hand—the only way in which he could express his thanks.

"I turned to look at him. Mariano's eyes were shining with joy. A radiant, childlike smile lit his tortured face, like that of a man unexpectedly called back to life, whose sufferings were finished and who was now recovering consciousness in the midst of his friends and rescuers.

"I stroked his hand, and if I had not been embarrassed in front of so many people, I would have stooped down and kissed this happy man. A lump rose in my throat: I was so moved that I could not say a single word." And he continues: "One of our stokers came up to me, sweating, with blackened face, just as he had come from the engine-room: 'So, in spite of everything, they've been saved!' he said, smiling. I was not at all surprised to see the white streaks that tears of joy had drawn through the coal-dust on his face.

"Under the care of Dr. Shrednievsky, Mariano was taken to the sick-bay. Zappi, whom I had invited to come with me to the saloon, staggered rather shakily across the bridge, and going down the companion-way he stumbled, like a man who has forgotten how to walk after a long illness. When we arrived at the saloon he dropped into an armchair. I sat down beside him, and he at once began to tell me about his privations—how he had eaten nothing for the last thirteen days. I interrupted him: 'And Malmgren? Where is Malmgren?' '*C'était un homme!*' replied Zappi: 'He died a month ago.' And after a short pause he added: 'Give me something to eat—I am very hungry!' "

Zappi and Mariano had been picked up by the *Krassin* at 7 a.m. on July 12th, at 80° 30' of latitude N. and 26° 7' of longitude E. Samoilovitch at once gave me the news in the following telegram:

Commander Zappi and Mariano are on board the *Krassin*. We are going on towards the Viglieri group. Please give me the latest position of the tent.

In fact, an hour after taking Zappi and Mariano on board, the *Krassin* had continued on its way to the Red Tent. About eleven o'clock, while the ice-breaker was off Foyn Island, the officer on watch noticed two men waving from the coast: they were Captain Sora and his companion van Dongen. On June 18th Sora, van Dongen and the Dane Warming, with a sledge and nine dogs, had started from Beverley Strait, with the intention of getting to Foyn Island and thence to the Red Tent. But at Cape North Warming, having fallen ill, had left the group. The other two had gone on, and on July 4th had reached Foyn Island. Here they had stopped, because their provisions had run out, and also because they had no idea how to find the Red Tent, not knowing its position.

Samoilovitch and Orass discussed whether the *Krassin* should stop to pick them up, but they wisely decided to push straight on to the tent without wasting time. They could fetch Sora and van Dongen on the way back. But there was no need. That same evening the Swedish expedition, warned by the *Krassin*, sent 3 seaplanes to the spot—one of them being the Finnish trimotor piloted by Sarko, which found the men and brought them to safety. The only living being left on the island was a dog, the sole survivor of a team of nine. Of the rest, one had died and the others had been eaten.

In the face of such marvellous events we could only thank God and express our gratitude to the heroic rescuers, trying to help them in the least things, as we could not do in the greater.

And that was what I did.

Scarcely had I received the news that the Russians were making for the tent, when I took up the matter of communications, called the chief wireless operator to my cabin, and pointed out the necessity of keeping in constant touch with the tent and the *Krassin*. Our base-ship had to act as intermediary, forwarding any news which either needed to send to the other. The wireless operator objected that he could not possibly do this, as the Captain had ordered him to transmit some long telegrams to Rome.

I sent for Romagna. At first he backed up the wireless operator in his objections. I pointed out that at this moment no wireless service could be more urgent or more important than the one I was speaking about. The *Krassin* might easily overshoot the tent without noticing it, especially if a fog came down. . . . Eventually Romagna gave way, and we decided to get into touch with the tent once every hour.

Having come to this decision, I had it communicated to my men:

From this moment until you are in contact with the *Krassin* we will call you at the 55th minute of every hour. When you see the *Krassin* tell us where you sight it and how far away; then we shall be able to help them find the tent.

This telegram was transmitted at 2.55 p.m. An hour later I added:

When the *Krassin* approaches, if the weather is bad, it would be advisable to light smoke-signals.

As if to confirm the wisdom of these minor precautions, the tent telegraphed at 4.55 p.m.:

We have sighted the *Krassin* about 6 miles SW.

What had happened was exactly what I had foreseen: the ice-breaker had passed the tent without noticing it.

Naturally, the news was sent at once to the *Krassin*, which was then able to change its course and reach the tent.

At 8 p.m. on board the *Krassin* a great column of smoke was seen rising from a wide field of ice. The sailors cheered exultantly. It was the field where Lundborg had landed twice, and to which the tent had been shifted on the day after his aeroplane capsized. Both the tent and the machine could be clearly seen through a telescope.

Half an hour later the *Krassin*, having approached the icefield, moored about a hundred yards from the tent. Several men disembarked. It was a large field, almost rectangular in shape and about 350 × 120 yards. Here and there multicoloured flags had been spread out as a signal to airmen. The field was covered with snow—soft snow on the point of melting; footprints in it made large holes, quickly filled with water. There were tracks in all directions around the camp. Quite near the tent there was a large rubber dinghy: about 40 yards farther away was the Swedish aeroplane—or what was left of it after the men had used its plywood wings to make a raised platform on which to pitch the tent. The skeleton of the aeroplane lay tilted at an angle, with its tail and skis in the air. On the fuselage one could see three crowns painted inside a circle, and the number 31. Between the aeroplane and the tent, anchored by wire guy-ropes, was the wireless mast.

At 8.45 Viglieri, Behounek, Trojani, Cecioni and Biagi were on board the *Krassin*: our anxiety for them was at an end.

They told me afterwards that, almost as soon as he set foot on the ice-breaker, Behounek had asked Samoilovitch: "May I go on with my scientific work on board the *Krassin*?" "Of course!" Samoilovitch had replied, smiling. "We too are making scientific observations, and we shall be glad to help you."

The last to come had been Biagi. He had stopped to send a wireless message written by Viglieri. It got lost on the air, conveying among other things: "Greetings and good wishes to our beloved General Nobile."

This, of course, pleased me very much, as I was pleased when Behounek, saying good-bye to me some days afterwards, added that he was proud to have shared in my expedition.

But I was still more deeply moved, on our return to Italy, when, at the moment of parting in the train, Viglieri, Trojani and Biagi embraced me with emotion and said: "Thank you for taking us with you." Without realizing it, they were repeating the very words that Wisting had used two years earlier, upon the arrival of the *Norge*—and that Malmgren had stoically pronounced in that terrible moment just after the crash: "*Thank you for the trip.*"

Simple words—but expressive of deep feeling.

Meanwhile, I had been thinking what must be done to find the last group of castaways. This was the best moment to explore the environs of the tent, where I thought the airship must have descended or fallen. If we lost this chance, the search would afterwards become very difficult, because on the drifting pack it would have been impossible to find the site of the tent, once the *Krassin* had left it and there was no one remaining on the spot to check and report on the rapidly changing position of the tent.

So I had the following telegram prepared for Samoilovitch, and by my decided action got it off, in spite of difficulties that were put in my way:

I do not know how to thank you, on this day when my heart is full of rejoicing over your generous and splendid achievement. May I now ask you whether, in your present state, you can go another 10 or 15 miles eastward to look for the dirigible?, extending your search in the sector between 80° and 140° of the compass, centred on the tent. Perhaps I am asking too much, but I know you will forgive me. If this search is undertaken now, it will be made in the best possible conditions.

Next day at 2 p.m. Samoilovitch replied:

Cordial thanks for what you say. I only did what had to be done. If we are to search for the airship group, I think it is useless to try it without first reconnoitring by aeroplane. If the *Krassin* has to make the search by itself, we need coal for 3 or 4 weeks; so, before beginning, we should have to coal up at Advent Bay and then come back here.

A few hours later (5.25 p.m.) growing steadily more convinced that it was opportune to make the search at once, he telegraphed again:

Please tell me if you are going to search for the airship group with flying-boats. In that case we will wait here by the tent.

I begged Captain Romagna to have the flying-boats prepared. It was vital not to let this chance slip. This was the right moment to look for the last six men. Other favourable opportunities had already been missed: first, by not undertaking the search during the exceptional period of fine weather in June, while I was still on the pack; and later, by continual hesitation and procrastination, waiting for the perfect weather conditions that could no longer be expected. We must not lose this last chance. With the Russian ice-breaker in the pack, on the actual site of the tent, the search would be much easier and the risk to the pilots reduced to a minimum, since the *Krassin* could come to their help in case of an accident.

These reasons were so self-evident that nobody should have hesitated for a moment. But, alas! hesitation there was—and to justify it an extraordinary story of the catastrophe was spread on board the *Città di Milano*, according to which the search would certainly be in vain, and it was therefore useless to risk the flying-boats in other flights. Hesitations ... doubts ... fears ... as a result of which the *Krassin* was induced to turn back.

So, by transforming a possibility into a certainty, the search for the six men who had disappeared into the fog with the *Italia* on the morning of May 25th, 1928, was given up, at the very moment when it could have been made with the least risk and the greatest chances of success.

Over a month later, in the second half of August, in quite unsuitable weather, the Italian Navy took it up again, sending the whaler *Braganza* to the Seven Islands group, with two aeroplanes on board piloted by Penzo and Crosio. But this search yielded no result—nor could it have done, because by this time no one knew where the wind and the currents had swept the mass of ice on which the airship had presumably come down.

It was a grave error not to have listened to me when I had insisted that the search should be made while the *Krassin* was still beside the Red Tent. Aldo Pontremoli, Ugo Lago, Ettore Arduino, Attilio Caratti, Callisto Ciocca, Renato Alessandrini—my six comrades who on the dark May morning disappeared in the Polar sky on board the *Italia*, had fearlessly risked their lives for the honour and glory of their country. Even if there were no longer any chance of finding them alive, it was the duty of the Italian Government to make every effort to ascertain how they had died; while as it is, today, nearly a third of a century after the event, the Polar ice still holds the tragic secret of their fate.

Mariano and Zappi

Zappi had telegraphed to me from the *Krassin*:

Malmgren, having one foot frozen and being at the end of his strength, gave up the march on June 14th. We have been picked up at the last gasp, after 12 days without food. Mariano's condition is pretty fair, my own good.

Naturally I was very much upset by this abandonment of Malmgren. But I understood how the two Italian officers might have been placed in such a crucial position that they had been obliged to accept the separation.

Then other particulars arrived, given by Zappi himself. Having left us on May 30th, Malmgren, Mariano and Zappi made for Broch Island, which Malmgren expected to reach in a day or two. But the state of the pack made the march very difficult. Their progress was not much over half a mile a day, instead of the six they had foreseen. To make things much worse, the drift carried them in the opposite direction, so that after fourteen exhausting days on the march they were even farther from the island than when they started. This tragic situation must have weighed heavily on Malmgren's spirits, since when he left me he had declared that he expected to reach Cape North in a fortnight.

In these circumstances it is not surprising that Malmgren, by this time convinced of the futility of their attempt, should have confessed himself beaten. On the fourteenth day of the march, according to Zappi, at the end of his strength, he let himself drop in the snow, declaring that he could go no farther, and asking the others to go on alone to try and reach land. "Leave me to die here in peace," he had said, insisting that Mariano and Zappi should take his share of provisions. He made them dig him a shallow trench in the ice, and lay down in it, after having given Zappi a little magnetic compass with the request that it should be sent to his mother.

The two Italians, after walking about a hundred yards, sat down to rest, hoping that Malmgren would change his mind and come to join them. They waited there about 24 hours, and then

Malmgren, raising his head from the trench, called to them: "Why don't you go? Go on quickly: don't waste time!" This was the last time that Mariano and Zappi saw their companion. It was June 16th. They set off again on their march.

But they did not get very far. Mariano was attacked by snow-blindness and became almost blind. Holding his hand, Zappi tried to guide him across the crevasses, and up and down the blocks of ice—but it was impossible. They stopped, dug themselves a trench and sheltered in it for some days, waiting for death. On June 20th, when the drift had carried them quite near Broch Island, suddenly they heard the hum of an aero-engine over their heads: a large flying-boat was passing over them. They shouted and waved their arms to attract the pilot's attention, but in vain. The airman did not notice those two tiny greyish dots against the infinite whiteness of the pack. Their disappointment was terrible, but they had at least the comfort of knowing that rescue expeditions were at work.

As Mariano was somewhat better, they tried to continue towards Broch Island. It was no use. The pitiless drift wiped out all their progress. The pack continued to zigzag, now in one direction now in another, according to the wind and the currents. Once they were so near the coast of Broch Island that Zappi thought he could have crossed the 700 or 800 yards that separated them from it; but Mariano was again snowblind. Zappi had the idea of going on alone, and Mariano himself urged him to do it. Fortunately for them, the ice conditions were so bad that Zappi had the feeling that, with the heavy knapsack on his back, he could not even have made those few hundred yards. A day or two later they were in the neighbourhood of Cape Leigh Smith. The coast was very near, and for the second time Zappi thought of trying his luck to reach land; but soon afterwards the drift again changed its direction, carrying the two men away from North-East Land, first towards Broch Island and then towards Cape Brunn.

On June 30th, said Zappi, they finished the last of their food. The 120 lb. of pemmican, chocolate, malted milk and butter, with which they had left the Red Tent, had lasted 30 days. Each man had eaten, on an average, 1 lb. 10 oz. a day of these concentrated foods.

On July 4th Broch Island was again very near. Mariano told Zapppi not to bother about him, but to go on. However, in the state to which Zappi was now reduced, and without any food whatever, it was too much of an undertaking. There was nothing more to be done, and they settled down resignedly to wait for death.

On the evening of July 10th, again they suddenly heard engines overhead: it was Tchuknovsky flying towards the Red Tent. Zappi jumped out of the ice-trench and began desperately waving a rag to attract attention. The pilot saw him and made several turns around them, to see them better; then he went on his way. They anxiously awaited his return for several hours. But the aeroplane did not come back, and once more they were plunged into despair.

All at once, on the morning of July 12th, the silence of the pack was broken by the prolonged whistling of a siren. It was the *Krassin*. Their terrible Odyssey was at an end. They were saved.

And so might Malmgren also have been saved, if, once he had realized the futility of continuing their march, he had persuaded his companions to stop where they were, conserving their strength and waiting for a providential rescue.

A few days later Zappi and Mariano were on board the *Città di Milano*. Theirs was a curious fate! They had set out firmly convinced that our wireless was nothing but lumber, which at best might serve for firewood—yet it was to this very wireless that they owed their miraculous salvation.

As soon as he arrived, Zappi came down to my cabin to greet me. I was struck by the overstrung condition in which his fearful adventure had left him: a desperate march, one companion dead and the other incapacitated by a frozen foot, the provisions finished, and aeroplanes passing overhead without noticing the rags that they had spread out on the snow to form the letters HELP US. Truly, he had shown marvellous energy in standing up to this terrible test.

A few days later, still on the *Città di Milano*, I was at last able to go and see Mariano, who had unfortunately been obliged to have his foot amputated. He was lying in bed, with the traces of indescribable sufferings clearly visible in his face. He told me about their march, and the recital of such dreadful adventures made my heart ache.

Samoilovitch

When the *Krassin* arrived at King's Bay with the rescued men on board, Professor Samoilovitch, with Tchuknovsky and Captain Orass, came down to my cabin. Samoilovitch embraced me affectionately. He said he was sorry I had been unable to join the *Krassin*. The Moscow Government had given him orders to take me on board any time I asked him: "We waited for you, north of Virgo Bay, as we couldn't get into it."

I asked him if they were going on looking for the airship group. Yes! The *Krassin* was bound, first of all, for Stavanger, for repairs, but would return to the north of the Svalbard once she was refitted. Samoilovitch would be glad if I could share in this second search: no doubt I could give him useful information and advice.

I answered that I was very keen to do this, and I made the request to the Italian Navy, but permission was not granted me.

Homo Homini Lupus

On July 22nd, obeying orders from Rome, the *Città di Milano* left King's Bay for Narvik, where my companions and I were to be landed. Shortly before we left, Penzo came to see me again. He frankly said how sorry he and Maddalena were that they had been placed in a situation that prevented them from doing all that they, in their enthusiasm, would have wished.

On July 26th we arrived at Narvik, where two railway-carriages had been specially sent from Paris to meet us and take us right through to Italy. A gangway from the ship allowed us to pass straight into the train.

And thus concluded my stay on the *Città di Milano* after I was brought off the pack: one of the worst periods of my life—thirty-two interminable days of indescribable torment.

Imprisoned in the four wooden walls of that tiny cabin, my life had become sheer hell, as I looked on helplessly—unable to defend myself in any way—at the shameful campaign of slander launched against me, and at the sabotage of the expedition. This had been quite unconcealed—to the point that Captain Romagna had forbidden one of the journalists on board to send a radiogram in which Behounek spoke of the scientific results achieved. The pretext had been that orders had been received from Rome "not to write up the scientific value of the expedition." I had borne all this stoically, because I was quite determined not to abandon my place in the struggle, but to carry out to the end my duties as leader.

In the train at Narvik, as if to round off the fearful ordeal, they brought me a bundle of newspapers. There I read everything that had been printed in the European Press during the last month against the *Italia* expedition. The full, brutal, unexpected revelation showed me, as if in a mirror, the spectacle of a world which, after having sympathized with our disaster and vied in efforts to save us, had then tried almost as eagerly to demolish with the vilest calumnies a daring scientific enterprise, which was fine and noble even if unfortunate. The most ignominious things had been written about me and my companions. They had even gone so far as to represent as an act of petty cowardice what had been obedience to an order, the fulfilment of a high and definite duty. Everything had served as material for calumny, insinuations, insults. I felt crushed under the avalanche of abuse hurled at me by mean spirits throughout the world, whilst I had been unable to defend myself during that terrible month on the *Città di Milano*, fighting with all my might for the rescue of the castaways. A great sadness took possession of me, a profound disgust with life and humanity.

Then at Vindeln, the first Swedish station where the train stopped, a little fair-haired, blue-eyed girl came towards me, smiling sweetly, to offer me a bunch of flowers. Choked with emotion I thanked her, stammering.

After all, there were still pure and gentle spirits among mankind. Not all were beasts of prey.

Ebba Håggström. . . . I memorized her name and impressed it on my heart, never to forget it again.

The Return to Italy

From Vindeln to Malmö we crossed the whole length of Sweden, amidst countless demonstrations of sympathy from the people, who gathered in ever-increasing numbers at the stations as we passed. In Sweden the soul of the masses had not been poisoned by the horrible accusations in the newspapers. They felt the atrocious injustice that had been done us, and instinctively did their best to make amends.

The crowd at the stations, serious and restrained like all northern crowds, looked out for me, wanted to see me, to salute me—felt the need of showing, somehow or other, their sympathy and fellow-feeling. . . . Flowers, simple phrases of greeting, kind letters. One anonymous letter woke me in the dead of night, saying: "With affectionate, cordial sympathy, an immense number of people are following your journey through our country. To bear up gallantly against undeserved misfortune is often braver than to die. Accident and bad luck are no dishonour. God, Who has sent the storm, will let the sun shine out again."

At last we arrived in Italy. Despite official opposition, the people spontaneously swarmed into the stations, invaded the squares, to tell us their affection. Soon there was scarcely room to sit down in my compartment for the flowers that filled it.

At station after station the same moving scenes were repeated. Boys with tear-reddened eyes caught me by the arm, kissed my hands, crying: "Only command us! We are ready to die for you!" This phrase passed from town to town, from mouth to mouth, almost like a watchword.

And so we came to Rome. We returned there on the evening of July 31st, after four months of terrific adventures. Two hundred thousand people were waiting at the station. A delirious crowd: a crowd which, hour by hour, had lived through the Italia expedition; had suffered the anguish of silence, the strain of suspense, the uncertainties of the rescue work; a crowd which had lived through all our tragedy, shared all our sufferings, felt all the infamies committed against us and our enterprise.

With these popular demonstrations the *Italia* expedition came to an end. The rest does not count. Above the contemptible trifles, the base intrigues, the passions of the moment, was raised the admonitory voice of Pius XI, who, singling out our enterprise as worthy of universal admiration, described it as: "one of those feats which attain the highest beauty and sublimity that can be encountered in this life".

APPENDIX TO PART I

The Danger of Icing

THE agreement made on September 1st contained a clause by which it only became definite after the Aeroclub of Norway had paid the first instalment of the price agreed for the dirigible. That is why the work could not be begun before October. But meanwhile, losing no time, as soon as I returned from Norway I started to investigate the effects that the low temperatures which we would certainly meet would have on our airship. It was a question of vital importance, because up till then no dirigible had flown in the Arctic regions. I carried out many experiments, which convinced me that no ill-effects upon the resistance of the materials of which the ship was constructed, or upon the functioning of its working parts, were to be expected from temperatures of between $-4°$ and $-12°$ F.

I also had to consider the possibility that when the ship was passing through a cloud-layer of higher temperature than itself, the condensation of water-vapour on its surface would give rise to icing: a serious danger, because even a thickness of one-tenth of a millimetre would increase its weight by half a ton. But none of my research showed me any effective defence against this. The only thing I could do was to strengthen the outer walls within the radius of the plane of rotation of the airscrews; having foreseen that (as did in fact happen) pieces of ice flung from the blades might strike and tear them.

Another serious danger was that, when drawing off gas in order to balance the ship, ice might form on the valve-seats, making it impossible to close them and so causing an involuntary loss of gas. This had happened several times to our dirigibles, when they were flying in winter or at a great height, and also to

English airships. I had been studying the phenomenon since 1916, without being able to put my finger on its causes. I had not succeeded in determining in what measure the intrinsic humidity of the hydrogen and that of the surrounding air contributed towards ice formation. The best thing to do was to provide against both, so far as it was possible. This was done, partly by using hydrogen compressed to the density of several tens of atmospheres, and partly by covering each group of valves (which were placed on the back of the ship) with a light cap which protected it against the external humidity.

The Airship "N.1"

Here is a very brief description of the airship that was destined to achieve the first Polar crossing.

The silvery body, of a very graceful streamlined shape, was 106 m. long, and, in the principal section, 18 m. high. It was partitioned into 10 airtight compartments, containing the hydrogen from which it obtained its lift. Each compartment was provided with a group of valves, which could either be operated manually from the control cabin, or automatically when the pressure increased beyond a certain safety limit.

Below this, the hull was stiffened throughout its whole length by a triangular-section framework, with its apex pointing downwards, made of girders in latticed steel, connected by articulated joints also made of steel. In the larger inner space of the framework were placed the petrol and oil tanks, the tanks for water-ballast, the controlling machinery, navigation accessories and equipment, provisions and spare clothing. A narrow wooden cat-walk, running from one end to the other, gave easy access to the tanks and to the tail-fins, and also, by means of a ladder in the nose-cap, out on to the top of the airship.

The control-cabin, which was—so to speak—an expansion of this framework, communicated directly with it.

From the body of the airship were suspended, by means of metal cables, 3 duralumin engine-boats, each containing a 250 h.p. piston engine which actuated an airscrew. By a simple manœuvre this could be made to rotate in the opposite direction, which was very useful when landing. There was room in each engine-boat for 2 mechanics.

Of the 3 boats, one was placed towards the stern, in the plane of symmetry of the airship, and was reached from the hull by means of a ladder; the other 2 were hung, level with each other, midway along the hull. A catwalk with a handrail enabled the mechanics to get from each of the boats into the hull, and *vice versa*.

The Landing-sack

Landing a dirigible is always a tricky business, and, if the wind is strong, a very difficult one, even when it is done with the help of an experienced ground-crew, or adequate mechanical means prepared in advance. But to land in unknown or desert places, as we had to be ready to do in Alaska, at the end of our voyage, was not only difficult but actually dangerous. This was, therefore, one of the major problems to be solved, and I devoted a good deal of study to it, and many experiments on the Lake of Bracciano with the little *Mr* airship—a semi-rigid of only 1,000 cubic metres; to which I attribute not a little merit in the success of our enterprise.

I will not go into details—always dull, even if important—of the devices which I tested and used on the airship; but I must mention the landing-sack which played an essential part in the manœuvre carried out when we arrived at Teller, thanks to which I succeeded in bringing the dirigible down on the ice without the slightest damage, while the wind was blowing a gale.

This sack, made of strong cloth, was cylindrical in shape, with a diameter of 30 cm. and a length of 7 m. It was like a sausage-skin, closed at one end and open at the other; on the outside, around the walls of the cylinder were sewn at brief intervals strong hemp ropes (which later, on the *Italia* expedition, I replaced by steel cables). These ropes were intended as a protection to the material when it was dragged along the ground. At the bottom end of the sack were attached one or more anchors, which, forced by its weight to lie flat on the ground, were in the best position to exert a braking action by their drag.

INDEX

I. GENERAL

Names of Ships and Aircraft are in italic type. Details of the *Norge* and *Italia* expeditions will be found in an itemised entry under NOBILE, Umberto. Names of places are indexed separately (II. GEOGRAPHICAL).

Abruzzi, Duke of, 19, 108
Academy of Sciences, Leningrad, 42
Aeroclub of Norway, 16, 17, 18, 22, 29, 36, 52, 53, 92, 95, 100, 273
Agent of Foreign Affairs (*see* Weinstein)
Air Ministry (English), 18, 36
Albertini, Gianni, 111
Alessandrini, Renato, 25, 27, 28, 44, 47, 54, 57, 58, 64, 66, 68, 78, 81, 82, 103, 108, 121, 125, 130, 143, 147, 154, 155, 265
American Army, 28, 29
American Navy, 29, 49
Amundsen, Gustave, 53
Amundsen, Roald, 9, 15, 16, 17, 24, 31, 43, 44, 48, 49, 50, 53, 54, 55, 59, 67, 75, 77, 79, 81, 82, 83, 88, 89, 91-96, 99, 100, 108, 215, 219, 250, 251, 255
Anderson, Capt. Wm. R., 10
Andrée, Salomon A., 60, 234
Aponte, Salvatore, 234
Arduino, Ettore, 25, 26, 28, 54, 57, 65, 82, 95, 103, 107, 125, 130, 143, 154, 162, 265
Arild (Master Builder), 112

Babushkin, M. S. (air pilot), 255
Baccarani, Ugo, 240
Balbo, Italo, 100, 101, 102, 111, 235-236
Behounek, Dr. Francis, 52-53, 105, 107, 125, 129, 140, 143, 150, 154, 157, 161, 162, 162, 171, 172, 173, 176, 183, 184, 188, 189, 190, 193, 196, 197, 199, 217, 221, 222, 224, 225, 226, 227, 228, 229, 263, 270
Bellocchi (Italian workman), 53
Bennett, Floyd, 50
Biagi, Giuseppe, 105, 108, 125, 130, 140, 143, 151, 157, 159, 161, 162, 163, 165-166, 167, 171, 172, 173, 174, 176, 181, 183-184, 185, 188, 189, 192, 194, 195, 196, 198, 199, 200, 201, 202, 204, 217, 218, 219, 221, 222, 224, 226, 228, 229, 230, 239, 240, 241, 242, 252, 263
Biancamano (ship), 90
Bombieri (Consul), 19, 39
Bonzani (General), 29

Braganza (ship), 246, 250, 254, 255, 256
Brazy, Gilbert, 215
Breinkopf, August, 258, 259
Byrd, Richard E., 49-50, 59

Caratti, Attilio, 25, 26, 28, 54, 57, 82, 95, 103, 108, 125, 130, 143, 155, 156, 265
Cecioni, Natale, 25-26, 27, 28, 52, 54, 55, 57, 61, 69, 80, 81, 82, 104, 105, 107, 125, 130, 143, 150, 152, 153, 154, 155, 156, 157, 161, 162, 163, 164, 165, 170, 172, 173, 174, 175, 176-177, 178, 182, 183, 184, 186, 187-188, 189, 190, 191, 192, 195, 197, 199, 204, 210, 217, 220, 221, 224, 225, 226, 228, 229, 252, 253, 255, 263
Chantier (ship), 49
Christell, Einar, 231, 232, 234
Ciocca, Calisto, 103-104, 108, 125, 130, 143, 155, 265
Città di Milano (ship), 103, 112, 118, 123, 124, 151, 159, 160, 162, 163, 167, 168, 170, 171, 174, 191, 193, 199, 200, 201, 202, 203, 209, 211, 212, 216, 217, 219, 220, 223, 224, 225, 228, 232, 233, 234-257, 261-265, 268, 269, 270
Corbino, Prof. Orso M., 106
Coolidge, Calvin (President, U.S.A.), 89-90
Crosio, Lieut. Jullio, 265

De Cuverville, Lieut. Albert, 215
De Martino (Ambassador), 90
De Martoin, Nicola, 112

Dietrichsen, Leif, 215
Dornier Wal (seaplane), 15

Eiffel Tower R/T Station, 198
Ellsworth, Lincoln, 17, 31, 48, 50, 53, 54, 55, 81, 82, 83, 86, 89, 92
Eredia, Filippo, 36

Fascist Government (*see* Italian Government)
Fram (ship), 109
French Air Ministry, 31

Geodetic Institute, U.S.A., 58
Gianfranceschi, Father, 141
Gibson, Miss, 30
Giles, Cornelius, 137
Gottwaldt, Bürger, 23, 24, 28, 38, 57, 58, 65, 76, 83, 93-94
Gran, Major Tryggve, 95, 110
Guilbaud, René, 215, 255

Håggström, Ebba, 270-271
Harris, R. A. (Coast & Geodetic Survey, Washington), 67
Heimdal (ship), 48, 49, 95
Hoare, Sir Samuel, 35
Hobby (ship), 112, 118, 123, 135, 207, 214, 250
Hoel, Prof. A., 95, 109, 110
Horgen, Emil, 23, 24, 28, 38, 48, 54, 57, 58
Huggins (Rigger), 36

Institute of Aerial Communications (Leningrad), 42
Isaachsen, Commander, 110
Italia (airship) (*see* under NOBILE, Umberto)
Italian Admiralty, 104
Italian Air Ministry, 29, 243
Italian Army, 15

Italian Government, 16, 29, 100, 101, 198, 233, 235-236, 265
Italian Navy, 15, 16, 20, 265, 269
Italian Royal Geographical Society, 102
Italian University Students' Association (see S.U.C.A.I.)
Italy, King of, 28-29, 91, 114
Italy, Queen of, 33, 178
Ivanov, Semjen, 259

Japanese Navy, 89, 100
Johnsen, F. Storm- (see Storm-Johnsen)

Kamenev (Soviet Vice-Commissar), 236
Karpinsky, Prof., 42
Kerensky, Alexander F., 40
Krassin (icebreaker), 208, 237, 238, 244, 246, 247-249, 254, 255, 256, 257-265, 266, 268

La Fortune, Father, 86-87
Lago, Ugo, 108, 130, 140, 150, 154, 265
Larsen, Hjalmar Riiser (see Riiser-Larsen)
Latham 47 (flying-boat), 215, 250, 255
Lebedenko (Russian journalist), 44, 53
Ledochovski, Father V., 86
Liljequist, Prof. G. H., 50
Lippi (Helmsman), 47, 53
Litvinoff (Asst. Sec. for Foreign Affairs, U.S.S.R.), 19
Lundborg, Einar, 228-233, 235, 236, 238, 242, 244, 245, 246, 248, 251, 252, 253, 254, 255, 262
Lützow-Holm, Finn, 214, 250

Maddalena, Umberto, 207, 216, 217-218, 219, 220, 221, 236, 241-242, 245, 269
Makaroff, Vera, 41, 42
Malmgren, Dr. Finn, 24, 28, 53, 54, 55, 57, 58, 105, 106-107, 115, 118, 119, 122, 124, 125, 126, 129, 130, 135, 137, 139, 140, 141, 143, 144, 146, 147, 149-150, 154, 156, 157, 158-159, 161, 163, 164, 165, 166, 169, 170, 171, 172, 173, 176, 177, 178, 180, 181, 182-183, 184-185, 186, 188, 191, 193, 194, 208, 244, 245, 251, 255, 259, 260, 263, 266-268
Malyghin (icebreaker), 208, 255
Manzoni, Count, 19
Marconi, Guglielmo, 36
Mariano, Adalberto, 104, 107, 111, 125, 130, 150, 153, 154, 157, 159-160, 161, 162, 163, 166, 167, 170, 171, 172, 173, 175, 176, 177, 178, 180-182, 184, 185, 189, 191, 220, 231, 250, 255, 259-260, 266-269
Matteoda, Sergio, 111
Maud (ship), 24
Mercanti, Arturo, 236
Mercier, Lieut., 31, 36
Milan, City of, 102, 147
Milan, Mayor of, 102
Milan, University of, 106, 107
Mr. (airship), 15-16
Mussolini, Benito, 17, 29-31, 33, 100, 102, 114

N.1. (Norge) (airship) (see NOBILE, Umberto)
N-type airships, 16

Nansen, Fridtjof, 16, 19, 108-109, 110

Nautilus (submarine), 10

Nielsen, Capt., 95

Nobile, Dr. Amedo(brother), 22, 48, 49, 52, 56, 112, 118

Nobile, Carlotta (wife), 32-33, 34, 89, 119, 188-189

Nobile, Maria (daughter), 32, 33, 34, 89, 119, 151, 188, 189

NOBILE, Umberto
Norge Expedition
first contacts with Amundsen, 9, 15-16
preliminary agreements, 16-17
visit to Russia, 18-19
reconstruction of airship, 20-21
preparation of bases, 21-22
choice of crew, 23-28
contacts with Mussolini, 29-31
Rome—King's Bay Flight
start from Rome, 31-34
halts: Pulham, 35-36; Oslo, 37-39; Gatschina, 39-44; Vadsö, 46
crossing Barents Sea, 47
at King's Bay, 48
Polar Flight
preparations, 50-52
personnel, 53-54
start, 55-56
from King's Bay to Pole, 57-61
icing troubles, 61-61, 65-69
at the Pole, 63-64
over unexplored territory, 65-69
sighting land, 69-70
over Bering Straits, 71-72
astray in fog, 72-73
over Alaskan coast, 74-75
in trouble above Kivalina, 75-76

landing at Teller, 79-83
stay at Teller, 82-86; at Nome, 86-88; at Seattle, 88
lecture tour in U.S.A., 89
reception by President Coolidge, 89-90
dispute with Amundsen, 91-96
technical details of airship, 274-275
Italia Expedition
choice of airship, 100-101
programme, 101-102
financial backing, 102
crew, 103-105, 107-108
scientists, 105-106
preparatory work, 108-111
flight: Milan—Stolp, 144-117; Stolp—Vadsö, 119-121; Vadsö—King's Bay, 121-123
first Arctic flight, 124-126
in snowstorm at King's Bay, 126-128
flight to Severnaya Zemlya, 129-137
equipment for Polar flight, 140
flight to North Pole, 141-146
at the Pole, 146-147
return journey, 148-154
disaster, 154-156
last sight of airship, 157
marooned on the ice, 157ff
his injuries in crash, 156, 157-158
organises the camp, 166, 190
discussions with Mariano, Malmgren and Zappi, 170-176, 180-189
first wireless contact with base, 200-202

wireless messages to base,
202-206, 211-212, 219-220,
224
rescued by Lundborg, 227-
230
at Swedish base, 231-232
on Città di Milano, 234-269
messages to Red Tent, 234,
237, 244-245, 248, 262
troubles with Romagna, 235,
237, 244-245, 248, 262
talks with rescue pilots, 234,
237, 241-242
meeting with Riiser-Larsen,
250-251; with Zappi and
Mariano, 268-269; with
Samoilovitch, 269
reception in Sweden, 270
return to Rome, 271
Norway, Crown Prince of, 35
Norway, King of, 37
Norwegian Naval Attaché, 36
Norwegian Navy, 47

Ojetti, Ugo, 87
Olomkin, Genadii, 24, 28, 39, 54
Omdal, Oscar, 23, 28, 33, 54, 55,
57
Orass, Capt. Paul, 261, 269
Oslo Institute, 186

Paonessa, Captain, 36
Peary, Robert E., 59, 108, 144
Pedretti, Ettore, 105, 108, 130,
140, 240
Penzo, Pier Luigi, 207, 220-221,
236, 241, 242-243, 269
Petersen, Capt., 84, 99
Pius XI, 112-114, 147, 195, 272
Polet, 86
Pomella, Vincenzo, 25, 26, 28, 54,
57, 82, 103, 108, 125, 130,
143, 149, 155, 162, 185

Pontremoli, Dr. Aldo, 105, 106,
107, 125, 126, 129, 130,
137, 140, 143, 147, 149,
150, 154, 156, 265
Pope, The (see Pius XI)
Post, Father, 86-87
Pouziewsky, Prof., 39
Prague Meteorological Office, 115
Prague, University of, 107

Quattrini, Antonio, 31, 37, 44
Quest (ship), 232, 233, 246, 253,
254

Ramm, Fredrik, 24, 28, 37, 53,
54, 59
Riiser-Larsen, Hjalmar, 16, 23, 24,
28, 38, 48, 49, 50, 54, 55,
57, 58, 62, 75, 76, 77, 78,
79, 80, 81, 93, 94, 99-100,
207, 214, 215, 216, 217,
220, 250-251
Roma (airship), 28
Romagna, Capt. Giuseppe, 203,
206-207, 234, 235, 246,
247, 249, 252, 254, 255,
256, 262, 264, 270
Ross, Capt., 86
Rossi, Giuseppe, 36, 43, 46-47
Russian Geographical Society, 42
Russian Government (see Soviet
Government)
Russian relief expedition (see
Krassin and Samoilovitch)
Rutherford, Sir Ernest, 106
Rynin, Prof., 42

S.55 (flying-boat), 207
S.U.C.A.I., 111
Salizy, 40, 41
Samoilovitch, Prof. Rudolf, 247,
255, 258, 260, 261, 263,
264, 269

San Paolo R/T Station, 165, 168, 171, 174, 175, 198, 199, 200, 201, 202, 211, 212, 240, 256

Sarko, Olavi, 237, 241, 242

Scaroni, Capt., 90

Schmidt, Nicholas, 198

Schokalsky, Prof., 42

Schyberg, Birger, 229, 230, 252

Scott, Major G. H., 31

Scott, Capt. Robert Falcon, 109

Shrednievsky, Dr. Anton, 259, 260, 261

Sirianni, Admiral, 103

Sora, Capt. Gennaro, 111, 112, 220, 255

Soviet Embassy, 18, 198

Soviet Government, 19, 40, 199, 269

Spanish Navy, 29

Stekloff, Vice-President, 42

Storm-Johnsen, Frithjof, 54, 57, 58

Sverdrup, Otto, 108, 109, 110

Swedish Government, 233

Swedish Rescue Expedition, 207, 223-233, 246, 251, 252, 253, 254, 255, 261

Tchuknovsky, Boris, 256, 258, 268, 269

Thommessen, Dr., 29, 34, 37, 95, 100

Titina (dog), 31, 32, 35-36, 41-42, 77, 90, 108, 160, 189, 193-194, 218

Tomaselli, Francesco (Cesco), 31, 36, 37, 53, 56, 108, 130, 140

Tornberg, Capt. Egmont, 231-232, 233, 251-252, 253, 254

Trojani, Felice, 105, 107, 123, 125, 130, 143, 150, 152, 154, 157, 161, 162, 163, 171, 172, 173, 176, 181, 182, 184, 185, 186, 187, 190, 193, 195, 196, 197, 199, 200, 201, 204, 208, 209, 217, 219, 223, 225, 226, 229, 244, 263

Tromsö Geophysical Institute, 119, 120, 121, 122, 124, 125, 126, 139, 141, 186, 243

Turku (flying-boat), 241, 253

Under-Secretary for Air (see Balbo)

Uppsala, University of, 106

Valette, Emile, 215

Vallini, Major Mario P., 43, 44, 48

Van Dongen, Joseph, 111, 261

Vangensten, Ove L. L. (Norwegian Legation), 34

Victor Emmanuel III (see Italy, King of)

Victoria (ship), 87-88

Viglieri, Alfredo, 104, 107, 125, 130, 140, 141, 152, 154, 157, 161, 162, 163, 172, 173, 176, 182, 183, 184, 188, 189, 190, 191, 193, 195, 196, 199, 217, 219, 221, 223, 225, 226, 227, 228, 229, 230, 236, 242, 243, 244, 252, 256, 257, 261, 263

Vorobieff, Prof., 39

Warming, L., 261

Weinstein (Agent for Foreign Affairs, U.S.S.R.), 19, 39

Wilkins, George H., 70

Wireless Institute, Prague, 107

Wisting, Oscar, 23, 24, 28, 52, 54, 57, 58, 76, 79, 82, 263

Zappi, Filippo, 104, 107, 125, 130, 147, 150, 153, 154, 156, 157, 161, 163-164, 167, 170, 171, 172, 173, 175, 176, 177, 178, 180-182, 184, 185, 189, 191, 255, 258-261, 266-269

Zeppelin Goodyear Corporation, 94

Zeppelins, 16

Zinovieff, General, 18, 19, 39

II. GEOGRAPHICAL

Abel Is., 136
Admiralty Strait, 88
Advent Bay, 264
Akron, 89
Alaska, 9, 10, 16, 20, 33, 58, 64, 67, 70, 71, 72, 73-88, 101, 110, 133
Albert Armitage Is., 134
Alcazar, 235
Aleutian Is., 45, 74, 88
Alexandra Lane, 133
Alfred Harmsworth Is., 134
America, 11, 16, 17, 21, 48, 83, 87-90, 92, 95, 124, 139
Amsterdam Is., 60, 142
Andrée Land, 131
Angers, 35
Antarctic, 50, 88, 95
Archangel, 198, 199, 200, 207, 239
Arctic (Arctic Circle, Arctic Ocean), 10, 11, 12, 15, 16, 19-20, 27, 44, 52, 58, 61, 67-68, 83-84, 88, 89, 91, 99-102, 107, 114, 181, 195, 207, 215
Argentine, 29, 100
Arthur Is., 134
Asia, 73
Atlantic, 36
Austria Strait, 134

Baltic, 38, 115
Barents Sea, 17, 20, 43, 44, 47, 74, 96, 119, 120, 136, 144, 215
Barren Cape, 125, 132
Barrow Point, 16, 44, 57, 70

Bear Is., 20, 46, 47, 120, 121, 141
Benadir, 240
Bergen, 106, 247
Bering Straits, 11, 20, 58, 71, 84
Beverley Strait, 261
Bohemia, 115
Bologna, 108
Boston (U.S.A.), 89
Bothnia, Gulf of, 120
Brescia, 26
Breslau, 117
Bridgmann, Cape, 142, 143, 146
Broch Is., 173, 190, 192, 194, 266, 267, 268
Brünn, 115, 116, 117
Brunn, Cape, 136, 176, 267
Buenos Ayres, 100

Canada, 101, 144
Canal du Midi, 34
Candle, 77
Caudebec-en-Caux, 215
Cassino, 108
Channel, English, 35
Charles Alexander Land, 134
Charles XII Is., 169, 173, 245, 258
Chicago, 89
Chigi Palace, 29
Ciampino, 28, 30, 32, 34
Cleveland, 89
Colville River, 70
Courcelles, 85
Czechoslovakia, 115, 116

Dane Is., 60, 132
Dundee Bay, 48

England, 18, 29, 31, 35, 233
Eschscholtz Bay, 77
Esthonia, 38, 39
Europe, 17, 85, 87, 112

Falsepasse, 88
Fiesole, 107
Finland, 38, 39, 119, 207, 235
Fligely, Cape, 34
Florence, 25, 83, 107
Forli, 107, 147
Fort Clarence, 78
Foyn Is., 111, 173, 178, 180, 187,
190, 192, 193, 194, 196,
199, 209, 212, 213, 214,
216, 219, 230, 261, 265
France, 34, 43, 103, 215
Franz Josef Land, 20, 89, 113, 129,
133, 135, 169, 194, 200,
204
Frederick Jackson Is., 134

Gatschina, 18, 23, 27, 36, 39-44,
46
Germany, 103, 115, 119, 207
Gillis Land, 133, 137
Glatz, 116, 117
Goodhope Bay, 77
Great Is. (Grosse Is.), 136, 245
Green Harbour, 49
Greenland, 9, 101, 124, 139, 141,
142

Haakon VII Land, 60, 132, 142
Hansteen, Cape, 132
Helsingfors, 236
Helsinki, 37
Hinlopen Strait, 137
Hope Point, 71

Icefjord, 48
Iceland, 141
Icy Cape, 71

Italy, 15, 16, 22, 46, 48, 74, 82,
83, 87, 90, 100, 102, 103,
108, 200, 207, 235, 269, 271

Japan, 11, 29, 89, 100, 102
Jesseritz, 117

Kalmjoki, 120
Karst, 115
Kesi, 120
King Charles Is. (see Charles XII
Is.)
King's Bay, 9, 16, 17, 18, 21, 22,
36, 43, 46, 48, 49, 52, 53,
56, 59, 64, 78, 93, 100,
103, 104, 111, 112, 118,
121, 122, 123, 124, 126,
129, 136, 144, 149, 152,
154, 168, 186, 191, 200,
203, 207, 216, 217, 236,
246, 250
Kirkenes, 46
Kivalik, 77
Kivalina, 76, 77, 93-94
Körmend, 115
Kotzbue Bay, 71, 75, 77
Kukpuk River, 73

Ladoga Lake, 45, 51
Latvia, 38
Leigh Smith, Cape, 136, 196, 197,
209, 244, 248, 251, 252,
257
Lenin Land (see Severnaya Zem-
lya)
Leningrad, 17, 18, 20, 27, 37, 40,
42, 100, 118
Lindenberg, 115, 117
Linneus, Cape, 70, 72
Lithuania, 39
London, 20, 35, 36
Los Angeles, 89
Lubiana, 115

Mackenzie, River, 110, 124, 141, 146
Madrid, 235
Malmö, 271
Marino di Pisa, 15
Medicina, 108
Mediterranean, 11, 236
Mercato Saraceno, 107
Milan, 104, 107, 112, 114, 117, 129
Mitre, Cape, 59, 142
Modena, 108
Moffen Is., 125, 132, 151, 207
Mogadiscio, 240
Moscow, 19
Mossel Bay, 207
Murchison Bay, 231, 246

Naples, 28, 47, 90
Narvik, 269, 270
Nassau, Cape, 136
Neva, River, 45
Nevsky Prospect, 45
New Friesland, 137
New York, 83, 89, 90
Nicholas II Land (see Severnaya Zemlya)
Nome, 45, 58, 70, 71, 73, 75, 77, 78, 79, 83, 86-88, 92
North, Cape, 125, 130, 132, 135, 171, 175, 176, 180, 186, 191, 194, 203, 207, 214, 215, 216, 220, 247, 248, 250, 255, 261, 266
North-East Land, 111, 132, 136-137, 152, 169, 171, 186, 208, 209, 244, 246, 248, 250, 256, 258, 267
North Pole, 9, 10, 11, 15, 16, 20, 27, 29, 30, 32, 33, 48, 49, 50, 54, 56, 58, 59, 61, 62, 63, 64, 65, 67, 68, 83, 84,

88, 91, 100, 101, 110, 124, 133, 139-147, 148, 160, 169
Norway, 16, 18, 20, 21, 30, 35, 37, 46, 48, 103, 120, 121, 207, 235, 273
Noto, 108
Novaya Zemlya, 20
Ny Aalesund, 123, 141

Onega, Lake, 51
Oppeln, 117
Oslo, 16, 18, 20, 21, 36, 37-39, 100, 106, 109, 247, 250

Pacific Ocean, 74, 83
Paris, 236, 269
Pekkala, 120
Petrosavodsk, 45
Philadelphia, 89
Pittsburgh, 89
Platen, Cape, 176, 258
Po, River, 115
Point Barrow (see Barrow)
Posen, 117
Prague, 107, 116
Prince Charles Land, 48, 122, 247
Prince of Wales Cape, 77
Prince Rudolph Is., 134
Providence, 89
Pulham, 18, 23, 31, 35-36, 37

Quale Hoek, 48

Ravarino, 108
Reval, 38
Rhodes, 170
Riga, 39
Rivarolo Canavese, 107
Rochefort, 35
Rochester, 89

Rome, 11, 15, 16, 17, 18, 20, 21,
23, 31, 34, 47, 83, 87, 88,
90, 100, 101, 107, 108, 112,
163, 165, 167, 234, 235,
241, 257, 262, 269, 270,
271-272
Ross Is., 154, 248
Rovaniemi, 120
Rovato, 108
Russia, 17, 18-19, 24, 27, 31, 36,
39-44, 51, 120, 207, 235

Sadobrava, 115
Salisbury Is., 134
Salizy, 40, 41, 97
San Francisco, 89, 99
Santa Barbara, 89
Sarichef, 77
Sarzana, 107
Scandinavia, 38, 99, 119
Scoresby Is., 176
Seattle, 45, 70, 88, 89, 95, 99, 250
Serpentine River, 77
Seven Islands, 248, 255, 265
Severnaya Zemlya, 9, 11, 101,
124, 125, 129, 134, 137,
139, 140, 208
Seward Peninsula, 71
Shishmaref Bay, 72
Siberia, 101, 144
Silesia, 115, 117
Sopron, 115
Sorkap, 47
Spezia, 112
Spitsbergen (The Svalbard), 9, 10,
15, 16, 17, 20, 21, 24, 33,
36, 43, 44, 46, 47, 52, 56,
57, 58, 60, 68, 84, 101,
110, 112, 117, 118, 120-
121, 122, 129, 133, 136,
137, 141, 153, 167, 168,

171, 198, 200, 208, 231,
247, 257, 269
Stavanger, 269
St. Elia Fiumerapido, 108
Stockholm, 37, 119, 231
Stolp, 104, 112, 117-119, 123
Sudetes, 115, 116
Svalbard (see Spitsbergen)
Sweden, 185, 207, 235, 271
Syracuse, 108

Taymir, Is., 135
Teller, 9, 27, 31, 42, 52, 70, 72,
83-86, 87, 94, 99, 250
Tiber, 15
Tokio, 99, 100
Torell Land, 48
Trieste, 115
Tripoli, 31
Tromsö, 112, 118, 120, 215, 250
Trondheim, 18
Turin, 107, 108
Tyrrhenian Sea, 83

U.S.A. (see America)
U.S.S.R. (see Russia)
Uppsala, 106, 107

Vadsö, 21, 22, 36, 43, 44, 46, 47
50, 100, 112, 120-121
Valga, 39
Vardö, 47
Vatican, 114
Venice, 108
Verona, 26, 107
Vienna, 115
Viminal, 102, 111
Vindeln, 270, 271
Virgo Bay, 232, 233, 234, 246
247, 250, 253, 269

Vissinger Hoft, Cape, 136
Vogel Hoek, 78

Wainwright, 70, 71

Washington, 89

Yokahama, 89

Zelantya, Cape, 136